FLORENTINE CODEX

Florentine Codex

General History of the Things of New Spain

FRAY BERNARDINO DE SAHAGÚN

Book 12 – The Conquest of Mexico

Translated from the Aztec into English, with notes and illustrations
(Second edition, revised)

By

Arthur J. O. Anderson
School of American Research

Charles E. Dibble
University of Utah

IN THIRTEEN PARTS

PART XIII

Chapter heading designs are from the Codex

Published by

The School of American Research and The University of Utah

Monographs of The School of American Research

Number 14, Part XIII   Santa Fe, New Mexico   1975

ISBN-10: 0-87480-096-x (Book 12)
ISBN-13: 978-0-87480-096-8

ISBN-10: 0-87480-082-x (Set)
ISBN-13: 978-0-87480-082-1

Published and distributed by
The University of Utah Press
Salt Lake City, Utah 84112

To

Msgr. Angel María Garibay K. and Byron
McAfee, who helped us in translating the text,
and Don Rafael García Granados and Lic.
Jorge Gurría Lacroix, who helped us in matters
of historical accuracy,
we affectionately dedicate this book

CONTENTS

TWELFTH BOOK

LIST OF ILLUSTRATIONS

following page 46

Note. — Although spaces were provided, illustrations are lacking in the last five chapters of Book XII. The eight figures reproduced following Plate 161 are some of the many ornamental designs found in this Book.

VALLEY OF MEXICO

Chart showing two-fold division of the island and
four-fold division of Tenochtitlan

KEY TO MAP OF TENOCHTITLAN-TLATILULCO

1. Palace of Moctezuma
2. Totocalco
3. Quauhquiauac
4. Tecpantzinco
5. Acatl yiacapan
6. Tezcacoac
7. Temple of Uitzilopochtli
8. Palace of Moctezuma the Elder
9. Teoayoc
10. Cuicacalco
11. Uitzillan
12. Xoloco
13. Fort Xolloco
14. Acachinanco
15. Tecpancaltitlan
16. Tecpantzinco
17. Tzapotlan
18. Atenchicalco
19. Mixcoatechialtitlan
20. Tolteca canal
21. Petlacalco
22. Popotlan
23. Copulco
24. Nextlatilco
25. Iliacac
26. Ayauhcaltitlan
27. Yauhtenco
28. Market of Tlatilulco
29. Teteuhtitlan and Tlaixcuipan
30. Atecocolecan
31. Coyonacazco and Amaxac
32. Copalnamacoyan
33. Ayacac
34. Atliceuhyan
35. Totecco
36. Quauecatitlan
37. Apauazcan
38. Tlacochcalco
39. Tetenanteputzco and Atactzinco
40. Xochicalco and Quauhquechollan
41. Yacacolco
42. Tlilhuacan and Atezcapan
43. Colhuacatonco
44. Xocotitlan or Cihuatecpan
45. Tetzontlalamacoyan
46. Atzacualco
47. Tetamaçolco

(After Orozco y Berra, with modifications suggested mainly by reference to Alfonso Caso, *Los barrios antiguos de Tenochtitlan y Tlatilulco*. The locations of many of the places are provisional.)

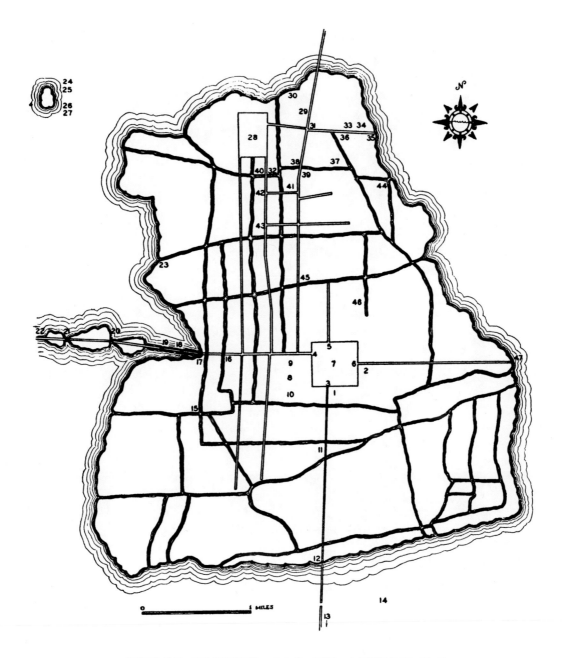

TENOCHTITLAN-TLATILULCO

BOOK TWELVE --THE CONQUEST

EL DOZENO LIBRO
tracta de como los es
pañoles conquis
taron a la ciu
dad de Me
xico.

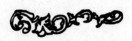

De la Conquista Mexicana

| TWELFTH BOOK, WHICH TELLETH HOW WAR WAS WAGED HERE IN THE CITY OF MEXICO.[1] | INJC MATLACTETL OMUME AMOXTLI, ITECHPA TLATOA IN QUENJN MUCHIUH IAUIOTL IN NJCAN IPAN ALTEPETL MEXICO. |

First Chapter, in which it is told how there appeared, how there were seen the signs, the omens of evil, before the Spaniards had come here to this land, before they were known to the natives here.[2]

Ten years before the Spaniards arrived here,[3] an omen of evil first appeared in the heavens. It was like a tongue of fire, like a flame, like the light of dawn. It looked as if it were showering [sparks],[4] as if it stood piercing the heavens. It was wide at the base, it was pointed at the head. To the very midst of the sky, to the very heart of the heavens it stood reaching; to the very midpoint of the skies it stood stretched as it was seen. It was there to the east when it thus came

Injc ce capitulo vncã mjtoa in nez, in mottac in machiotl yoã in tetzavitl, in aiamo valhuj españoles, in njcan tlalli ipan, in aiamo no iximachoa in njcã chaneque.

In aiamo vallaci españoles, oc matlacxivitl, centlamãtli tetzavitl achto nez, ilhujcatitech, iuhquj in tlemjiaoatl, iuhquj in tlecueçalutl, iuhqujn tlavizcalli, pipixauhticaca injc necia, iuhq'n ilhujcatl qujçoticac: tzimpatlaoac, quapitzaoac: vel inepantla in ilhujcatl; vel yiollo in aciticac ilhujcatl, vel ilhujcaiollotitech aciticac, in iuh ittoia vmpa tlapcopa: in oalmoquetzaia, oiuh onqujz ioalnepantla in necia tlatviliaia, ipan tlatvia, q'n iehoatl qujoalpoloaia in tonatiuh, in

1. In Book XII, especially toward the end, the reader may detect a pro-Tlatilulcan and an almost anti-Tenochtidanian bias to the *Florentine Codex*'s account of the Conquest. Since Tlatilulco, an independent entity, had been annexed to Tenochtitlan a scant fifty years by the time of Cortés's final success, any underlying Tlatilulcan distaste for their victorious neighbors is perhaps understandable. At any rate, the version of the Conquest in the *Florentine Codex* owes much to Tlatilulco, and so does the subsequent 1585 "Relacion de la Conquista," in Carlos Ma. de Bustamante, ed., *La Aparicion de Ntra. Señora de Guadalupe de Mexico, Comprobada con la refutacion del argumento negativo que presenta D. Juan Bautista Muñoz, fundandose en el testimonio del P. Fr. Bernardino de Sahagun* (Mexico, D.F.: Ignacio Cumplido, 1840; hereafter referred to as Bustamante, *Aparicion*), to which we shall frequently refer for statements differing in detail from those in the *Florentine Codex*. (See esp. p. 1 of Bustamante, *Aparicion*.)

Because we treat this history of the Conquest as a native account, we call upon other sources mainly to clarify the Nahuatl text. The student of the Conquest will still need to consult such contemporary accounts as those of Cortés, Bernal Díaz, Aguilar, Cervantes de Salazar, etc., for a more complete and consistent narrative.

Other basic sources to which we are indebted for comparable or differing versions are Bernardino de Sahagún, *Historia general de las cosas de Neuva España*, ed. Angel María Garibay K., 4 vols. (Mexico, D.F.: Editorial Porrúa, S.A., 1956; hereafter referred to as Sahagún, Garibay ed.) and Eduard Seler, *Einige Kapitel aus dem Geschichtswerk des Fray Bernardino de Sahagun aus dem Aztekischen übersetzt*, ed. Caecilie Seler-Sachs, Walter Lehmann, and Walter Krickeberg (Stuttgart:

Strecker und Schroeder, 1927; hereafter referred to as Seler, *Einige Kapitel*).

2. The same Nahuatl text appears as Chap. 6 of Book VIII. See Arthur J. O. Anderson and Charles E. Dibble, trans., "Kings and Lords," *Florentine Codex, Book VIII* (Santa Fe: School of American Research and University of Utah, 1954; hereafter referred to as Anderson and Dibble, *Book VIII*). Except for variations in spelling and punctuation, the texts are identical. The corresponding Spanish text in Book VIII varies somewhat from that of Book XII. A third Nahuatl text is inserted in Book II of the *Real Palacio MS*. See "Memoriales en 3 columnas," in Fr. Bernardino de Sahagún, *Historia de las cosas de Nueva España*, ed. Francisco del Paso y Troncoso (Madrid: Hauser y Menet, 1906; hereafter referred to as *Real Palacio MS*), Vol. VII, p. 93. Marginal notes in Sahagún's hand read: "Esto q̃ se sigue esta puesto en el primero capitulo del libro q̃ tracta de la guerra q̃ vbo entre los indios y los españoles"; "Este es el primero capitulo del quinto libro q̃ tracta de la guerra." There are three Spanish versions of the Nahuatl text by Sahagún: two in the *Florentine Codex* and the subsequent revised version as published by Bustamante in 1840.

3. Two years, in Bustamante, *Aparicion*, p. 9. Eduard Seler, in *Einige Kapitel*, p. 453, n. 1, reads: "D. h. zwei Jahre vor der Ankunft der Spanier (eins Rohr = A. D. 1517). Die Angabe oben, dass diese Lichterscheinung zehn Jahre vor der Ankunft der Spanier gesehen worden sei, stimmt also nicht zu der Angabe hier."

4. Corresponding Spanish text (Book VIII): "y que echaba de si centellas de fuego."

forth at midnight; it looked as if day had dawned, day had broken. Later, the sun destroyed it when he arose. For a full year [the sign] came forth. (It was [in the year] Twelve House that it began.) And when it appeared, there was shouting; there was the striking of the palm of the hand against the mouth. There was fear; there was inactivity.

A second evil omen came to pass here in Mexico. Quite of its own accord, the house of the demon Uitzilopochtli burned; it flared greatly. No one had set fire to it; only of itself it burst into flames. It was called Itepeyoc,[5] at the place called Tlacateccan. When [the fire] appeared, already the wooden pillars were burning. From within emerged the flame,[6] the tongue of fire, the blaze. Speedily it ate all the house beams. Thereupon there was an outcry. [The priests] said: "O Mexicans, hasten here! Let [the fire] be put out! [Bring] your water jars!" But when they cast water upon it, when they tried to put it out, all the more did it flare up. It could not be put out; it all burned.

A third evil omen: a temple was struck by lightning; a thunderbolt struck it. It was only a straw hut, a place called Tzonmulco, Xiuhtecutli's temple. It was not raining hard; only drizzling. Thus it was considered an evil omen. So, it was said, it was a mere[7] summer flash; nor was there a thunder-clap.[8]

A fourth evil omen: there was yet sun when a comet fell. It became three parts. It began there in the west, and it traveled there to the east as if showering glowing coals. For a great distance it went extending a tail; far did its tail go reaching. And when it was seen, great was the outcry. It was as if [the din of] shell rattles was overspread.[9]

A fifth evil omen: the [lake] water foamed up. The wind did not make it foam up. It was as if the water boiled up, as if it boiled up with a cracking sound. Very far did it go as it rose upward. And it reached the bases of the houses, and it flooded, it crumbled the houses.[10] This is the great lake which stretches about us here in Mexico.[11]

A sixth evil omen: often was heard a woman going weeping, going crying out. Loudly did she cry out at night. She walked about saying: "My beloved sons,

jquac oalqujçaia: vel ce xivitl in oalmoquetzaia (ipan matlactli omume calli in peuh). Auh in jquac necia tlacaoacaia, netenvitecoia, neiçaviloia, tlatemmachoia.

Injc vntetl tetzavitl muchiuh, njcan mexico: çan monomavi in tlatlac, cuetlan, aiac ma qujtlecavi, çan monoma tlecavi in jcal diablo vitzilobuchtli: mjtoaia, iteioc itocaiocan Tlacateccan: in nez ie tlatla in tlaquetzalli, in jtec, oalqujça in tlemjiaoatl, in tlenenepilli, in tlecueçalutl, cenca çan iciuhca compalo in ixqujch calquavitl: njman ie ic tlacaoaca, qujtoa. Mexicae ma vallatotoca, tla ceviloz, amaapilol: auh in jquac caatequjaia, in qujceviznequja, çan ie ilhujce mopitza, aocmo vel ceuh, vel tlatlac.

Injc etetl tetzavitl: vitecoc ipan tlatlatzin teucalli, çan xacalli catca, itocaiocan tzūmulco: iteupan in xiuhtecutli, amo tilaoaia, çan aoachqujavia in juh tetzammachoc: iuh mjtoa in ça çan tonalhujtecoc, amono caqujztic in tlatlatzinjliztli.

Injc nauhtetl tetzavitl: oc vnca in tonatiuh in xivitl vetz ieteieia, vmpa oalpeuh in tonatiuh icalaqujampa; auh vmpa itztia in jqujçaianpa, iuhquj in tlesuchtli pipixauhtiuh, veca mocujtlapiltitiuh, veca acitiuh in jcujtlapil: auh in oittoc cēca tlacaoacac, iuhqujn oiovalli ōmoman.

Injc macujltetl tetzavitl: poçon in atl, amo iehecatl qujpoçonalti, iuhqujn momomoloca, iuhqujn xixittemomoloca, cenca veca in ia, injc macoquetz: auh in calli tzitzintla cacic, auh capapachiuh, xixitin in calli: iehoatl in vei atl totlan manj njcan mexico.

Injc chiquacentlamantli tetzavitl: mjecpa cioatl cacoia chocatiuh, tzatzitiuh, ioaltica cenca tzatzi; qujtotinemj. Nonopilhoantzitzin, ie ic çan ie tonvi: in

5. Itepeyoc: cf. *Real Palacio MS.*

6. Book VIII of the *Florentine Codex* has *iitic* in a similar passage. In the *Real Palacio MS* it reads: *ytic y valquiça.*

7. *Ca çan* appears in the *Real Palacio MS.*

8. In Bustamante, *Aparicion*, p. 10: "y deciase ... *El sol ha encendido este templo, porque no hemos visto relámpago, ni tampoco trueno.*"

9. See Anderson and Dibble, *Book VIII*, p. 18, n. 5.

10. In the *Real Palacio MS*, this passage reads: "*auh ȳ calli tzitzintla caçic Auh ceq' papachiuh cequi xixitin.*"

11. In *ibid., manj* is followed by "*Auh ynic mocuep ynic ceceuh çā no vmpa ya ȳ vmpa vatztia ȳ vey apāpa.*"

now we are about to go!"[12] Sometimes she said: "My sons, whither am I to take you?"

A seventh evil omen: once [when] the water folk were hunting or snaring game they caught an ashen bird like a brown crane. Then they went to the Tlillan calmecatl to show it to Moctezuma.[13] It was past noon, still early. On its head was as it were a mirror, round, circular, as if pierced in the middle.[14] There appeared the heavens, the stars — the Fire Drill [constellation]. And Moctezuma took it as an omen of great evil when he saw the stars and the Fire Drill. And when he looked at the bird's head a second time, he saw, a little beyond,[15] what was like people coming massed, coming as conquerors, coming girt in war array. Deer bore them upon their backs. And then he summoned the soothsayers, the wise men.[16] He said to them: "Do you not know what I have seen there like people coming massed?" But when they would answer him, that which they looked at vanished. They said nothing more.[17]

An eighth evil omen: often were discovered men — thistle-men having two heads [but] only one body. They took them there to the Tlillan calmecatl. There they showed them to Moctezuma. When he had beheld them, then they vanished.

quenmanjan qujtoa. Nonopilhoantzitzin, campa namechnoviqujliz.

Injc chicuntlamantli tetzavitl: ceppa tlatlamaia, manoço tlamatlaviaia in atlaca; centetl cacique tototl nextic, iuhqujn tocujlcoiotl: njmã qujttitito in Motecuçoma, tlillan, calmecac: ommotzcalo in tonatiuh, oc tlaca, iuhq'n tezcatl icpac manj, malacachtic, tevilacachtic, iuhqujn xapotticac: vmpa onnecia in ilhujcatl, in cicitlaltin, in mamalhoaztli. Auh in motecuçoma, cenca qujmotetzavi in jquac qujmjttac cicitlaltin, yoã mamalhoaztli. Auh injc vppa ontlachix in jcpac tototl, ene qujttac, iuhquj on in ma acame, moquequetztivitze, tepeuhtivitze, moiaochichiuhtivitze, qujnmama mamaça. Auh njman qujnnotz in tlaciuhque, in tlamatinjme: qujmjlhuj: Amo anqujmati in tlein onoconjttac, iuhqujn acame moquequetztivitze: auh ie qujnanqujlizquja, in conjttaque, opoliuh, aoc tle qujtoque.

Injc chicuetetl tetzavitl: mjecpa motenextiliaia, tlaca, tlacanetzolti, ontetzontecomeque, çan çe in intlac, vmpa qujmõvicaia in tlillan calmecac, vmpa qujmjttaia in motecuçoma, in oqujmjttac njmã polivia.

---

12. Cf. *ibid.*, where *çã yeh tiui* appears.

13. In Bustamante, *Aparicion*, p. 10, this is explained: *"la llevaron á presencia de Moctheuzoma, el cual por entonces estaba en unos palacios que se llamaban* Tlillancalmecatle *(quiere decir, palacios teñidos de negro) y parece que como tenía otros palacios para alegrarse, ricamente edificados, este* Tlillancalmecatle *tenía para recogerse en el tiempo de adversidad y tristeza."*

14. A *tlachieloni* (instrument for seeing), attribute of Tezcatlipoca and the fire god (Seler, *Einige Kapitel*, p. 455, n. 4).

15. In the *Real Palacio MS*, a similar phrase is written: *"Ene q'mittac, yuhq'n acame moquequetztivitze."* On *moquequetztivitze*, see

Rémi Siméon, *Dictionnaire de la langue nahuatl ou mexicaine* (Paris: Imprimerie Nationale, 1880) — *quequetza*. In corresponding Spanish passages, Sahagún translates as *"muchedumbre de gente junta"* or *"mucha gente junta."*

16. *Tlaciuhque*: see Angel María Garibay K., "Paralipómenos de Sahagún," *Tlalocan*, Vol. II, No. 2 (1946), p. 171. *Astrólogo* is favored as translation: *"La raiz* ciuh, *parece denotar fenómenos meteorológicos."*

17. In the *Real Palacio MS*, following *opoliuh*, we read: *"aoc tle vel q'toq[ue], oc ceppa q'milhvi y tlaciuhq[ue] in tlamatinime, tle ynin tototl quilhviq[ue] amo nel yehoatl yn quatezcatl."*

Second Chapter, in which it is told how the first boat which came arrived, which, as they say, was only one boat.

And when were seen those who came to the seashore, already they were traveling by boat. Then in person went Pinotl of Cuetlaxtlan, the high steward. He took with him still other stewards. The steward of Mictlanquauhtla — Yaotzin — [was second]. Third was the steward of Teocinyocan, named Teocinyacatl. Fourth was Cuitlalpitoc, who was only an underling,[1] a guide. Fifth was Tentlil,[2] likewise a guide.

For the time being these went only to look at [the Spaniards]. They went as if to sell [goods] in order to go to spy upon them, to find out about them. They went to offer them precious capes, precious goods: indeed capes pertaining to Moctezuma alone, which no one else wore. They were his alone, his prerogative.

It was in boats that they went in order to go to see them, in order that they might do this. Pinotl said: "Let us not deceive the lord Moctezuma, for no longer would you live. Let us indeed go, lest we die, in order that he may be truthfully informed." (Moctezuma[3] was his princely name, and *tlacatecutli* was his title as ruler.)

Thereupon they went into the water. They entered the boats; they took to the water. The water folk rowed them.

And when they had drawn near to the Spaniards, then before them they performed the earth-eating ceremony at the prows of the boats:[4] they thought it was Quetzalcoatl Topiltzin who had come to arrive.

The Spaniards called out to them: they said to them: "Who are you? Whence have you come? Where is your home?"

Then [the others] said: "It is from there in Mexico that we have come."

Injc vme capitulo, vncan mjtoa in quenjn acico, in achto acalli oalla: in juh qujtoa ca çan centetl in acalli.

Auh in oittoque, in aqujque ovallaque ilhujcaatenco, in acaltica ie onotinemj. Niman inoma ia in cuetlaxtecatl pjnotl, vei calpixquj, q'nvicac oc cequjntin calpixque: Mictlan, quauhtla calpixquj, Jaotzin. Injc ei, Teuciniocan calpixquj: itoca Teuciniacatl. Injc navi iehoatl in cujtlalpitoc, çan tetlan nenquj tlaiacanquj. Injc macujlli Tentlil, çan no tlaiacanquj;

çan oc iehoantin in, in qujmjttato, çan iuhqujnma qujntlanamaqujltito, injc qujnnaoalittato, injc qujnnemjlito: qujnmacato tlaçotilmatli, tlaçotlanquj, çan vel itech itilma in Motecuçoma, in aoc ac oc çe qujquemj, çan vel ineixcavil, vel itonal:

acaltica in iaque injc qujmjttato, injc iuh qujchiuhque in: qujto in pinotzin. Ma tiqujztlacaviti in tlacatl Motecuçomatzin, ca iaocmo annenca ma çan tehoantin tivia, ma tonmjqujti, injc vel melaoac qujmocaqujtiz (in motecuçomatzin ipiltoca, auh Tlacatecutli in jtlatocatoca:[)]

njman ie ic vi in atl itic ommacalaqujque, ommatoctique, qujntlanelhujque atlaca.

Auh in ointech ompachivito españoles: njman imjxpan ontlalquaque acaliacac, in momatque, ca iehoatl in Quetzalcoatl topiltzin, in oacico,

qujnoalnotzq̃ in españoles: qujmjlhujque. Acamjque campa oanvallaque, can amochan?

Çan njman qujtoque, ca vmpa in mexico tioallaque.

---

1. Corresponding Spanish text: "*criado de vno destos calpisques.*"

2. Fernando de Alva Ixtlilxochitl, in *Décima tercia relación de la venida de los españoles y principio de la ley evangélica* (Mexico, D.F.: Editorial Pedro Robredo, 1938), p. 8, mentions Teopili, or Teuhtlile, *gobernador de Mocthecuzoma, que era de Cotaztlatl, o Cuetlachtlan,* who brought the news to the ruler when Cortés landed later (1519).

3. Motecuçomatzin: reverential form of well-known Nahuatl names

is generally not expressed in our translation unless demanded by the context. With others we usually follow the Nahuatl text.

4. Cf. Arthur J. O. Anderson and Charles E. Dibble, trans., "The Ceremonies," *Florentine Codex, Book II* (Santa Fe: School of American Research and University of Utah, 1951; hereafter referred to as Anderson and Dibble, *Book II*), p. 182. Seler, *Einige Kapitel,* p. 457, translates the phrase thus: "*assen sie Erde vor ihnen vorn am Kanu.*"

[The Spaniards] answered them: "If in truth you are Mexicans, what is the name of the ruler of Mexico?"

They said to [the Spaniards]: "O our lords, his name is Moctezuma."

Thereupon they offered them all the various things which they bore with them, the precious capes like those which are here named: the one with the sun design, the blue-knotted one, the one with the jar design, the one with eagle down, the one with the serpent face, the one with the wind jewel, the one with the turkey blood design, or the one with the whirlpool design, the one with the smoking mirror.

All these various things they presented to [the Spaniards. These] gave them gifts in return. They offered them green and yellow necklaces which resembled amber.[5]

And when they had taken [the gift], when they had seen it, much did they marvel.

And [the Spaniards] addressed them; they said to them: "Go! For the time being we depart for Castile. We shall not tarry in going to reach Mexico."

Thereupon [the Spaniards] went. Thereupon also [the others] came back; they turned back.

And when they had come to emerge on dry land, then they went direct to Mexico. Day by day, night by night[6] they traveled in order to come to warn Moctezuma, in order to come to tell him exactly of its circumstances; they came to notify him.[7] Their goods had come to be what they had gone to receive.

And thereupon they addressed him: "O our lord, O my noble youth, may thou destroy us. For behold what we have seen, behold what we have done, there where thy grandfathers stand guard for thee before the ocean. For we went to see our lords the gods in the midst of the water. All thy capes we went to give them. And behold their noble goods which they gave us. They said: 'If in truth ye have come from Mexico, behold what ye shall give the ruler Moctezuma by which he will know us.'"

Thus they told him all of how [the Spaniards] had spoken to them in the midst of the water.

And Moctezuma said to them: "You have suffered fatigue; you have become exhausted. Rest. What I have seen has been in secret. No one shall speak any-

Qujnoalnanqujlique: intla nelli anmexica tle itoca in tlatoanj mexico?

Qujmonjlhujque. Totecujovane ca Motecuçoma itoca.

Njmã ie ic qujnmaca in jzqujtlamantli qujtqujque tlaçotilmatli: iuhquj in, iehoatl in, in njcã moteneoa. Tonatiuhio xiuhtlalpilli: tecomaio, xaoalquauhio, coaxaiacaio, ecacozcaio, Tolecio, anoço amalacaio, Tezcapocio:

in jzqujtlamãtli in in qujmõmacaque, qujnoalcuepcaiotilique, qujnoalmacaque cozcatl, xoxoctic, coztic: iuhqujnma in apoçonalnenequj:

auh in oconcujque, in oqujttaque, cenca tlamaviçoque,

yoan qujnoalnaoatique qujnoalilhujque: xivian oc ie tivi in castilla, amo tivecaoazã tacitivi in mexico:

njmã ie ic vi, njman ie no ic vitze, oalmocuepque.

Auh in otlalhoacca qujçaco, njman oallamelauhque in Mexico, cecemjlhujtl, ceceioal in oalnenenque, injc qujnonotzaco in motecuçoma, in melaoac in jveliaca qujlhujco, qujcaqujtico: intlatquj oalmochiuhtia in oqujcujto.

Auh njman ie ic qujnonotza. Totecujoe, notelpotzine, ma xitechmotlatlatili ca izcatquj otiqujttaque, izcatquj oticchiuhque, ca in vmpa mitzonmotlapielilia in moculhoan, in teuatl ixco. Ca otiqujmjttato in totecujoan, in teteu in atl itic: in jxqujch motilmatzin otiqujnmacato: auh izcatquj techmacaque intlatqujtzi. Qujtoque; intla nelli vmpa oanoallaque mexico, izcatquj anqujmacazque in tlatoanj Motecuçoma, ic techiximatiz:

much iuh qujlhujque, in juh qujmjlhujque atl itic.

Auh in Motecuçoma qujmjlhuj, oanqujhiovique, oanqujciauhque: ximocevicã, ca onontlachix in topco, petlacalco: aiac tle qujtoz, aiac tle contenqujxtiz,

5. Spanish text: "los españoles dieron a los indios cuёtas de vidrio, vnas verdes y otras amarillas."

6. Ibid.: "en vn dia, y en vna noche."

7. Seler, Einige Kapitel, p. 458, has ivel ioca, translated "first of all." Garibay (Sahagún, Garibay ed., Vol. IV, p. 84) translates the passage thus: "Día y noche vinieron caminando para comunicar a Motecuzoma, para decirle y darle a saber con verdad lo que él pudiera saber."

thing [of this]. No one shall let it escape his lips. No one shall let any of it out. No one shall loose a word of it. No one shall mention it. It is only within you."

aiac tle conchitonjz, aiac tle concamacaoaz, aiac quj-teneoaz, çan amjtic.

Third Chapter, in which it is told what Moctezuma commanded when he heard the account of those who saw the boat which first came.

Moctezuma thereupon commanded [Pinotl] of Cuetlaxtlan and all of them. He said to them: "Command that watch be kept everywhere at the water's edge [at the places] thus named: Nauhtlan, Toztlan, Mictlanquauhtla — wheresoever [the strangers] would come to land."

The stewards then departed in order to command that watch be kept.

And Moctezuma assembled his lords: *ciuacoatl* Tlilpotonqui, the *tlacochcalcatl* Quappiaztzin, the *tiçociauacatl* Quetzalaztatzin, the *uitznauatlailotlac* Ecatenpatiltzin.[1] He informed them of the account, and he showed them, he laid before them the necklaces which [the stewards] had brought.

He said to them: "We have marveled at the fine, blue turquoises. They shall be well watched. The guards will watch them well. If they lose one of them, [their houses, their children, their women with child will be] our houses, our children, our women with child."[2]

And then the year changed to the companion to follow, Thirteen Rabbit. But the year [Thirteen][3] Rabbit was about to come to an end, was at the time of closing, when [the Spaniards] came to land, when they were seen once again.[4]

And then [the stewards] hastened to come to inform Moctezuma. When he heard of it, then he speedily sent messengers. Thus he thought — thus was it thought — that this was Topiltzin Quetzalcoatl who had come to land. For it was in their hearts that he would come, that he would come to land, just to find his mat, his seat.[5] For he had traveled there [eastward][6] when he departed. And [Moctezuma] sent

---

Injc ei capitulo: vncan mjtoa in tlein ic tlanaoati Motecuçoma in jquac oqujcac intlatol, in iehoantin in qujttaque acalli in achto valla.

In motecuçoma, njman ie ic q'nnaoatia in Cuetlaxtecatl, yoan in jzqujntin: qujmjlhuj. Xitlanaoaticã, ma tlapielo, in noviã atenco; injc mjtoa. Nauhtlan Toztlan, mjctlanquauhtla: in campa ie qujçaqujvi:

njmã ic iaque in calpixque, tlanaoatique injc tlapieloia.

Auh in motecuçoma: qujncentlali in jtecuioan, Cioacoatl, Tlilpotonquj, Tlacochcalcatl, Quappiaztzin, Ticociaoacatl, Quetzalaztatzin, Vitznaoatlailotlac, hecatenpatiltzin: qujncaqujti in tlatolli, yoan qujmjttiti, qujmjxpanti in qujoalcujque cozcatl:

qujmjlhuj. Ca oticmaviçoque in matlalteuxivitl, vel mopiaz, in tlatlatique vel qujpiazque: intla centetl qujchitonizque tocacal, topipilhoan, titeheoan.

Auh njman ie mocuepa in xivitl, ie imonamjcioc in matlactli omei tochtli: auh ie tlamjznequj, ie itzonqujzian in xivitl omei tochtli, in qujçaco, in ie no ceppa ittoque.

Auh njman qujnonotztivetzico in Motecuçoma, in oqujcac, njman iciuhca tlaioa, in iuh qujma, in iuh moma, ca iehoatl in topiltzin Quetzalcoatl in oqujçaco: ca iuh catca iniollo in çan oallaz, in çan qujçaqujuh, qujoalmatiz in jpetl, in jcpal: ipampa ca vmitztia, in jquac ia. Auh in qujmjoa macujltin, in qujnamjqujtivi, in qujtlamamacativi: in teiacantia Teuoa, in jtecutoca, in jpiltoca Joalli ichan. Injc vme

---

1. Cf. Bernardino de Sahagún, *Historia general de las cosas de Nueva España* (Mexico, D.F.: Editorial Pedro Robredo, 1938; hereafter referred to as Sahagún, Robredo ed.), Vol. II, p. 330; also James Cooper Clark, *Codex Mendoza* (London: Waterlow & Sons, 1938), Vol. I, p. 96. For many of these titles a satisfactory English equivalent is difficult to suggest.

2. Cf. Seler, *Einige Kapitel*, p. 460; also corresponding Spanish text: *"pagarla an los que tienen cargo de guardar la recamara."*

3. Before *omei* in the Aztec text, read *matlactli*.

4. Arrival of Cortés in 1519.

5. Garibay (Sahagún, Garibay ed., Vol. IV, p. 86) translates the passage thus: *"Así estaba en su corazón: venir sólo, salir acá; vendrá para conocer su sitio de trono y solio."*

6. Cf. corresponding Spanish text.

five [emissaries] to go to meet him, to go to give him gifts. The first was the *teohua*, whose lordly name, whose princely name was Yoalli ichan. Second was the ruler of Tepoztlan. Third was Tiçaua. Fourth was the ruler of Ueuetlan. Fifth was Ueicamecatl eca.[7]

Tepuztecatl. Injc ei, tiçaoa. Inic navi vevetecatl. Injc macujlli Veicamecatl heca.

---

7. Sahagún, Garibay ed., Vol. IV, p. 86: "*Los guiaba un sacerdote, el que tenía a cargo y bajo su nombre el santuario de Yohualichan. El segundo, el de Tepoztlan; el tercero, el de Tizatlan; el cuarto el de Huehuetlan y el quinto, el de Mictlan grande.*"

Fourth Chapter, in which is told that which Moctezuma commanded[1] when he knew how the Spaniards had just returned. They came the second time with Don Hernando Cortés.

He said to them: "Come, O ye brave ocelot warriors, come! It is said that our lord hath at last come to land. Meet him. Listen well; use your ears well. What he will say you will bring back well in your ears. Behold wherewith you will arrive [before] our lord."

[First was] the array of Quetzalcoatl:[2] a serpent mask of turquoise [mosaic] work;[3] a quetzal feather head fan;[4] a plaited neck band of green stone beads, in the midst of which lay a golden disc;[5] and a shield with [bands of] gold crossing each other, or with [bands of] gold crossing [bands of] seashells, [with] spread quetzal feathers about the [lower] edge and with a quetzal feather flag;[6] and a mirror upon the small of the back,[7] with quetzal feathers; and this mirror for the small of the back was as though provided with a shield of turquoise [mosaic]—encrusted with turquoise, glued with turquoise; and there were green stone neck bands, on which were golden shells; and then the turquoise spear thrower, which was entirely of turquoise with a sort of serpent's head; it had the head of a serpent;[8] and there were obsidian sandals.

Secondly they went to give him the array of Tezcatlipoca: a headpiece of feathers, with stars of gold;[9]

Injc nauj capitulo: vncan mjtoa in tlein ic tlaonaoati Motecuçoma, in oqujma in quenjn çan oalmocuepque Españoles, injc vppa oallaque, iehoatl in don hernando Cortes.

Qujmjlhuj tla xioalhujan moceloqujchtle, tla xioalhujan qujl iequene oqujçaco in totecujo tla xicnamjqujti, vel xitlacaqujcan, vel xinacaçocan, tlein qujtoz, vel nacaztli in anqujoalcujzque: izcatquj ic itech amacizque in totecujo,

iehoatl in jtlatquj Quetzalcoatl: coaxaiacatl, xiuhtica tlachioalli, quetzalapanecaiotl, chalchiuhcozcapetlatl nepantla mantiuh teucujtlacomalli, yoan centetl chimalli, teucujtlatica nenepanjuhquj, anoço teucujtlatica epnepanjuhquj, quetzaltençouhquj, yoã quetzalpanio; yoan tezcacujtlapilli quetzallo: auh inin tezcacujtlapilli, iuhqujn xiuhchimallo tlaxiuhtzacutli, xiuhtica tlatzacutli, tlaxiuhçalolli, yoan chalchiuhcuecuextli, teucujtlacoiollotoc: njman ie iehoatl xioatlatl, çan motqujtica xivitl, iuhqujn coatzontecometica, coatzontecome, yoan itzcactli.

Injc vntlamantli qujmacato, iehoatl in jtlatquj catca Tezcatlipuca: hivitzoncalli, coztic teucujtlatica

---

1. *Tlaonaoati:* read *tlanauati.*

2. Seler, *Einige Kapitel,* p. 461, says: "*In Wahrheit ist dies die Tracht Xiuhtecutlis.*"

3. Cf. Eduard Seler, *Gesammelte Abhandlungen zur Amerikanischen Sprach- und Alterthumskunde* (Berlin: A. Asher und Co., 1904), Vol. II, p. 413, where a figure corresponds to the description in the corresponding Spanish text: "*una mascara labrada de mosayco de turquesas tenja esta mascara labrada de las mjsmas piedras vna culebra doblada y retorcida cuya dublez era el pico de la nariz y lo retorcido yua hasta la frente era como lomo de la nariz luego se diujdia la cola de la cabeça y la cabeça con parte del cuerpo yua por sobre el vn ojo de manera que hazia ceja y la cola con parte del cuerpo yua por sobre el otro ojo y hazia otra ceja.*"

4. Corresponding Spanish text: "*Estaua esta mascara enxerida en vna corona alta y grãde llena de plumas ricas largas y muy hermosas de manera que ponjendose la corona sobre la cabeça se ponja la mascara en la cara.*" See the name-glyph for Apanecatl in Codex Boturini.

5. The corresponding Spanish text reads: "*lleuaua por joel vna medalla de oro redonda y ancha estaua asida con nueue sartales de piedras preciosas que echadas al cuello cubrian los hombros y todo el pecho.*"

6. *Ibid.:* "*lleuauã tanbien vna rodela grande bordada de piedras preciosas con vnas vandas de oro que llegauan de arriba abaxo por toda ella: y otras vandas de perlas atrauesadas sobre las de oro de arriba abaxo por toda ella y los espacios que haziã estas vandas los quales eran como mallas de red yvan puestos vnos sapitos de oro tenja esta rodela vnos rapacejos en lo baxo yva asido en la rodela vna vandera que salia deste la manjxa de la rodela hecha de plumas ricas.*"

7. *Ibid.:* "*vna medalla grande hecha de obra de mosaico que la lleuaua atada y ceñjda sobre los lomos.*"

8. *Ibid.:* "*vn cetro como cetro de obispo todo labrado de obra de mosayco de tosquesas [sic] y la buelta de arriba era vna cabeça de vna culebra rebuelta o enroscada.*"

9. *Ibid.:* "*vna cabellera hecha de pluma rica que colgaua por la parte detras hasta cerca de la cintura estaua sembrada toda de estrellas de oro.*"

and his golden shell earplugs;[10] and a necklace of seashells; and the breast ornament decorated with small seashells, with a fringe sown with them; and a sleeveless jacket all painted with a design, with eyelets on its border and a feathered fringe;[11] and a cape with blue knots, called *tzitzilli*, grasped by the corners in order to tie it across the back;[12] also over it, a [mosaic] mirror lying on the small of the back;[13] and — still another thing — golden shells bound on the calves of the legs; and one [more] thing, white sandals.

Third was what was called the adornment of the lord of Tlalocan: the heron feather headdress all of quetzal feathers, entirely of quetzal feathers — rather blue-green, overspread blue-green — and over it [a band of] shells crossing [a band of] gold; and his green stone serpent-shaped earplugs;[14] his sleeveless jacket with a design of green stone; his neck ornament, a plaited, green stone neck band, also with a golden disc; also with a mirror at the small of the back, as was said; and likewise with rattles; the cape with red rings on the border[15] which was tied on; and golden shells for the ankles; and his serpent staff of turquois [mosaic] workmanship.

Fourth, what likewise was the array of this Quetzalcoatl was yet another thing: a peaked ocelot skin cap with pheasant feathers; a very large green stone at the top, fixed at the tip;[16] and round, turquoise [mosaic] earplugs,[17] from which were hanging curved, golden seashells; and a plaited green stone neck band in the midst of which there was also a golden disc; and a cape with a red border which was tied on; likewise, the golden shells required for his ankles; and a shield with a golden disc in the center, and spread quetzal feathers along its [lower] rim, also with a quetzal feather flag;[18] and the curved staff of the wind god, hooked at the top,[19] overspread with white green stone stars;[20] and his foam sandals.

cicitlallo, yoan itecujtlacoiolnacoch: yoan chipolcozcatl; elpan cozcatl, cilin ic tlatlatlamachilli, ic tenchaiaoac; yoan xicolli, çan tlacujlolli, in jtenjxio, hivitica tenpoçonquj: yoan centetl tilmatli, xiuhtlalpilli, motocaiotiaia, tzitzilli, qujoalnacazvitzana injc mocujtlalpia; no ipan mantiuh tezcacujtlapilli: yoã oc no centlamãtli, teucujtlacoioilli, itlanjtzco molpiaia, yoã centlamantli, iztac cactli.

Injc etlamantli, iehoatl in jnechichioal catca, Tlalocã tecutli: quetzalaztatzontli, çã moca quetzalli, motqujtica quetzalli, iuhqujn xoxoqujvi, xoxoqujuhtimanj: auh in jpan teucujtlatica epnepanjuhquj: yoan ichalchiuhcoanacoch: ixicol, tlachalchiuhcujlolli: in jcozquj chalchiuhcozcapetlatl no teucujtlacomallo, no tezcacujtlapile, in juhquj omjto, no tzitzile; tenchilnaoacaio in tilmatli injc molpia: yoan icxicoiolli teucujtlatl: yoan icoatopil, xiuhtica tlachiuhtli.

Injc nauhtlamantli çan ie no iehoatl in jtlatquj catca Quetzalcoatl, ie ne centlamantli: ocelocopilli, coxoliio; veitepul in chalchivitl yicpac ca ic quatzacutica; yoan xiuhnacochtli, malacachtic, itech pilcatica teucujtlaepcololli; yoan chalchiuhcozcapetlatl, çan no teucujtlacomalli in jnepantla mantia; yoan tilmatli tentlapallo injc molpia; çan no teucujtlacoioilli in jcxi itech monequja: yoan chimalli teucujtlatica itixapo, quetzaltençouhquj, no quetzalpanio: yoã hecaxonecujlli, quacoltic, iztac chalchivitl injc citlallotoc yoan ipoçolcac.

---

10. *Ibid.*: "*vnas orejeras de oro que lleuauã colgados vnos cascauellitos de oro y sartales de cãracolitos marinos blancos y hermosos destos sartales colgaua vn cuero que era como peto y lleuauanle cenjdo* [sic] *de manera que cubria todo el pecho hasta la cintura, lleuaua este peto muchos caracolitos sembrados y colgados por todo el.*"

11. *Ibid.*: "*vn cosete de tela blanca pintado la orilla de abaxo deste cosete yva bordada com plumas blancas tres listas por todo el rededor.*"

12. *Ibid.*: "*vna manta rica la tela della era vn açul claro y toda labrada encima de muchos labores de vn açul muy fino llamause esta manta tzitzilli esta manta se ponja por la cintura atada por las esqujnas al cuerpo.*"

13. *Ibid.*: "*vna medalla de mosayco, atada al cuerpo sobre los lomos.*"

14. *Ibid.*: "*vnas orejeras de chalchiujtl, anchas que tenja dẽtro vnas culebritas de chalchiujtes.*"

15. *Tenchilnaoacaio*: read *tenchilnauaio*.

16. Corresponding Spanish text: "*vna mjtra de cuero de tigre, y colcagaua* [sic] *d ela mjtra, sobre las espaldas, vna capilla grande, hecha de plumas de cueruo, lleuaua la mjtra vn chalchiujtl grãde: y redondo, en la punta.*"

17. *Ibid.*: "*de mosayco de turquesas.*"

18. *Ibid.*: "*la qual rodela estaua bordada com plumas ricas en lo baxo de la rodella* [sic] *salia vna vanda de plumas ricas.*"

19. *Ibid.*: "*vn baculo labrado de mosayco de turquesas y en la buelta de arriba puestas vnas piedras ricas o perlas enmjnentes en lo alto de arriba.*"

20. Literally, white green stone. The term *chalchiuitl*, often translated "jade" or "jadeite," included various kinds of stones. Hence our translation has adopted the term "green stone."

These were all the things called the gods' array, which became the things carried by the messengers, and there were still many more things which they bore as their greeting [gifts] — the shell-shaped headpiece of gold, with pendant parrot feathers;[21] the golden conical cap,[22] etc.

Thereupon baskets were filled; wooden frames for carrying burdens on the back were arranged. And Moctezuma thereupon commanded the five [messengers] mentioned; he said to them: "Go! Linger nowhere! Pray to our lord the god; say unto him: 'Thy governor Moctezuma hath sent us. Here is what he giveth thee, for [the god] hath come to reach his humble home in Mexico.'"

And when they had gone to reach the coast, [the water folk] ferried them across; they took them by boat across to Xicalanco. Once again they departed from there by boat; the water folk took them. Everything was placed, was heaped in the boats; they filled the boats with goods. And when the boats were filled with things, thereupon they departed. They betook themselves to the water; they went to reach the [Spaniards'] boat; they approached their boat.

Then [the Spaniards] addressed them: "Who are you? Whence have you come?"

Then [the messengers] thus answered them: "We have come from there — Mexico."

Again [the Spaniards] addressed them: "Perhaps not. Perhaps you only flee from there. Perhaps you only pretend it. Perhaps you make sport of us."

But when they were assured, when they were satisfied, then they hooked the prow of the boat with an iron pole, in order to draw [the messengers] toward them. Then also they set out a ladder.

Oca izqujtlamãtli in, in moteneoa teutlatqujtl in intlatquj mochiuhtia titlanti, yoan oc cenca mjec tlamantli in qujtqujque in intenamjquja Teucujtlaquatecciztli toztlapilollo, teucujtlacopilli, etc.

Niman ie ic tlatanatemalo, tlacacaxchichioalo. Auh in omoteneuhque macujltin; njman ie ic qujnnaoatia in Motecuçoma: qujmjlhuj. Tla xivian, ma cana anvecauhti, xicmotlatlauhtilican in totecujo in teutl: xiqujlhujcan, ca otechalioa in motechiuhcauh Motecuçoma: izcatquj mjtzalmomaqujlia, ca omaxitico in jchãtzinco mexico:

Auh in oacito atenco, qujmõpanavique, acaltica qujmonvicaque in xicalanco: ie no ceppa vncan oneoaq̃ acaltica qujnvicaque in atlaca, moch onmacalaquj, onmacalten, conacaltenque in tlatqujtl. Auh in ontlaacaltemaloc, njman ie ic vi, ommatoctique, itech onacito in jmacal, itech compachoque in jmacal.

njmã qujnoalilhujque. Ac ameoan? campa anoallaque?

njman iuh qujnnanqujlique. Ca vmpa tioallaque in Mexico:

oc ceppa qujnoalilhujque. Acaçomo, aço çan vmpa anmotlamja, aço çan anqujpiquj, aço çã toca anmocacaiaoa.

Auh in ovel yiollo macic, in oiniollopachiuh. Niman ic qujoaliacatzopinjque in acalli, tepuztopiltica, ic qujnoaltilinjque: njman no quioalquetzque ecaoaztli.

---

21. *Ibid.*: "*vna mjtra de oro hecha a manera de caracol marisco cõ vnos rapacejos de plumas ricas que colgauan hazia las espaldas.*"

22. *Ibid.*: "*otra mjtra llana.*"

Fifth Chapter, in which it is told what came to pass when Moctezuma's messengers entered there into Don Hernando Cortés's boat.

Thereupon they climbed up. In their arms they each carried the array [of the gods]. When they had proceeded to climb up into the boat, each one of the group separately ate the earth before the Captain. Thereupon they prayed to him; they said to him:

"May the god deign to hear: his governor, Moctezuma, who watcheth over Mexico for him, prayeth unto him. He sayeth: 'The god hath suffered fatigue; he is weary.'"

Thereupon they arrayed the Captain. They put him into the turquoise [mosaic] serpent mask with which went the quetzal feather head fan, and with which went, with which were inserted, with which went suspended the green stone serpent earplugs. And they put him into the sleeveless jacket; they clad him in the sleeveless jacket. And they put the necklace on him — the plaited green stone neck band in the midst of which went the golden disc. To his back they bound the mirror for the small of the back; also on his back they placed the cape named *tzitzilli*. And about [the calf of] his leg they placed the green stone band with the golden shells.[1] And they gave him, they laid upon his arm[2] the shield with [bands of] gold crossing [bands of] shells, on whose lower rim went quetzal feathers outspread; on which went a quetzal feather flag. And before him they laid the obsidian sandals.

And the other three adornments, the array of the gods, they only placed in order, placed in rows before him.

And when this had been done, the Captain said to them: "Are these all your [gifts of] greeting, your [gifts for] approaching one?"

They answered [the Spaniards]: "These are all with which we have come, O our lord."

Then the Captain commanded that they be bound. They put irons on their ankles and their necks. This

Injc macujlli capitulo: vncan mjtoa in tlein muchiuh, in jquac ititlanoan motecuçoma in vmpa callacque in jacalco don hernando Cortes.

Niman ie ic tleco, qujnanapalotivi in tlatqujtl: in otlecoto acalco ceceniaca ontlalquatimanj yixpan in capitan: Niman ie ic contlatlauhtia: qujlhujque:

Ma qujmocaqujlti in teutl: ca qujoalmotlatlauhtilia in jtechiuhcauh Motecuçoma in cõmotlapielilia mexico; ca conjtoa. Oqujmjhiovilti, oqujmociavilti in teutl:

njman ie ic qujchichioa in capitan vel iehoatl conaqujque in xiuhcoaxaiacatl, itech ietiuh in quetzalapanecaiotl, yoan itech ieietiuh, itech aactiuh, itech pipilcatiuh chalchiuhcoanacochtli: yoan conaqujque xicolli, conxicoltique, yoan concozcatique in chalchiuhcozcapetlatl nepantla mantiuh in teucujtlacomalli, ic conxillancujtlalpique in tezcacujtlapilli, no ic contzinapanque in tilmatli in jtoca tzitzilli, yoan icxic contlalilique in chalchiuhtecuecuextli teucujtlacoiollo: yoan conmacaque imac cõmanjlique chimalli teucujtlatica nenepanjuhquj, yoan epnepanjuhcaio, quetzaltençouhtiuh quetzalpaniotiuh: yoan ixpã contemjlique itzcactli.

Auh in oc etlamantli nechichioalli, teutlatqujtl, çan ixpan contecpãque, convipanque:

auh in ie iuhquj, qujmjlhuj in capitã. Cujx ie ixqujch in, in amotenamjquja, in amotetechacia?

qujnnanqujlique ca ie ixqujch injc tioallatiaque totecue.

Niman tlanaoati in capitan injc ilpiloque, tepoztli imjcxic qujntlalilique, yoan inquechtlan: in ie iuh-

---

1. Described earlier as a wrist ornament.   2. The left arm, in the corresponding Spanish text.

done, they then shot the great lombard gun. And the messengers, when this [happened], indeed fainted away and swooned; they each fell; each one, swaying, fell; they knew no more. And the Spaniards raised each one, raised each one so that he sat; they made them drink wine. Thereupon they gave them food; they made them eat. Thus they restored them; thus they regained strength.

And when this had come to pass, then the Captain said to them: "Hear! I have known, I have heard that it is said that these Mexicans are very strong, very brave, great overthrowers. If there is one Mexican, he can pursue, drive on, overcome, turn back even ten or even twenty of his foes. And now I wish to be satisfied; I wish to see you; I wish to test you—how strong you are, how powerful you are."

Then he gave them leather shields, and iron swords, and iron lances.

"And very early in the morning, when the dawn is about to form, we shall contend against one another, we shall fight one another as equals. By comparing we shall know who will already fall down."

They replied to the Captain; they said to him: "May the lord hear: his governor Moctezuma hath by no means commanded us to do this. We have come only to greet, to salute [our lord]. What the lord requireth is not our charge. And if we should thus act, would not Moctezuma therefor be mightily wrathful? Would he not destroy us?"

Then the Captain said: "No; for it will come to pass. I wish to see, I wish to marvel at [your prowess]. For it hath gone to be known in Castile that it is said that you are very strong, you are very brave. Eat while it is yet early dawn; while it is yet early dawn I also shall eat. Indeed prepare yourselves."

quj njman ic qujtlazque in tomaoac tlequjqujztli: auh in titlanti in jquac in vel iolmjcque, yoan çoçotlaoaque, vehuetzque, nenecujliuhtivetzque, aocmo qujmatque: auh in españoles qujmeeuhq̄ qujmeeoatitlalique, qujmonjitique vino: njmã ie ic qujntlamaca, qujntlaqualtique, ic imjhio qujcujque, ic oalihiocujque:

auh in ie iuhquj in, njman qujmjlhuj in capitan. Tla xiccaqujcan, onjcma, onjccac, qujlmach in iehoantin mexica cenca chicaoaque, cenca tiacaoan, cenca maiavinj, intla ce mexicatl vel qujntocaz, vel qujntopeoaz, vel qujnpanaviz, vel qujnteputztiz in manel matlactin, in manel noço centecpantin in jiaovan. Auh in axcan noiollo pachiviznequj, namechittaznequj, namechieiecoznequj, in quenjn anchicaoaque, in quenjn antlapalivi:

njmã ic qujnoalmacac eoachimalli, yoan tepuzmacquavitl, yoã tepuztopilli:

auh inin vel oc iovatzinco, tlavizcalpan in muchioaz, in titomaiztlacozque, titoneneuhcavizque, tinevivican tlamatizque, ac ie tlanj vetziz:

qujnanqujlique in Capitan: qujlhujque. Tla qujmocaqujtin tlacatl, achcamo ic technaoati in jtechiuhcauh in Motecuçoma; ca çan tiqujxcavico in tictociauhquechilico, in tictotlapalhujco, ca amo tonaoatil in qujmonequjltia tlacatl: auh intla iuh ticchioazque, cujx amo cenca ic qualaniz in Motecuçoma, amo ic techtlatlatiz.

Niman qujto in capitan ca amo ca ça mochioaz njqujttaznequj, njcmaviçoznequj ca in omachiztito in castillan qujl cenca anchicaoaque, antiiacaoan, ma oc veca ioac in xitlaquacan, oc no ioan in njtlaquaz, ma vel ximochichioacã.

Sixth Chapter, in which it is told how Moctezuma's messengers returned here to Mexico. They came to relate to Moctezuma that which they had seen.

Thereupon [Cortés] left them; [the Spaniards] let them descend to their boats. And when they had climbed down to their boats, then they rowed vigorously. Each one rowed as hard as he could; some paddled with their hands.

With all their force they fled. They came saying to one another: "O warriors, [exert] all your strength! Row vigorously! Let us not be forced to do something [evil]; let nothing [evil] befall us!"

Speedily in the midst of the water they came hastening to the place called Xicalanco; there they no more than quickly restored their strength, so that once again they might hasten along with all their force. Then they came to reach Tecpantlayacac. Thereupon also they hastened along, they fled along. They came hastening to Cuetlaxtlan. Likewise they quickly left, [having] there restored their strength.

And the ruler of Cuetlaxtlan said to them: "Rest yet but a brief day! Restore your strength!"

But they said to him: "No, we shall only go hastening on. We shall warn the lord, the ruler Moctezuma. We shall tell him what we have seen, which is very terrifying, of which the like hath never been seen. Wilt thou perchance already be the first to hear it?"

Then speedily they set forth to go quickly to reach Mexico. It was deep night when they came to reach it; they entered it quite by night.

And while this was happening, [Moctezuma] enjoyed no sleep, no food. No one spoke more to him. Whatsoever he did, it was as if he were in torment. Ofttimes it was as if he sighed, became weak, felt weak. No longer did he enjoy what tasted good, what gave one contentment, what gladdened one.

Wherefore he said: "What will now befall us? Who indeed standeth [in command]? Alas, until now, I. In great torment is my heart; as if it were washed in chili water it indeed burneth, it smarteth. Where in truth [may we go], O our lord?"

Then [the messengers] demanded of those who

Injc chiquacen capitulo: vncã mjtoa, in quenjn ititlanoan Motecuçoma, oalmocuepque in njcan mexico qujlhujco in motecuçoma in qujttaque.

Niman ie ic qujncauh, qujnoaltemovique in jmacalco: auh in ovaltemoque acalco, njman ie ic tequjtlaneloa, ontetemj in tlaneloa, cequjntin matlaneloa.

centlaquauh oalmotlaloa, qujmolhujtivitze, tiacaoane ixqujch amotlapal, xitequjtlanelocan, ma itla njcan taxti ma itla njcan topan muchiuh

iciuhca acitivetzico in atl iitic in jtocaiocan xicalanco, çan tequjtl vncan oalihiocujtiqujzq̃, ic ie no ceppa centlaquauh oaltotoca: njman acico in tecpan tlaiacac, njman ie no ic oalmeoaltia, oalmotlaloa, acitivetzico in cuetlaxtlan, çan no oalqujztiqujzque, vncan ihiocujque.

Auh in cuetlaxtecatl qujmjlhuj ma oc cemjlhujtzintli ximocevicã ma oc amjhio xiccujcan.

Auh qujlhujque, ca amo ca çan ticiuhtivi tictononochilizque in tlacatl tlatoanj Motecuçoma, tictolhujlizque in tlein otiqujttaque, in cenca temamauhti, in aic iuhquj omottac, cujx ie cuel ie teachto, toconcaqujz:

njman iciuhca oalpeuhque, acitivetzico in mexico, çan ioaltica in acico, çan oalioalcalacque.

Auh in jquac in aoqujcochiz, aoqujtlaqual qujmatia, aoc ie qujlhujaia in çaço tlein qujchioaia, ça iuhqujn nentlamatia, iuhqujn achica elcicivi, mociauhquetza, mociauhpoa, aoc tle velic, aoc tle tepac, aoc tle teavialti ipan qujmatia,

ipampa in qujtoaia, tlein ic topan muchioaz, ac nel icac, ha ieppa nehoatl, vel patzmjquj in noiollo, iuhqujnma chilatequjlo, vel toneoa chichinaca campa nel totecue.

Niman qujmõnaoatique in qujpia in qujtzontlan

guarded; they said to those who stood watch over his principal possessions: "Even if he sleepeth, tell him: 'They whom thou hast sent into the midst of the water have come.'"

But when they went to tell him, he then said: "I shall not hear it here; I shall hear it there in the Coacalli.[1] There let them go." And he gave a command: he said: "Let two of the captives be covered with chalk."

And then the messengers went there to the Coacalli. Moctezuma also [went].

Thereupon before them the captives were slain; [they] cut open the captives' breasts; with their blood they sprinkled the messengers. For this reason did they do so, that they had gone to very perilous places; that they had gone to see, to look into the faces, the heads of the gods — had verily spoken to them.

tlapia qujmonjlhujque intla mocochitia xicmolhujlican ca ovallaque in tiqujnmotitlanj atl itic.

Auh in oconjlhujto: njman qujoalito. Amo njcan njccaqujz, vmpa njccaqujz in coacalco, ma vmpa vian, yoan oallanaoati: qujoalito: ma ontetiçavilo in mamalti.

Auh njman vmpa iaque in coacalco in titlanti: no iehoatl in motecuçomatzin,

njmã ie ic imjxpan mjcoa qujmeltetequj in mamalti, in jmezio ic qujmonatzelhujaia in titlanti (ipampa in juh qujchiuhque in, ca cenca ovican in ovia ca oqujmjttato, imjxco imjcpac otlachiato, vel oqujnnotzque in teteu.

1. Cf. Anderson and Dibble, *Book VIII*, p. 44.

Seventh Chapter, in which is related the account by which the messengers who had gone to see the boats reported to Moctezuma.

And when this was done, they thereupon reported to Moctezuma; so they told him how they had gone marveling, and they showed him what [the Spaniards'] food was like.

And when he had so heard what the messengers reported, he was terrified, he was astounded. And much did he marvel at their food.

Especially did it cause him to faint away when he heard how the gun, at [the Spaniards'] command, discharged [the shot]; how it resounded as if it thundered when it went off. It indeed bereft one of strength; it shut off one's ears. And when it discharged, something like a round pebble came forth from within. Fire went showering forth; sparks went blazing forth. And its smoke smelled very foul; it had a fetid odor which verily wounded the head. And when [the shot] struck a mountain, it was as if it were destroyed, dissolved. And a tree was pulverized; it was as if it vanished; it was as if someone blew it away.

All iron was their war array. In iron they clothed themselves. With iron they covered their heads. Iron were their swords. Iron were their crossbows. Iron were their shields. Iron were their lances.

And those which bore them upon their backs, their deer, were as tall as roof terraces.

And their bodies were everywhere covered; only their faces appeared. They were very white; they had chalky faces; they had yellow hair, though the hair of some was black. Long were their beards; they also were yellow. They were yellow-bearded. [The Negroes' hair] was kinky, it was curly.[1]

And their food was like fasting food[2] — very large, white; not heavy like [tortillas]; like maize stalks, good-tasting as if of maize stalk flour; a little sweet, a little honeyed. It was honeyed to eat; it was sweet to eat.[3]

Ic chicome capitulo: vncan mjtoa in tlatolli injc qujnonotzato in Motecuçoma, in titlanti in qujttato acalli.

Auh in ie iuhquj, njman ie ic qujnonotza in Motecuçoma iuh qujlhujque in juhquj oqujmaviçoto, yoan qujttitique in juhquj intlaqual.

Auh in oqujcac in juh tlanonotzque in titlanti cenca momauhti, mjçavi, yoan cenca qujmaviço in intlaqual:

oc cenca iehoatl in qujiolmjcti in oqujcac in quenjn vetzi in jnnaoatil in tlequjqujztli, iuhq'n tlatlatzinj ic caqujzti in jquac vetzi, vel teçotlauh, motzatzaqua in tonacaz. Auh in jquac vetzi iuhqujn telolotli oalqujça yitic, tlepipixauhtiuh, chichitocatiuh: auh in jpocio cenca hiiac, xoqujiac, vel tetzonvitec: auh in qujmotla tepetl iuhq'n xitinj, xixitica: auh in quavitl qujmotlatetextia, iuhqujn atetlachialti, iuhqujn aca conilpitza:

çan muchi tepuztli in iniautlatquj, tepuztli in cõmaquja, tepuztli in conaquja intzontecon, tepuztli in inmaquauh, tepuztli in intlavitol, tepuztli in inchimal, tepuztli in intopil,

auh in qujnmama in inmaçaoa, iuhqujn tlapantli ic quaquauhtique.

yoan novian qujmjlivi in innacaio, çanjo neci in inxaiac, cenca iztac, ixtetenextique, tzoncoztique, tel cequj tliltic in intzon, viiac in intentzon no coztic, tētzōcoztique, cocototztique ocolochtic:

auh in intlaqual iuhqujn tlacatlaqualli, veitepul, iztac, amo etic iuhqujn tlaçolli, iuhqujn ovaquavitl, iuhqujn ovaquauhtextli injc aviac, achi tzopelic, achi nenecutic monecticticaqua, motzopelicaqua:

---

1. Corresponding Spanish text: *"tenjan las caras blancas, y los ojos garços, y los cabellos rojos, y las barbas largas: y de como venjã algunos negros entre ellos, que tenjã los cabellos crespos, y prietos...."*

2. In a footnote in Seler, *Einige Kapitel*, p. 469, Lehmann and Krickeberg suggest that the natives marveled at the Spaniards' food be-cause if they were gods their fare should have been blood and human hearts. *Tlacatlaqualli* can also be translated as "human food" (cf. Sahagún, Garibay ed., Vol. IV, p. 93). Seler, *Einige Kapitel*, p. 470, has *Fürstenspeise.*

3. *Monecticticaqua*: read *monecuticaqua.*

And their dogs were very large. They had ears folded over; great dragging jowls. They had fiery eyes — blazing eyes; they had yellow eyes — fiery yellow eyes. They had thin flanks — flanks with ribs showing. They had gaunt stomachs. They were very tall. They were nervous; they went about panting, with tongues hanging. They were spotted like ocelots; they were varicolored.

And when Moctezuma so heard, he was much terrified. It was as if he fainted away. His heart saddened; his heart failed him.

auh in jmjtzcuioan veveipopul, nacazcuecuelpachtique, tenvivilaxpopul, ixtletletique, ixtletlesuchtique, ixcocoztique, ixtlecocoztique, xillanvicoltique, xillāoacaltique, xillancapitztique vel quaquauhtique, amo tlaca manj, neneciuhtinemj, nenenepilotinemj, ocelocujcujltique, mocujcujloque.

Auh in oiuh qujcac in Motecuçoma, cenca momauhti iuhqujn iolmjc, moioltequjpacho, moiollacoma.

Eighth Chapter, in which it is told how Moctezuma sent magicians,[1] wizards,[2] sorcerers[3] so that they might bring about [evil] to the Spaniards.

Then at that time Moctezuma sent emissaries. He sent all evil men — soothsayers, magicians. And he sent the elders, the hardy [warriors], the brave [warriors] to secure [for the Spaniards] all the food they would need: turkey hens, eggs, white tortillas, and what they might desire. And in order that their hearts might be well satisfied, they were to look to them well. He sent captives so that they might be prepared: perchance [the Spaniards] would drink their blood. And thus did the messengers do.

But when [the Spaniards] beheld this, much were they nauseated. They spat; they closed their eyes tight, they shut their eyes; they shook their heads. And [the emissaries] had soaked the food in blood, they had covered it with blood. Much did it revolt them; it nauseated them. For strongly did it reek of blood.

And Moctezuma had acted thus because he thought them gods, he took them to be gods, he worshipped them as gods. They were called, they were named "gods come from heaven." And the black ones were said to be dirty gods.[4]

Later they ate white tortillas, maize kernels, eggs, turkey hens, and all manner of fruit — custard apple,[5]

Injc chicuei capitulo: vncan mjtoa in quenjn iehoatl motecuçoma, qujmjoa in nanaoalti in tlatlacateculo, in tetlachivianjme, injc itla impan qujchioazque in Españoles.

Niman iquac tlaioa in Motecuçoma in qujmjoa mocheoantin in atlaca, in tlaciuhque, in nanaoalti: yoan qujmjoa in achcacauhti, chicaoaque, in tiacaoã in jpan tlatozque in jxqujch intech monequjz in qualonj in totoli in totoltetl, in jztac tlaxcalli: yoã in tlein qujtlanjzque, yoan injc ça oc vel pachiviz in iniollo, vel qujmjttazque, qujmjoa in mamalti, ic monemachti, cujx qujzque in jmezço: auh iuh qujchiuhque in titlanti.

Auh in jquac oqujttaque: cenca motlaeltique, chichicha, ixtetenmotzoloa, ihicopi, motzontecõvivixoa: auh in tlaqualli eztica catzelhujque, queezvique, cenca invic eoac, qujntlaelti: iehica ca cenca xoqujiac in eztli.

Auh injc iuh qujchiuh motecuçoma, ca qujnteuma, teteu impan qujnma qujnteutocac: ic notzaloque, ic tocaiotiloque, teteu ilhujcac vitze: auh in tliltique teucacatzacti mjtoque,

qujn iehoatl qujquaque iztac tlaxcalli, tlatzincujtl, totoltetl, totoli, auh in ie ixqujch xochiqualli, quauh-

---

1. In "Paralipómenos de Sahagún," *Tlalocan,* Vol. II, No. 2 (1946), p. 170, Garibay refers to the "'*duplicación de la persona*' o el '*desdoblamiento*'" in regard to *naualli.* The term may be related etymologically to *naui* (4) — a quadruple personality; an archaic verb *nauali, nauala* (to fool or dissimulate, as in magic tricks); or Maya-Quiche *na, nao, naua* (wisdom, science, magic). Garibay favors the second possibility (*nauali, nauala*).

2. *Tlacatecolo:* concerning the term *tlacatecolohuia,* Garibay refers to an *arte de hombre pernicioso,* and quotes Sahagún's phrase (in Sahagún, Robredo ed., Vol. III, p. 33) — "*tiene pacto con el demonio*" (*tlacatecolotl*) ("Paralipómenos de Sahagún," Vol. II, No. 2, p. 174). In "Paralipómenos de Sahagún," *Tlalocan,* Vol. I, No. 4 (1944), p. 309, he refers to *tlacatecolotl* as "*brujo,*" "*mago,*" "*hombre que perjudica a la gente, hombre pernicioso*"; "*presagiaban y procuraban la muerte.*" There is a discussion of the etymology of the term.

3. *Tlaciuhqui:* we have previously used the term "soothsayer." In "Paralipómenos de Sahagún," Vol. 2, No. 2, p. 171, Garibay, noting that Molina translates the term as *astrólogo,* states: "*La raíz* ciuh, *parece denotar fenómenos meteorológicos,*" and notes the relationship of the term to *teciuhtlazqui,* one who prevents hail from falling. He cites *La población del valle de Teotihuacán,* Vol. II, p. 404.

4. In Seler, *Enige Kapitel,* p. 471, this passage is translated "*die Schwarzen nannte man 'wirklich Schmutzige'*"; Garibay, in Sahagún, Garibay ed., Vol. IV, p. 94: "*los negros, fueron dichos: 'divinos sucios.'*"

5. *Quauhtzapotl:* anona (*Annona cherimolia* Mill.) in Francisco Hernández, *Historia de las plantas de Nueva España* (Mexico, D.F.: Imprenta Universitaria, 1942–46), Vol. I, p. 274. Cf. also Robert L. Dressler, "The Pre-Columbian Cultivated Plants of Mexico," *Botanical Museum Leaflets,* Harvard University, Vol. 16, No. 6 (1953), p. 123.

mamey,[6] yellow sapota,[7] black sapota,[8] sweet potato,[9] manioc,[10] white sweet potato,[11] yellow sweet potato,[12] colored sweet potato, *jícama*,[13] plum,[14] *jobo*,[15] guava,[16] *cuajilote*,[17] avocado,[18] acacia [bean],[19] *tejocote*,[20] American cherry,[21] tuna cactus fruit,[22] mulberry,[23] white cactus fruit,[24] yellow cactus fruit,[25] whitish-red cactus fruit,[26] *pitahaya*,[27] water *pitahaya*.[28] And the deer food was *pipillo*[29] [and] *tlachicaztli*.

And it is said that for this reason did Moctezuma send the magicians, the soothsayers: that they might see of what sort [the Spaniards] were; that they might perhaps use their wizardry upon them, cast a spell over them; that they might perhaps blow upon them, enchant them; that they might cast stones at them; that they might with some words of wizardry utter an incantation over them, so that they might take sick, might die, or else because of it turn back.

But these, when they performed their charge, their duty against the Spaniards, had no power whatsoever. They could do nothing.

Then they hastened to return; they came to tell Moctezuma what they were like, how strong they

tzaputl, teçontzaputl, atztzaputl, totolcujtlatzaputl, camutli, quauhcamutli, poxcauhcamutli xochicamutli, tlapalcamutli, xicama, maçaxocotl, atoiaxocotl, xalxocotl, in quauhxilotl, aoacatl, oaxi, texocotl, in capoli, in nochtli, in amacapuli, iztac nochtli, coznochtli, tlatocnochtli, tzaponochtli, anochtli: auh in maçatlaqualli, pipillo, tlachicaztli:

Auh qujl injc qujmjoa Motecuçoma in nanaoalti, in tlaciuhque, injc qujmjttazque in quenamjque in aço vel qujntlacateculovizque, qujntlachivizque, in aço vel qujmjpitzazque qujnxoxazque in aço oc itla ic qujnmotlazque, in aço itla tlacateculotlatolli, ic qujntlanonochilizque, injc aço cocolizcujzque, mjmjqujzque, in anoce ic ilotizque.

Auh in iehoantin in qujchiuhque in intequjuh, in innaoatil in intechpa españoles, çan njmã avelitque, atle vel qujchiuhque:

niman ic oalmocueptivetzque qujnonotzaco in Motecuçoma injc iuhque, injc chicaoaque, amo tite-

---

6. *Teçontzaputl: mamey (Lucuma mammosa* Gart.) in Sahagún, Garibay ed., Vol. IV, p. 358. In Bernardino de Sahagún, *Histoire générale des choses de la Nouvelle-Espagne*, trans. D. Jourdanet and Rémi Siméon (Paris: G. Masson, 1880), p. 733, n. 2, this explanation appears: "*Les premiers Espagnoles d'Amérique confondirent* [with various sapotas] *le fruit beaucoup plus gros du tetzontzapotl ou lucuma mammosa, de la famille des zapote, qu'ils appellent aujourd'hui* mamey. *C'est probablement le même fruit que les Aztèques connaissaient sous le nom de* tecotzapotl." *Calocarpum mammosum* (L.) Pierre in Dressler, "Pre-Columbian Cultivated Plants," p. 125. Cf. also Sahagún, Garibay ed., Vol. IV, p. 358.

7. *Atztzapotl*: probably the same as *atzapotl*. In Hernández, *Historia de las plantas*, Vol. I, pp. 267–68, this is *Lucuma salicifolia* Kunth. The *atzatzapotl* (yellow sapota) is now generally known as *zapote borracho* (personal communication, Rafael García Granados). Cf. also Sahagún, Garibay ed., Vol. IV, p. 323.

8. *Totolcuitlatzapotl: zapote negro (Diospyros ebenaster* Rotz — Sahagún, Garibay ed., Vol. IV, p. 360).

9. *Camotli*: sweet potato, batata *(Ipomoea batatas* Poir, in Hernández, *Historia de las plantas*, Vol. II, p. 521; *Convolvulus batata* Lam. in Sahagún, Garibay ed., Vol. IV, p. 326).

10. *Quauhcamotli: Manihot esculenta* Crantz in Paul C. Standley, "Trees and Shrubs of Mexico," *Contributions from the United States National Herbarium*, Vol. 23, Pt. 3 (Washington, D.C.: U.S. Government Printing Office, 1920), p. 643. Cf. also Hernández, *Historia de las plantas*, Vol. II, p. 524.

11. *Poxcauhcamotli*: probably sweet potato of white or red skin and interior (Hernández, *Historia de las plantas*, Vol. II, p. 521).

12. *Xochicamotli*: reddish or yellow sweet potato (*ibid.*).

13. *Xicama: Pachyrrhizus erosus* (L.) Urban in Dressler, "Pre-Columbian Cultivated Plants," p. 140. *Pachyrhizus angulatus*. Azteq. "jícama" (Sahagún, Garibay ed., Vol. IV, p. 368).

14. *Maçaxocotl*: plum — *Spondias mombis* sp. (Sahagún, Garibay ed., Vol. IV, p. 341).

15. *Atoyaxocotl: Spondias purpurea* L. in Francisco J. Santamaría,

Diccionario de mejicanismos (Mexico, D.F.: Editorial Porrúa, S. A., 1959), p. 96; *atoyajocote, jobo*. See also Standley, "Trees and Shrubs of Mexico," Pt. 3, p. 656 *sqq*.

16. *Xalxocotl: Psidium pomiferum* L. (*mirtáceas*) in Sahagún, Robredo ed., Vol. III, p. 335; *Psidium guajava* L. in Dressler, "Pre-Columbian Cultivated Plants," p. 145.

17. *Quauhxilotl: Parmentiera edulis* DC. in Hernández, *Historia de las plantas*, Vol. II, p. 451.

18. *Auacatl: Persea americana* Mill. Gard. (Standley, "Trees and Shrubs of Mexico," Pt. 2, p. 290).

19. *Uaxin: Leucaena esculenta* Moc. & Ses. (*ibid.*, Pt. 2, p. 368).

20. *Texocotl: Crataegus mexicana* Moc. & Ses. in Santamaría, *Diccionario de mejicanismos*, p. 1022.

21. *Capuli: Prunus capuli* (Standley, "Trees and Shrubs of Mexico," Pt. 2, p. 340).

22. *Nochtli*: fruit of *Opuntia* sp. (Sahagún, Robredo ed., Vol. III, p. 335).

23. *Amacapuli: Morus celtidifolia* (Standley, "Trees and Shrubs of Mexico," Pt. 2, p. 340).

24. *Iztac nochtli*: white cactus fruit (*Opuntia* sp.) in Hernández, *Historia de las plantas*, Vol. III, pp. 934, 936. Cf. also Rafael Martín del Campo, "Las cactáceas entre los mexica," *Cactáceas y suculentas mexicanas*, Vol. II, No. 2 (Mexico, D.F., 1957), p. 28.

25. *Coznochtli: Opuntia* sp. of yellow fruit in Hernández, *Historia de las plantas*, Vol. III, pp. 934, 936.

26. *Tlatocnochtli*: "*tuna blanca tirando a bermejo*"; *Opuntia* sp. in *ibid*.

27. *Tzaponochtli (zaponoscle, pitahaya* — Santamaría, *Diccionario de mejicanismos*, p. 1146); *Opuntia ficus-indica* in Martín del Campo, "Las cactáceas entre los mexica," p. 30.

28. *Anochtli*: possibly *tuna de agua, pitahaya del agua (Pereskiopis aquosa* Britt & Rose); cf. Santamaría, *Diccionario de mejicanismos*, p. 1094.

29. *Pipillo*: possibly *Asclepias scandens* PB.; cf. *ibid.*, p. 858.

were: "We are not their equals; we are as nothing."

Then Moctezuma sternly commanded, charged, enjoined, ordered on pain of death the stewards and all the lords, the elders, to see to, to care for everything [the Spaniards] might need.

And when the Spaniards came forth to dry land, [when] finally they so came, when already they were to move, when already they moved, when already they followed the road, they were well cared for, they were held in esteem. It was completely in [the emissaries'] hands that they went along, that they followed the road along. Much was done for their sake.

namjcoan, iuhqujn atitleme:

niman ic tetlaquauhnaoati in Motecuçoma, vel qujncocolti, vel qujntenjzti, qujnmjqujznaoati in calpixque: auh in jxqujch in tecutli, in achcauhtli in qujttazque, in qujmocujtlavizque in jxqujch intech monequjz.

Auh in ovallalhoacaqujzque iequene ic vitze: in ie oalolinjzque, in ie oalolinj, in ie oalotlatoca, cenca necujtlaviloque, mavizmachoque, çan temac in oallatiaque, in oalotlatocaque, cenca inca nechioaloc.

Ninth Chapter, in which it is told how Moctezuma wept, and [how] the Mexicans wept, when they knew that the Spaniards were very powerful.

And Moctezuma loudly expressed his distress. He felt distress, he was terrified, he was astounded; he expressed his distress because of the city.

And indeed everyone was greatly terrified. There were terror, astonishment, expressions of distress, feelings of distress. There were consultations. There were formations of groups; there were assemblies of people. There was weeping — there was much weeping, there was weeping for others. There was only the hanging of heads, there was dejection. There were tearful greetings, there were tearful greetings given others. There was the encouragement of others; there was mutual encouragement. There was the smoothing of the hair; the hair of small boys was smoothed. Their fathers said: "Alas, O my beloved sons! How can what is about to come to pass have befallen you?" And their mothers said: "My beloved sons, how will you marvel at what is about to befall you?"

And it was told, declared, shown, announced, made known to Moctezuma, it was fixed in his heart, that a woman from among us people here brought them here; she interpreted for them. Her name was Marina. Her home was Teticpac. There on the coast they had first come to take her.[1]

And then at that time [this] began — that no more was there the placing of themselves at [the Spaniards'] feet. The emissaries, those who had interceded for them for everything, everywhere, that they might need, just went, turning their backs.

And at just this same time [the Spaniards] came enquiring about Moctezuma: "What sort [of man is he]? Is he perchance a youth? Is he perchance mature? Is he perchance already old? Is he perchance already advanced in years? Is he perchance an able old man? Is he perchance already an aged man? Is

Injc chicunavi capitulo: vncã mjtoa in quenjn chocac Motecuçomatzin, yoan in chocaque mexica, in jquac oqujmatque, ca cenca chicaoaque in Españoles.

Auh in motecuçoma cenca tlatenma, motenma, momauhti, mjçavi, qujtlatenmachili in altepetl;

yoan in ie ixqujch tlacatl, cenca momauhtique, nemauhtiloc neiçaviloc, tlatēmachoc, netenmachoc, nenonotzalo, nececentlalilo, neohololo, nechoqujlilo, nechochoqujlilo, techoqujlilo, ça tlaquechpilivi, ça tlaquechvi, nechoqujztlapalolo, techoqujztlapalolo, teellaquaoalo, neellaquaoalo, tepepetlalo, pepetlalo in pipiltzitzinti: in tetaoan qujtoa: Veh nopilhoãtzitzine, quen vel ameoantin in oamopan muchiuh, in tlein ie muchioaz: auh in tenanoan qujtoa. Nonopilhoantzitzin, que ço uel amehoanti in anqujmaviçozque in tlein ie topan muchioaz:

yoan ilhujloc, ixpantiloc, machtiloc, nonotzaloc, caqujtiloc, yiollo itlan tlaliloc in Motecuçoma: ce cioatl njcan titlaca in qujnoalhujcac, in oalnaoatlatotia: itoca Malintzi teticpac ichan, in vmpa atenco, achto canaco.

Auh njman iquac peuh: in aocmo onnecxitlalilo, in ça mocujtlacueptinemj in titlanti, in jpan ontlatoa in jzqujtlamantli, in jzqujcan icac in intech monequjz.

Auh çan njmã no iquac in qujtemotivitze Motecuçoma: quenamj cujx telpuchtli, cujx yiolloco oqujchtli, cujx ie veve, cujx ie tlachicalhuja, cujx ie veve tlamati, cujx ie veve tlacatl, cujx ie quaiztac? Auh qujnnanqujliaia in teteu in Españoles: ca yiolloco oqujchtli, amo tomaoac, çan pitzactõtli, çan pipitzac-

---

1. It appears well established that the birthplace of la Malinche (Marina, Malintzin) was Painalla, a town now disappeared, which was south of Coatzacoalcos. It is shown in the map in Francisco Javier Clavi-jero's *Historia antigua de México* (personal communication, Rafael García Granados).

he perchance already white-headed?" And they answered the gods, the Spaniards: "He is a mature man, not fat but rather slender; thin — rather thin."

And when Moctezuma had thus heard that he was much enquired about, that he was much sought, [that] the gods wished to look upon his face, it was as if his heart was afflicted; he was afflicted. He would flee; he wished to flee; he needed to flee; he would take himself hence. He would hide himself; he needed to hide himself; he would hide himself — he wished to take refuge from the gods. And he was determining for himself in secret, he determined for himself in secret; he was imagining to himself, he imagined to himself; he was inventing, he invented; he thus was consulting within his heart, he consulted within his heart; he was saying to himself, he secretly said to himself that he would somewhere enter a cave. And of those whom he much unburdened himself to, confided in, held especially easy conversation with, some told what they knew; they said: "[Some] know where Mictlan is, and Tonatiuh ichan, and Tlalocan, and Cincalco,[2] that one may be benefited. [Determine] in what place indeed is thy need."

And indeed he wished, he desired [to go] there to Cincalco. So was it well known; it was so rumored.

But this he could not do. He could not hide. He could not take refuge. No longer had he strength; no longer was there any use; no longer had he energy. No longer were verified, no longer could be accomplished the words of the soothsayers by which they had changed his mind, had misled him, had troubled him. Thus they were taking vengeance upon him when they were feigning to be wise in knowing [the way] there [to places] named.

[Moctezuma] only awaited [the Spaniards]; he made himself resolute; he put forth great effort; he quieted, he controlled his heart; he submitted himself entirely to whatsoever he was to see, at which he was to marvel.

tontli, çan cujllotic, cujllotcatontli.

Auh in juh qujcaquja in, Motecuçoma, in cenca temolo, in cenca matataco cenca ixco tlachiaznequj in teteu iuhqujn patzmjquja yiollo, iolpatzmjquja, cholozquja, choloznequja, mocholtiznequja, mocholtizquja, motlatizquja, motlatiznequja, qujnnetlatilizquja, qujnneinailiznequja in teteu. Auh qujmoiollotica, qujmoiollotiaia, qujmopictica, qujmopictiaia, qujiocuxca, qujiocoaia; ic moiolnonotzca, ic moiolnonotzaia yitic: qujmolhujca, yitic qujmolhujaia cana oztoc calaqujz, auh cêca intech moiollaliaia intech vel catca yiollo, intech tlaquauhtlamatia: cequjntin qujmomachiztiaia, in qujtoaia. Ca vmmati in mjctlan, yoan tonatiuh ichan, yoan tlalocã yoan cincalco injc vmpatiz in campa ie vel motlanequjliz.

Auh ie vel vmpa motlanequjliaia, motlanequjli in cincalco: vel iuh machoc, vel iuh tepan motecac.

Auh inin amo velit, amo vel motlati, amo vel mjnax, aoc ievat, aoc tle tic, aoc ievatix, aoc ie onneltic, aoc tle vel muchiuh in intlatol tlaciuhque, injc qujiolcuepca, inic qujiollapanca. injc qujiolmalacachoca, injc qujtlacuepilica, in qujmomachitocaca in ommati, in vmpa omoteneuh;

çan qujnmochielti, çan moiollotechiuh, moiollochichili, qujoalcentlamj, qujoalcentlanqua in jiollo, qujmocenmacac in çaço tlein qujttaz, qujmaviçoz.

---

2. Seler (*Einige Kapitel*, p. 474) identifies Mictlan with the north, Tonatiuh ichan with the east, Tlalocan with the south, and Cincalco with the west. The corresponding Spanish text, however, says concerning Cincalco: "*esta cabe a tlacujoaian detras de chapultepec donde ay fama que ay grãdes secretos en vnos destos lugares se podra vña magestad remediar escoxa vuestra magestad el lugar que qujsiere que* *alla le lleuaremos: y alli se consolara sin recibir ningun daño. Motecuçoma se inclino a yrse a la cueua de cincalco: y asi se publico por toda la tierra pero no vuo effecto este negocio njnguna cosa de lo que dixeron los nigromanticos se pudo verificar y ansi Motecuçoma procuro desforçarse y de esperar a todo lo que venjese, y de ponerse a todo peligro.*"

Tenth Chapter, in which it is told how quite slowly the Spaniards came forth to dry land, [how] they followed along the road, and how Moctezuma left the great palace; he went there to his princely home.

Then Moctezuma vacated his old house, the great palace. From there he traveled to, came to, moved to, visited his princely house.

And when at last [the Spaniards] came, when already they came, when already they moved along, a man of Cempoalla called a *tlacochcalcatl*, whom they had also first come to capture when they had gone to see the land [and] the city, also interpreted for them, established the road for them, eliminated [wrong] roads for them, showed them the way, guided them along, was their guide along the way.[1]

And when they came to reach Tecoac,[2] it was on Tlaxcallan land where their Otomís lived. And the Otomís met them in battle; they met them with shields. But the Otomís, the men of Tecoac, they completely annihilated. They completely destroyed them. They trampled upon them; there was trampling of them. They shot them with their guns; they shot them with iron bolts; they shot them with crossbows. Not just a few but great numbers of them were destroyed.[3]

And when Tecoac perished, the Tlaxcallans, when they heard of it, when they knew of it, when they were told, could not control themselves for fear. They were bereft of courage. Great wonder prevailed. They were frightened.

Then they gathered themselves together; they took counsel among themselves. The lords took counsel among themselves. The rulers took counsel among themselves. They considered the news among themselves.

Injc matlactli Capitulo: vncan mjtoa in quenjn Españoles çan jvian, oallalhoaccaqujzque, oallotlatocatiaque yoã in quenjn Motecuçoma qujcauh in vei tecpan, vmpa ia in jpilchan.

Niman qujoallalcavi in jvevechan in vei tecpan, vncan oallamattia, vncan oallama, qujoalma, qujoaltocac in jpilchan in iehoatl Motecuçoma.

Auh in iequene vitze, in ie vitze, in ie ovalmolinjque: ce tlacatl, cempoaltecatl, itoca tlacochcalcatl, no achto canaco; in jquac qujttato tlalli, in altepetl, no oalnaoatlatotia, q'noaloquechilitia, qujnoalotlaxilitia, qujnoallaixtlatitia, qujnoaliacan, qujnoaliacantia.

Auh in oacico Tecoac: intlalpan tlaxcalteca vncan onoque imotonoan. Auh in otomj iautica qujnnamjcque, chimaltica qujnnamjcque: auh in otomj in Tecoaca vel qujmjxtlatique, vel ixpoliuhque, qujnxixilque, texixilioac, qujntlequjqujzvique, qujntepuzmjvique, qujntlavitolhujque, amo çan quexqujchtin, vel ixachintin, in jxpoliuhque.

Auh in ontlalpoliuh tecoac, in tlaxcalteca in oconcacque in ocõmatque, in onjlhujloto, cenca mauhcaçonecque, mocuetlaxoque, cenca in tlania in maviztli, mavizcujque:

njmã mocentlalique mononotzque, motecuiononotzque, motlatocanonotzque, qujmoottitique in tlatolli:

---

1. The corresponding Spanish text reads: "*Desque los españoles partieron de la ribera de la mar para entrar la tierra dentro, tomaron a vn indio principal que llamauã Tlacochcalcatl, para que los mostrase el camino: al qual indio aujan tomado de alli de aquella proujncia los primeros naujos que vinjeron a descubrir esta tierra el qual indio el capitan don hernando cortes truxo consigo, y sabia ya de la lengua española algo. Este juntamente con marina erã interpretes de don hernãdo cortes, a este tomaron por guja de su camjno para venjr a mexico.*"

2. Tecoac: today Molino, in the northern part of the State of Puebla (personal communication, Rafael García Granados).

3. This battle lasted fourteen or fifteen days, according to Fray Francisco de Aguilar in *Relación breve de la conquista de Nueva España* (Mexico, D.F.: José Porrúa e Hijos, Sucs., 1954), pp. 33 *sqq*. Reference to important contemporary Spanish sources, like Aguilar, Díaz, Cervantes, Cortés, and others, is necessary for gauging passage of time and other points often not in the *Florentine Codex* and other Aztec accounts.

They said: "How shall we be? Shall we, perchance, meet with them? For the Otomí is a great man of war, a brave warrior. [The Spaniards] thought nothing of them, considered them nothing. In a moment, in but the flutter of an eyelid, they destroyed the vassals. And now let us only submit to [the stranger], let us only befriend him, let us only reconcile ourselves to him. Unfortunate are the common folk."

And thereupon the rulers of Tlaxcalla went in order to meet them. They took food with them — turkey hens, eggs, white tortillas, delicate tortillas.

They said to them: "You have suffered fatigue, O our lords."

[These] answered them: "Where is your home? Whence have you come?"

They said: "We are Tlaxcallans. You have wearied yourselves. You have come to attain, you have come to reach the land [of] your humble home, Quauhtlaxcalla."

(But in former times it was known as Texcalla; the common folk were called Texcallans.)[4]

qujtoque. Quen toiezque, cujx tiqujnnamjqujzque: ca vei oqujchtli vei tiacauh in otomjtl, atle ipan oqujttac, atle ipan oconjttac, çan ixqujch cavitontli in çan ixpeioctli in oconpopolo maceoalli. Auh in axcan ma çan itlan toncalaqujcã, ma çan tictocnjuhtican, ma çan titocnjuhtlacan, motolinja in maceoalli.

Auh njma ie ic vi in qujnamjqujzque in tlaxcalteca tlatoque: qujtqujque in tlaqualli, in totoli, in totoltetl in jztac tlaxcalli, in chipaoac tlaxcalli: qujmjlhujque. Oanqujmjhioviltique totecujoane:

qujnoalnanqujlique. Cana mochan? Campa oanoallaque?

Conjtoque. Titlaxcalteca, oanqujmociaviltique, oanmaxitico, otlaltech anmaxitico in amochantzinco quauhtlaxcalla

(auh in ie vecauh moteneoaia Texcalla, in maceoalti mjtoaia, texcalteca.)

---

4. The Spanish text reads: "*La ciudad q̃ agora se llama tlaxcalla, ante que viniesen los españoles se llamaua Texcalla.*"

Tlaxcalla did not exist as a compact urban center before the Conquest except for the four *barrios* — Quiahuiztlan, Ocotelolco, Tepeticpac, and Tizatlan — which made up the Republic of Tlaxcalla (personal communication, Rafael García Granados).

Eleventh Chapter, in which it is told how the Spaniards came to arrive there in Tlaxcalla, [then] called Texcalla.[1]

[The Tlaxcallans] went guiding them. They accompanied them there; they guided them there in order to go to leave them, to quarter them, in their palaces. They made very much of them. They gave them whatsoever they required; they attended to them. And then they gave them their maidens.

Then [the Spaniards] asked them: "Where is Mexico? What manner of place is it? Is it yet distant?"

[The Tlaxcallans] answered them: "It is by no means distant now; it may be reached in perhaps but three days. It is a very good place. And [the Mexicans] are very strong, very brave. They are conquerors; they go everywhere."

And the Tlaxcallans had formerly been at enmity with the Cholulans. There was regarding with rage, there was regarding with hatred; there was detesting. They were disgusted; they could have nothing to do with them. Wherefore they incited [the Spaniards] against them, so that they might harm them.

They said to them: "They are very wicked. They are our foes. The Cholulan is as strong as the Mexican. He is the Mexican's friend."

When the Spaniards had so heard, they then went to Cholula. The Tlaxcallans and the Cempoallans accompanied them. They went arrayed for war. When they went arriving, thereupon there was calling out, there was shouting [that] all the noblemen, the lords, those who led one, the brave warriors and the commoners should come. There was crowding into the temple courtyard.[2] And when all had come together, then [the Spaniards and their allies] closed off each of the entrances — as many places as there was entrance.

There was thereupon the stabbing, the slaying, the beating of the people. The Cholulan had suspected nothing; neither with arrows nor with shields had he contended against the Spaniards. Just so were they treacherously slain, deceitfully slain, unknowingly

Injc matlactli oce capitulo: vncã mjtoa in quenjn Españoles acico in vncã tlaxcalla: in mjtoa Texcalla.

Qujmõiacanato, qujnoalhujcaque, qujnoaliacantiaque, injc qujmoncaoato, injc qujncalaqujto in intecpanchan, cenca qujnmavizmatque, qujnmacaque in intech monequj inca mochiuhq̃ yoan njman qujnmacaque imjchpuchoan:

njman qujntlatlanjque canjn Mexico, quenamjcan? oc veca?

Qujnanqujlique, ca aocmo veca, aço ça eilhujtl axioaloz, cenca qualcã, yoã cenca chicaoaque, cenca tiacaoã, tepeoanjme, novian tepeuhtinemj.

Auh in tlaxcalteca, ieppa mochalanjticatca, moqualancaitzticatca, motlavelitzticatca, mococoliticatca, aimelmottaia, acã vel monepanoaia in chololteca: Ipampa in qujntenanaoatilique, injc qujnpoiomjctizque:

qujmjlhujque. Ca cenca tlaveliloc, ca toiaouh in chololtecatl iuhqujn mexicatl ic chicaoac, ca icnjuh in mexicatl:

in oiuh qujcacque in españoles: njmã ic vmpa iaque in chololla, qujnvicaque in tlaxcalteca yoan in cempoalteca, moiauchichiuhtiaque: in oacito njmã ie ic tenotzalo, tetzatzililo, ixqujchtin oallazque in pipilti, in tlatoque, in teiacana, in tiacaoan, yoan maceoalti, neteuitoaltemaloc. Auh in ie ocenqujzque ixqujchtin, njman qujoaltzatzacque in calacoaiã, in jzqujcampa calacoa,

njmã ie ic texixilioa, temjctilo, teviviteco, atle iniollo ipan catca in Chololtecatl: amo mjtica amo chimaltica qujnnamjcq̃ in Españoles, çan iuhqujn ichtacamjctiloque, çan tlaixpopoiomjctilti, çan tlachtacamjctilti, ca nel çan qujntenanaoatilique in tlaxcalteca.

---

1. Corresponding Spanish text: *"que entoce se llamaua texcalla."*

2. This was at the Temple of Quetzalcoatl, according to the corresponding Spanish text.

29

slain. For in truth the Tlaxcallans had incited [the Spaniards] against them.[3]

And of all which had come to pass, they gave, told, related all the account to Moctezuma. And all the messengers who arrived here all departed; they just went fleeing. No longer did there remain listening anyone to hear the news which was to be heard. And indeed everyone among the commoners went about overwrought; often they rose in revolt. It was just as if the earth moved; just as if the earth rebelled; just as if all revolved before one's eyes. There was terror.[4]

And when there had been death in Cholula, then [the Spaniards] started forth in order already to come to Mexico. They came grouped, they came assembled, they came raising dust. Their iron lances, their halberds seemed to glisten, and their iron swords were wavy, like a water [course]. Their cuirasses, their helmets seemed to resound. And some came all in iron; they came turned into iron; they came gleaming. Hence they went causing great astonishment; hence they went causing great fear; hence they were regarded with fear; hence they were dreaded.

And their dogs came leading; they came preceding them. They kept coming at their head; they remained coming at their head. They came panting; their foam came dripping [from their mouths].[5]

Auh in ixqujch muchioaia, muchi qujoalmacaia, qujoalilhujaia, qujoalcaqujtiaia in tlatolli in Motecuçoma. Auh in titlanti, ixqujch oalaci, ixqujch vmpeoa, çan mocujtlacueptinemj, aoc quenman cactoc in qujcaquj, in caqujtilo tlatolli: auh in ie ixqujch tlacatl maceoalli, ça mâcomantinemj, ça achcan mocomonja, ça iuhqujn tlallolinj, ça iuhqujn tlalli xoxoqujvi, ça iuhqujn tlaixmalacachivi, mavizcujoac.

Auh in ommjcoac cholollan: njmã oalpeuhque in ie ic vitze Mexico, ololiuhtivitze, tepeuhtivitze, teuhtli, qujquetztivitze, in intepuztopil, in intzinacantopil iuhqujn tlapepetlaca: auh in intepuzmaquauh, iuhqujn atl monecujloa, iuhqujn tlacacalaca in intepuzvipil, in intepuzquacalala. Auh cequjntin vel much tepuztli motqujtivitze, tetepuztin muchiuhtivitze, pepetlacativitze: ic cenca valmomavizçotitiaque, ic cenca oalmotlamauhtilitiaque: ic cenca mauhcaittoia, ic cenca imacaxoia.

Auh in jmjtzcujnoan iacattivitze, qujniacantivitze iniacac icativitze, iniacac onotivitze, hiicicativitze, intenqualac pipilcativitz.

---

3. Cf., however, Domingo Francisco de San Antón Muñón Chimalpahin Quauhtleuanitzin, *Annales*, ed. Rémi Simeón (Paris: Maisonneuve et Ch. Leclerc, 1889); the Septième Relation (p. 187) notes: *"cenca miequintin quinmictique in Chololteca ynic yaoyotica quinamicque capitan general, Hernando Cortes"* — they slew very many Cholulans when they met the Captain-general Hernán Cortés, in battle. Garibay (Sahagún, Garibay ed., Vol. IV, p. 99) translates the passage thus: *"No más con perfidia fueron muertos, no más como ciegos murieron, no más sin saberlo murieron.*
"No fué más que con insidias se les echaron encima los de Tlaxcala."

4. This paragraph, which interrupts the narrtive to describe conditions generally in the land, is paralleled by the corresponding Spanish text: *"todo el camjno andaua lleno de mensajeros de aca por alla, y de alla por aca, y toda la gente aca en mexico y donde venjan los españoles en todas las comarcas andaua la gente muy alborotada y desasosegada parecia que la tierra se mouja todos andaua espãtados y atonjtos."*

5. In Sahagún, Garibay ed., Vol. IV, p. 100, Garibay translates: *"Y sus perros van por delante, los van precediendo; llevan sus narices en alto, llevan tendidas sus narices: van de carrera: les va cayendo la saliva."*

Twelfth Chapter, in which it is told how Moctezuma sent a personage, a great nobleman, and many other noblemen besides, to go to meet the Spaniards, and that with which they greeted each one, with which they greeted the Captain, between Iztac tepetl and Popocatepetl.

And Moctezuma thereupon sent [and] charged the noblemen, whom Tziuacpopocatzin led, and many others besides of his officials, to go to meet [Cortés] between Popocatepetl and Iztac tepetl, there in Quauhtechcac. They gave them golden banners, precious feather streamers, and golden necklaces.

And when they had given them these, they appeared to smile; they were greatly contented, gladdened. As if they were monkeys they seized upon the gold. It was as if there their hearts were satisfied, brightened, calmed. For in truth they thirsted mightily for gold; they stuffed themselves with it; they starved for it; they lusted for it like pigs.

And they went about lifting on high the golden banners; they went moving them back and forth; they went taking them to themselves. It was as if they babbled. What they said was gibberish.

And when they saw Tziuacpopocatzin, they said: "Is this one perchance Moctezuma?" They spoke to those who were among them, their watchers, the Tlaxcallans, the Cempoallans. Thus they secretly questioned them.[1] These said: "Not this one, O our lords. This one is Tziuacpopocatzin; Moctezuma is delegating him."

[The Spaniards] said to him: "Art thou perchance Moctezuma?" He replied: "I am your governor; I am Moctezuma."

And then these said to him: "Go thou hence. Why dost thou lie to us? Who dost thou take us to be? Thou canst not lie to us; thou canst not mock us; thou canst not sicken our heads; thou canst not flatter us; thou canst not make eyes at us; thou canst not trick

Injc matlactli omume capitulo: vncan mjtoa in quenjn Motecuçoma, qujoa ce tlacatl vei pilli: yoā oc cequjntin mjequjntin pipilti in qujnnamjqujto Españoles: yoan in tlein ic tlatlapaloque, injc qujtlapaloque Capitan, in jtzalan iztactepetl, yoan popocatepetl.

Auh in Motecuçoma: njmā ie ic qujmonjoa, qujmonjxquetza in pipilti, qujniacana in tzioacpopocatzin, yoan oc ceq'ntin cenca mjequjntin itechiuhcaoan cōnamjqujto, intzalan in popocatepetl, yoan iztactepetl, vncan in quauhtechcac, qujmōmacaque teucujtlapanjtl, quetzalpanjtl, yoā teucujtlacozcatl.

Auh in oqujmōmacaque iuhqujn yixvetzca, cenca papaquj, ahavia, iuhqujn cooçomatzitzquja in teucujtlatl, iuhqujn vncan motlatlalia, iuhqujn iiztaia, iuhq'n cecelia yiollo: ca nel iehoatl in cenca camjquj, qujpoçaoa, qujteucivi, qujpitzonequj in teucujtlatl.

Auh in teucujtlapanjtl qujhiiauhtivitze, qujtlatlavitzotivitze, qujmoottititivitze, iuhqujn tlapopoloca, in tlein qujmolhuja in popolochcopa.

Auh in jquac oqujttaque Tzioacpopocatzin: qujtoque. Cujx iee hin in Motecuçoma: Qujmjlhujque, in intlan mantivitze in intlachixcaoan, in tlaxcalteca, cempoalteca, injc qujmōichtacatlatlanjque: conjtoque ca amo ie iehoatl totecujioane. Inin tzioacpopocatzin, qujmjxiptlatica in Motecuçomatzin:

qujlhujque. Cujx ie te in tiMotecuçoma? Conjto. Ca nehoatl in namotechiuhcauh in njMotecuçoma.

Auh njmā qujlhujque. Nepa xiauh, tleica in titechiztlacavia, ac titechmati, amo vel titechiztlacaviz, amo vel toca timocaiaoaz, amo vel titechquamanaz, amo vel titechixmamatiloz, amo vel titechichchioaz, amo vel titechixcuepaz, amo vel titechixpatiliz, amo

1. In Sahagún, Garibay ed., Vol. IV, p. 101, the translation runs: "*Les dijeron los que andan con ellos, sus agregados lambiscones de Tlax-* *cala y de Cempoala, que astuta y mañosamente los van acompañando.*"

us; thou canst not turn aside our eyes; thou canst not make us turn back; thou canst not annihilate us; thou canst not dazzle us; thou canst not cast mud into our eyes; thou canst not touch our faces with a muddy hand — not thou.[2] For Moctezuma is there; he will not be able to hide from us; he will not be able to take refuge. Where will he go? Is he perchance a bird? Will he perchance fly? Or will he perchance plant his road underground? Will he somewhere enter a mountain hollowed within? For we shall see him; we shall not fail to look into his face. We shall listen to his words, which we shall hear from his lips."

Thus they only scorned him; they ignored him. Thus there came only to nothing still another of their meetings, of their welcomings.

Forthwith they quickly went straight on the direct road [to Mexico].

vel titechtlacuepiliz, amo vel titechixpopoloz, amo vel titechixmjmjctiz, amo vel titechixçoqujviz, amo vel titechixçoqujmatocaz? amo tehoatl ca vnca in Motecuçoma, amo vel technetlatiliz, amo vel mjnaiaz? campa iaz? cujx tototl, cujx patlanjz? cuj noço tlallan qujquetzaz yiovi, cujx cana ca tepetl coionquj yitic calaqujz ca tiqujttazque, ca amo maca ixco titlachiezque, ticcaqujzque in jtlatol, itenco titlacaqujzque,

ic çan contelchiuhque, atle ipan conjttaque ic çan onnenpoliuh in oc çequj in intenamjc, in intetlapalol:

ic njmã qujoalmelauhtivetzque in melaoac vtli.

2. Ibid.:" 'Tú no nos engañarás, no te burlarás de nosotros.
"Tú no nos amedrentarás, no nos cegarás los ojos.
"Tú no nos harás mal de ojo, no nos torcerás el rostro.
"Tú no nos hechizarás los ojos, no los torcerás tampoco.
"Tú no nos amortecerás los ojos, no nos los atrofiarás.
"Tú no echarás lodo a los ojos, no los llenarás de fango.'
"Tú no eres. . . ."

Thirteenth Chapter, in which it is told how Moctezuma sent still other sorcerers so that they might cast spells over the Spaniards,[1] and what befell them on the way.

And another company of messengers, the soothsayers, the magicians, and incense-offering priests had also gone; they also went in order to contend against [the Spaniards]. But nowhere were they successful. Nowhere could they face them. No more did they avail; no more did they prevail over them; no more were they sufficient.

First they came upon a drunk man in the road. They went to meet him. They were confused by him. They beheld him as a Chalcan; so was he arrayed. He was adorned as a Chalcan; he was like a Chalcan. He seemed to be drunk; he was like one besotted; he was like one who is drunk. With eight grass ropes was he bound about the chest.[2] He came facing them; he came ahead of the Spanish vanguard.[3]

And he just rose up against them. He said: "What have you still come to gain here? What do you yet require? What would Moctezuma still wish to do? Hath he then perchance come to his senses? Is he then perchance now overcome by a great fear? He hath committed a fault; he hath abandoned the common folk; he hath destroyed the people. Because of him, they have been struck on the head; because of him they have been wrapped [in wrappings for the dead]. They have been laughed at; they have been mocked!"[4]

And when they had thus seen this, when they had thus heard his words, yet to no purpose did they pay him attention when they humbly prayed to him. When they quickly set up his watching place, his earthen platform, and his straw bed, he no longer looked forth from there. Quite in vain was what had

Injc matlactli omei capitulo vncã mjtoa in quenjn Motecuçoma: qujmjoa oc cequjntin tetlachivianjme injc qujtlachivizquja Espanoles yoan in tlein vtlica impan muchiuh.

Auh ie no centlamantique titlanti: iehoan in tlaciuhq̃ in nanaoalti, yoan tletlenamacaque, no ic iaca, no ic iaque in tenamjqujzque: auh aoccã vel mochiuhque, aoccan vel teittaque, aocmo tlaipantilique, aocmo teipantilique, aocmo onieoatque:

çan ie ce tlaoanquj vtlica ica ommotzotzonato, qujmonamjctito, ica onmjxtilquetzato: injc qujttaq̃ iuhqujn chalcatl ic omochichiuh, mochalcachichiuh, mochalcanenequj: iuhqujn tlaoãquj, mjvincanenequj, motlaoãcanenequj: chicuei çacamecatl ic melilpi, qujmjxnamjctivitz hiiacac icativitz in Españoles.

Auh çan inca ieoac: qujmjlhuj. tle noma amaxtivitze in njcã? tlen oc anqujnequj? tle noma qujchioaznequj in Motecuçoma? cujx qujn omozcali? cujx qujn axcan ie momauhticapul? ca otlatlaco, ca oconcavili in maceoalli, ca otlacaixpolo teca omoquavitec, ca teca omoqujmjlo, ca teca omavilti, ca teca omocacaiauh.

Auh in oiuh qujttaque in, in oiuh qujcacque itlatol, oc nen itlan aquj, in qujmocnotlatlauhtilia, qujtlalilitivetzque ichiel itlalmomoz, yoan içacapepech, çan njmã aocmo vmpa qujoalittac: tel çan nenpanca in ommotlalica, in vncan oc nen qujtlalmomuztica:

---

1. *Espanoles:* the tilde is omitted in the Nahuatl text.
2. See Pl. 27.
3. The corresponding Spanish text reads: *"traya ceñjdo a los pechos ocho cabestros o sogas hechas de heno como de esparto, y venja de hazia donde estauan los españoles."*

4. In Sahagún, Garibay ed., Vol. IV, p. 102, the passage is thus translated: *"Ha cometido errores: ha llevado allá lejos a sus vasallos, ha destruído a las personas.*
"*Unos con otros se golpean; unos con otros se amortajan.*
"*Unos con otros se revuelven, unos de otros se burlan."*

been set up; in vain had they made the earthen platform there.

First, as if they had entered his mouth, he chid them, he taxed them. It was as if he spoke in a passion. He said to them:[5]

"Why in vain have you come walking here? Nevermore will there be a Mexico; it is already [gone] forever. Go hence; it is no longer there. Turn about; look at what cometh to pass in Mexico — what thus already cometh to pass!"

Then they turned about to look; they quickly turned about to look. They beheld that already all the temples, the *calpulli* [buildings], the *calmecac* [buildings],[6] all the houses in Mexico were burning; and it was as if already there was fighting.

And after the soothsayers had seen it, it was as if their hearts went [from them] somewhere; they no longer spoke clearly. It was as if someone had made them swallow something.

They said: "This was in no way for us to see; it was for Moctezuma to see what we have seen. For it was not just anyone [who accosted us]; he was the youth, Tezcatlipoca."

Thereupon he vanished. No more did they see him.

And the messengers went no further to encounter [the Spaniards]; they no longer went pressing on toward them. Right there the soothsayers, the incense-offering priests turned back. They came to notify Moctezuma. They and those who had earlier gone [with] Tziuacpopocatzin joined with one another.[7]

And when these messengers had come to arrive, they so related to Moctezuma what had come to pass, what they had beheld. Moctezuma, when he heard it, only bowed his head; he only sat with bowed head. He hung his head; he sat with head hanging down. No longer did he speak aloud; he only sat dejected for a long time, as if he had lost hope.

He only answered them in this way; he said to them: "What now, O my warriors? For already we

çan ie iuhqujn icamac ommaqujque, ie vncan qujmaoa, qujntequjaia, iuhqujn motititzatlatoa: qujmjlhuj.

Tle çã nen in njcan amjcativitze aoqujc iez in Mexico, ie ic cēmãia, nepa xivia, aocmo vncã, tla xommocuepacan, tla xontlachiacan in Mexico, tlein ie mochioa: in juh ie mochioa.

Nimã ic oallachixque, oallachixtivetzque, in quj-oalitta ie tlatlã in jxqujch teucalli, in calpulli, in calmecatl, yoan in jxqujch mexico calli, yoan iuhqujn ma ie cuel necaliva.

Auh in oiuh qujttaque in tlaciuhque, iuhqujn canjn ia, iniollo, aocmo onnaoatque, iuhqujn aca itla qujntololti:

qujtoque inin ca amo totech monequja in tiqujttazque, ca ie itech monequja qujttaz in Motecuçoma, in otiqujttaque: ca amo çan aca, ca iehoatl in telpuchtli Tezcatlipuca:

njman ic poliuh, aocmo qujttaque.

Auh in titlanti aocmo tenamjqujto, aocmo tevic qujçato, ça vncã oalilotque in tlaciuhque, in tletlenamacaque, qujnonotzaco in Motecuçoma: oalnepanjxtiaque in achto iaque in Tzioacpopocatzin.

Auh in oacico iehoantin titlantin, iuhquj povilique in Motecuçoma in juh mochiuh in juh qujttaque. In motecuçoma, in oiuh qujcac, ça oaltolo ça oaltolotimotlali, oalquechpilo, oalquechpilotimotlali, aocmo oalnaoat, çan ontlanauhtimotlali, vecauhtica in iuhquj ontlapolo,

ça ixqujch injc qujnoalnanqujli: qujnoalilhuj. Quennel mocechtle ca ie ic toncate, ca ie otictomaca-

***

5. *Ibid.*, p. 103: "*Aunque en vano le disponen, aunque allí en vano le hacen su adoratorio, ya no más de su boca se meten en el oráculo. Allí los espanta, los reprende con dureza, como si de lejos les hablara. Les dijo . . . .*"

6. *Calpulli, calmecatl* — tribal temple and priests' dwelling are translations of these terms, for which there are precedents. See Arthur J. O. Anderson and Charles E. Dibble, trans., *Florentine Codex, Books I–XII, passim.* Refer also to Arturo Monzón, *El calpulli en la organización social de los tenochca* (Mexico, D.F.: Instituto de Historia, 1949), *passim* (*calpulli*) and p. 77 (*calmecac*); or Alfonso Caso, "Instituciones

indígenas precortesianas," *Memorias del Instituto Nacional Indigenista*, Vol. VI (1954), pp. 20 *sqq.* (*calpulli*), 26 (*calmecatl*).

For recent studies on the *calpulli* see Alfonso Caso, "Land Tenure Among the Ancient Mexicans," *American Anthropologist*, Vol. 65, No. 4 (Aug., 1963), pp. 863–78, and Pedro Carrasco, "El barrio y la regulación del matrimonio en un pueblo del Valle de México en el siglo XVI," *Revista Mexicana de Estudios Antropológicos*, Vol. 17 (1961), pp. 7–24.

7. Sahagún, Garibay ed., Vol. IV, p. 103: "*Vinieron juntos con los que habían ido primero, con los de Tzioacpopoca.*"

are [at the end]; for already we have taken our medicine. Are there perchance mountains that we shall climb? And shall we perchance run away? For we are Mexicans. Will the Mexican state in truth be glorified? Unfortunate[8] are the poor old man, the poor old woman, and the child who hath no understanding. Where will they be taken? What now? What is to be done, in vain? What can be done? Where, in truth, [can we go]? For already we have taken our medicine. Whatsoever, wheresoever it is, we shall marvel at it!"

que, cujx cacah tepetl tictlecavizque: auh cujx ticholozque ca timexica, cujx nellaontimaliviz in mexicaiutl, motolinja in jcnoveve, in jcnoilama: auh in piltzintli, in aia qujmati, campa neviqujlilozque, quēnel, quēçannel nen, quēnoçonel, campa nel, ca ie tictomacaticate in çaço tlein, in çaço quenamj in ticmaviçozque.

8. From *motolinja* on, the passage is translated in Horacio Carochi, *Arte de la lengva mexicana* (Mexico, D.F.: Imprenta del Museo Nacional, 1892), p. 520.

Fourteenth Chapter, in which it is told how Moctezuma commanded that the road be closed, so that the Spaniards might not come to arrive here in Mexico.

And Moctezuma yet in vain had commanded that the road, the highway, be closed off. They planted the one which led direct here to Mexico with magueys. And there they let them look upon the road which went to, which entered Texcoco.

And there they had blocked the way with a wall of maguey plants. Then [the Spaniards] realized it; they saw that it only blocked [the way]. They scorned it. They took it up; they kicked each [plant] away; they made them burst out [of their places]; far did they cast the magueys.

They slept there at Amaquemecan.[1] Thereupon they came on; they came on direct; they came direct along the road; they came to reach Cuitlauac. That time they also slept there.

They assembled the rulers who held sway everywhere over the people of the floating gardens — Xochimilco, Cuitlauac, Mizquic. They spoke to them in just the same way that they had spoken to the Chalcan rulers. And these rulers of the people of the floating gardens at once also submitted to them.

And when the Spaniards had been satisfied, then they moved on; they came to settle themselves at Itztapalapan. Thereupon they summoned the rulers; they caused them to be summoned. They were known as the Four Lords — of Itztapalapan, of Mexicatzinco, of Colhuacan, of Uitzilopochco. In just the same manner as they had spoken to [the floating gardens peoples' rulers], so they interviewed them, as hath been told. And likewise peacefully, quietly they submitted to the Spaniards.[2]

And Moctezuma did not command that any make war against them, that any contend against them in battle. No one was to contend against them in battle.

Injc matlactli onnavi capitulo, vncan mjtoa in quenjn Motecuçoma tlanaoati in motzatzaquaz vtli injc amo vel aciqujvi Españoles, in njcã mexico.

Auh in Motecuçoma, oc nen tlanaoatica in qujtzatzaquazque in vtli, in vchpantli, qujmetecaque in oallamelauhticac njcã Mexico: auh ie vmpa qujmontlachieltiaia, in jpan vtli iaticac, calacticac tetzcucu.

Auh in vncan qujmetepãtzacca: njman qujmatque, qujttaque in çan oqujtzatzacque, atle ipan conjttaque, caanque, veca conxoxopeuhque, quioalchichitotzque, veca ica ommamaiauhque in metl:

vncã cochque amaquemecan, njmã ie ic vitze, tlamelauhtivitze, qujmelauhtivitze in vtli, acico in cuitlaoac, çan oc no vncan cochque:

in oqujncentlalique tlatoque, in jzqujcan tlatocachioa injc chinãpaneca in Suchmjlco in cujtlaoac, in mjzqujc: çan ie no ivi in qujmjlhujque, in juh qujmjlhujque chalcatlatoque. Auh in iehoanti chinanpaneca tlatoque, çan njmã no intlan oncalacque.

Auh in oiniollo vmpachiuh, in Españoles: njman ic oalolinque ommotlalico in jtztapalapan: njman ie no ic qujnnotza, qujnnenotzallanj in tlatoque: Nauhtecutli mjtoa. In jtztapalapan, Mexicatzinco, culhoacan, Vitzilobuchco: çã ie no ie in qujmjlhujque, injc qujntlatoltique (in oiuh mjto). Auh çan no ivian, iocuxca intlan oncalacque in Españoles.

Auh in Motecuçomatzin, amo tlanaoatiaia injc aca qujniauchioaz, injc aca iauiotica qujnnamjqujz, aiac iauiotica qujnnamjqujz, çan tlanaoatiaia, injc amo

---

1. Details are to be found in Chimalpahin, *Annales*, pp. 187–88.

2. In Sahagún, Garibay ed., Vol. IV, p. 104, the passage is thus rendered: "*Luego se les comunicó la disposición, con la cual se les dió el mandato, como se dijo, y desde luego se pusieron al lado de los españoles, en paz y calma.*"

He commanded only that they not be ignored, that much be done for them.

And when this had happened, here it was as if Mexico lay silent. No one went forth; no one was going forth. Mothers no longer let [their children] go forth. The roads were quite clean, they were wide open; the roads were wide open, as in early morning. No one went across; no one crossed it. There was an entering of the houses; there was preoccupation only with being afflicted.[3] The common folk said: "Let it be thus. Let it be accursed. What more will it be that you do? For already we are to die, already we are to perish. Yea, already we await our death."

çan tlacomachozque, ça cenca inca nechioaloz.

Auh in jquac y, in njcan Mexico, ça iuhqujn cactoc, aocac oalqujça, aocac oalqujztica. In tenanhoan aocmo oaltequjxtitlanj, ça chichipaoaticac in vtli, ichpelpul icac, ça ichpeliuhticac in vtli, ça iuhqujn tlalchipacpan, aocac ixtlapal iauh, aocac tlaxtlapaloa, necacaltemaloc, ça ixcavilo in tlaocuialo: qujtoaia in macevalli. Ma iuh tie, ma motelchioa, tle oc iez in anqujchioa, ca ie timjqujzq̃, ca ie tipolivizque, ca ie toconchixticate in tomjqujz.

3. *Ibid.*, p. 105: "*Estaban los caminos solitarios y limpios. Desamparados y sin gente, totalmente vacíos estaban los caminos. Tal como en honda noche: nadie pasaba a otros, nadie encontraba a otros. La gente estaba recogida en sus casas. No hacía otra cosa que dedicarse a su tristeza.*"

Fifteenth Chapter, in which it is told how the Spaniards[1] departed there from Itztapalapan in order to come to arrive in Mexico.

And thereupon they moved forth in order already to enter here into Mexico; thereupon they attired themselves, they arrayed themselves for war. They girt themselves; they bound on well their battle dress. Then their horses: thereupon they were, each one, disposed, arranged in rows, placed in order, put in line.

And four horse[men] came ahead; they came first, they came leading the others, they came constituting the vanguard of the others; they led the others.[2] They went continually turning about; they went turning about repeatedly. They went facing the people. They went looking hither and thither; they came scanning every side, they went looking everywhere among the groups of houses, they came examining things. They went looking up at the roof terraces.

Likewise their dogs: their dogs came ahead. They came sniffing at things. Each one came panting; each one came continually panting.

By himself came marching, came ahead, came marching alone one who bore the standard upon his shoulders. He came continually shaking it; he went making it circle; he went tossing it from side to side. It came continually stiffening [in the breeze]; it came rising like a warrior. Smartly did it twist; it came twisting as it raised itself; it came twisting and filling itself out.[3]

Then came following him the bearers of iron swords. Their iron swords each went flashing. They each bore on their shoulders, they went bearing on their shoulders, their shields — wooden shields, leather shields.

There came as the second group, as the second file, horses which came each carrying [a soldier] each [with] his cotton cuirass, his leather shield, his iron lance, and his iron sword, each hanging at the horse's

Injc caxtolli capitulo: vncan mjtoa in quenjn Espanoles, vmpa vallevaque in Itztapalapan injc acico mexico.

Auh njman ie ic oalolinj in ie ic oalcalaqujzque njcan Mexico; njman ie ic mocecencaoa, moiauchichioa; moolpia, vel qujilpia in iniautlatquj: njman ie iehoantin in in cavallos: njman ie ic motetecpana, mocuecuētilia, movivipana, mocecēpantilia.

Auh nauhteme in cavallos in iacattivitze, in attovitze, in teiacantivitze, in teiacaconotivitze, in te in teiacana; mocuecueptivi, ommocuecueptivi, onteixnamjctivi, havic tlachixtivi, nanacaztlachixtivitze, noviampa onjtztivi in cacaltzalan, tlaixtotocativitze, onacotlachixtivi in tlapanco:

no iehoan in chichime in jmjtzcujnoan, iacattivitze, tlatlanecutivitze, neneciuhtivitze, nêneneciuhtivitze;

yioca icativitz, iacattivitz, icel icativitz in quachpanjtl qujquechpanoa, qujtlatlavitzotivitz, qujmamalacachotivitz, havic qujtlatlaztivitz, mochichicauhtivitz, moqujchquetztivitz, vel mocolotilia, mocoloquetztivitz, mocolonectivitz;

qujoaltoqujlitivi tepuzmaquaveque, pepetlauhtivitz, in intepuzmaquauh, pepepetlacativitz, qujquequechpanoa, qujquequechpanotivitze, inchichimal, quauhchimalli, eoachimalli.

Injc vntlamantitivitze, injc vmpantitivitze cavallos temamativitze, imjichcavipil, imeeoachimal intetepuztopil, yoan intetepuzmaquauh inquezpā pipilcativitz in cavallosme, cocoiolloque, coioleque, coiollo-

---

1. *Espanoles*: the tilde is omitted in the Nahuatl text.

2. *In te in teiacana*: *in te* appears at the bottom of the folio (21*v*) and is probably repeated in error.

3. Cf. Seler, *Einige Kapitel*, p. 487, whose version varies somewhat from the foregoing.

neck.[4] Each horse had bells; they had bells; they came with bells. It was as if the bells each resounded; the bells resounded. The horses—the deer—neighed; there was neighing. Much did they sweat; it was as if water fell from them. And their flecks of foam from their mouths fell in large drops on the ground, they fell on the ground in drops like *amolli* soap [suds]. And as they advanced, heavily did their hooves beat; there was the beating of hooves. There was a pounding as if stones were cast at one. Then each [hoof] pierced holes; holes were dug in the ground there where they lifted their feet. Separately they each formed there where their hind legs, their forelegs went stamping.

The third group was of those with the iron crossbows. In the arms of the crossbowmen the iron crossbows went resting. They went testing them, they went wielding them, they went testing them. But some bore them upon their shoulders; they came shouldering the crossbows. And their quivers went hung at their sides or passed under their arms, each one well filled, crowded with iron bolts. Their cotton armor went reaching to their knees; it was very thick, firmly sewed, extremely dense, thick and close-woven. And their heads were covered in the same way with cotton armor. And from the top of each of their heads precious feathers arose; each one went dividing, outspread.

The fourth group likewise was of horse[men]; their array was the same as hath been told.

The fifth group were those with arquebuses, the arquebusiers. They carried the arquebuses on their shoulders. Some came with them extended. And when they had come to enter the great palace, the residence of the rulers, they fired them; they repeatedly fired the arquebuses. They each exploded, they each crackled, were discharged, thundered, disgorged. Smoke was spread, smoke was spread diffusely, smoke darkened, smoke massed all over the ground, spread all over the ground. By its fetid smell it stupefied one, it robbed one of one's senses.

And at the very last, directing from the rear, came the commander, who was considered the same as the *tlacateccatl*, the battle ruler, the battle director. Surrounding him, scattered about him, close to his side, knowing him, went his brave warriors, his insignia-bearers, his attendants, who were like [our] shorn

tivitze iuhqujn xaxamaca in coiolli, tlaxamacan coiolli in cavallosti; in mamaça pipitzca, tlapipitzca, cenca mjtonja, iuhqujn atl intechpa temo: auh in intepopuçoqujllo chachapaca tlalpan, iuhqujn amulli chachapanj; auh injc nenemj cenca tlatiticujtza, tlatetecujtza: tlacocomotza, iuhqujn tlatemotla, njman cocoionj, cocomolivi in tlalli in vncan qujquetza imjcxi, yioca momamana in vncan qujquequetztivi in jmjcxi, in inma.

Injqu epantin tepuztlavitoleque, tepuztlavitoloanj inmac onotivitz in tepuztlavitolli, tlaeiecotivitze, tlatlaieecotivitze, qujixcatzitztivitze. Auh in cequjntin qujquechpanoa, qujquequechpanotivitze in tepuztlavitolli: auh in inmjcon iniomotlan pipilcatiuh, inciacacpa qujqujztiuh, vel tetentiuh, cahcacatzcatiuh in mjtl, in tepuzmjtl, imjichcavipil, intlanquac ahacitiuh, vel titilaoac, vellatepizçotl, ixachi titilacpopul, iuhqujn tepetlatl: auh in intzontecon ic qujmjlivi çan no ie in jchcavipilli, yoan inquequetzal imjcpac conquequetztivi, xexeliuhtiuh, momoiaoatiuh.

Injc nappantin çan no iehoantin in cavallotin, çan ie no iuhquj in innechichioal in juh omjto.

Injc macujllamantli iehoātin in matlequjqujceque, in matlequjqujçoanj, qujquequechpanoa in matlequiqujztli; cequjntin qujtecativitze. Auh in jquac in ocalaqujco in vei tecpan, in tlatocan; qujtlazque, qujtlatlazque in matlequjqujztli, ie oncuecueponj, ie oncuecuepoca, xixitica, tlatlatzinj, oaoalaca, poctli moteca, poctli moteteca, poctica tlaioa in poctli centlalli momana cētlalli moteca: injc xoqujiac teixivinti, teiolmoiauh:

auh ça tlatzacutiuh, tetzinpachotiuh in iautachcauh in ma iuhquj tlacateccatl momati in iautlatoanj, in iautecanj, cololhujtivi, qujtepevitivi, qujtzcactitivi, qujtlamatilitivi, qujtzatzacutivi in jtiacaoan, in itlavicecaoan, in jmananqujlloā, in ma iuhquj quaquachictin, in ma iuhquj otomj in jchicavilloā, in

---

4. *Imjichcavipil*, etc.: these terms are actually distributive with plural possessing prefixes which we have ignored.

ones, like [our] Otomí [warriors]; the strong ones, the intrepid ones, the mainstay, the support of the state; its soul, its foundation.

Then the dwellers of the [farther] cities — the Tepoztecan, the Tlaxcallan, the Tliliuhquitepecan, the Huexotzincan — came along behind. They came arrayed for war, each in his cotton armor, each with his shield, each with his bow. Each one's quiver went filled, crowded with feathered arrows, some with barbed points, some blunted, some obsidian-pointed. They went with knees bent, loosing cries, loosing shrieks while striking their mouths with their hands, singing the Tocuillan song, whistling, shaking their heads.[5]

And some bore burdens, rations, upon their backs; some carried burdens [with a tump line about] their foreheads, [or with a band] about their chests; some bore burdens in carrying frames, some in cages, some in deep baskets. Some made bundles of things or bore bundles upon their backs. Some dragged the great lombard guns which went resting on wooden wheels. They came continually singing as they made them move.

jnechicaoalhoan, in jnetlaquechilhoan, in jtlaxilloan altepetl, in jiolloan, in jtetzonoan:

njman ie ixqujch in aoatepeoa, in tlateputzcatl, in tlaxcaltecatl, tliliuhqujtepecatl, in vexotzincatl: tlatoqujlitivitze, moiauchichiuhtivitze imjichcavipil, inchichimal, intlatlavitol, inmjmjcon tetentiuh, cacacatzcatiuh in totomjtl, cequj chichiqujlli, cequj tihpontli, cequj itzmjtl momamantivi, motenvitectivi, motenpapavitivi, tocujleuhtivi, tlatlanqujqujztivi, moquacuecuechotivi.

Auh in cequjntin tlamama, itacamama, cequjntin tlaixquamama, cequjntin tlaelpanmama, cequjntin tlacacaxvia, cequjntin tlaoacalhuja, cequjntin tlatompiavia, cequjntin tlaqujmjlhuja, manoço tlaqujmjlmamama, cequjntin qujvilana in vevei, in totomaoac tlequjqujztli, quauhtemalacac oonotiuh, qujcavatztivitze.

5. Sahagún, Garibay ed., Vol. IV, p. 107: "*Van tendidos en hileras, van dando gritos de guerra con el golpear de sus labios, van haciendo gran algarabía. Se revuelven como gusanos, van diciendo mil cosas, van agitando sus cabezas.*"

Sixteenth Chapter, in which it is told how Moctezuma peacefully, quietly went to meet the Spaniards there at Xoloco,[1] where now stands the house of Alvarado, or there at the place they call Uitzillan.[2]

And when this had happened, when [the Spaniards] had come to reach Xoloco, when already matters were at this conclusion, had come to this point,[3] thereupon Moctezuma arrayed himself, attired himself, in order to meet them, and also a number of great lords [and] princes, his ruling men, his noblemen [arrayed themselves]. Thereupon they went to meet them. In gourd supports they set out precious flowers — helianthus,[4] talauma,[5] in the midst of which went standing popcorn flowers,[6] yellow tobacco flowers,[7] cacao blossoms,[8] wreaths for the head, garlands of

Injc caxtolli occe capitulo: vncā mjtoa in quenjn Motecuçoma pacca, iocuxca qujnnamjqujto Españoles, in vmpa xoluco, in axcan ie vmpa manj ical albarado, in anoço vncan qujtoa Vitzillan.

Auh in ie iuhquj in oacico xoluco, in ie vncan tlantimanj ie vncan iaquetivitz. Niman ie ic muchichioa, mocencaoa in Motecuçomatzin injc tenamjqujz: yoan oc cequjntin veveintin tlatoque in tlaçopipilti, in jtlatocaiovan, in jpilloan: njmā ie ic vi tenamjqujzque, xicalpechtica cōmamāque in tlaçosuchitl, in chimalsuchitl, in iollosuchitl inepantla icatiuh in jzqujsuchitl, in coztic iiesuchitl, in cacaoasuchitl, icpacsuchitl, in suchineapantli: yoā qujtquj in teucujtlacozcatl, chaiaoac cozcatl, cozcapetlatl.

---

1. Xoloco or Xoluco served to identify the canal which ran along the Calzada de Chimalpopoca; this canal was crossed by a bridge given the same name. In times past they have been named Canal and Bridge of San Antón. Its exact location is the intersection of the Calzadas de San Antonio Abad and Chimalpopoca, the place of first meeting of Cortés and Moctezuma (personal communication, Rafael García Granados). Alfonso Caso, in "Los barrios antiguos de Tenochtitlán y Tlatelolco," *Memorias de la Academia Mexicana de la Historia,* Vol. XV (1956), pp. 14–15, identifies Xoloco as a *barrio* bounded N. by a line S. of Calle de José Ma. Izazaga; E., Pino Suárez and S. Antonio Abad; S., Lucas Alamán; and W., extension of 20 de Noviembre.

We reproduce unchanged the three maps of the Valley of Mexico and Tenochtitlan-Tlatilulco of our first edition of Book XII, and continue to base provisional locations of places mentioned in the Nahuatl text mainly on Caso's study. While we are aware that many of the locations are suspect, the continuing studies of Tenochtitlan topography by Edward E. Calnek are not yet sufficiently complete to permit our modifying the map of the island city consistently or indeed with confidence. See, however, Edward E. Calnek: "Settlement Pattern and Chinampa Agriculture at Tenochtitlan," *American Antiquity,* Vol. XXXVI (1972), pp. 104–15; "The Localization of the Sixteenth-Century Map Called the Maguey Plan," *American Antiquity,* Vol. XXXVII (1973), pp. 190–95; and "The Organization of Urban Food Supply Systems: the Case of Tenochtitlan," *Atti del XL Congresso Internazionale degli Americanisti, Roma-Genova* (in press). See also Edward E. Calnek: "Conjunto urbano y modelo residencial en Tenochtitlan," in Edward E. Calnek, Woodrow Borah, Alejandra Moreno Toscano, Keith A. Davies, and Luis Unikel, *Ensayos sobre el desarrollo urbano de México* (Mexico, D.F.: Secretaría de Educación Pública, 1974). Calnek's maps Nos. 1, 2, and 3 (pp. 16, 21, and 25) indicate contours of the island or islands which are somewhat different from their appearance in our maps.

2. Near the Church of S. Pablo, according to Sahagún's Spanish text in Chap. 30 of the MS; identified with Iznahuatonco or Huitznahuatonco in Caso, "Barrios antiguos," p. 25.

3. Corresponding Spanish text: "*En llegando los españoles a aquel rio que esta cabe las casas de albarado que se llama Xoluco.*"

4. *Chimalxochitl. Chimalacaxochitl* is mentioned in Hernández, *Historia de las plantas,* Vol. I, pp. 101–2 (fig., p. 102). Chimalacatl (*ibid.,* p. 100) "*tiene . . . flores redondas mayores (parece prodigio) de un palmo, amarillo rojizas con algo de amarillo más fuerte en su parte media*": Helianthus annuus L. Linn; *girasol, chimalatl, maíz de tejas. Chimalacaxochitl* is classifed as "*compuesta?*"

5. *Yolloxochitl: Talauma mexicana* Don (*yolosóchil*), according to Santamaría, *Diccionario de mejicanismos,* p. 1135. According to Emily Walcott Emmart, *The Badianus Manuscript (Codex Barberini, Latin 241), Vatican Library, an Aztec Herbal of 1552* (Baltimore: Johns Hopkins Press, 1940), p. 310 and Pl. 98, it is the Mexican magnolia and (citing Sahagún) "was reserved solely for the nobility, especially a kind known as *tlacaiolloxochitl.*"

6. *Izquixochitl: Bourreria formosa; B. huanita; B. littoralis* (Santamaría, *Diccionario de mejicanismos,* p. 508; *esquisúchil*). Popcorn flower (*Bourreria huanita* [La Slave and Lex] Hemsl.), according to Emmart, *Badianus Manuscript,* p. 276 and Pl. 69, a rare and coveted plant whose flowers were used to flavor cacao. In Sahagún, *Histoire générale,* p. 97, n. 2, it is noted that "*Cette fleur vient sur l'arbre* izquixochiquauitl, *moreliosa huanita, de la famille des styracinées.*"

7. *Yexochitl.* Nardo Antonio Reccho, in *Rervm medicarvm novae Hispaniae thesavrvs sev plantarvm animalivm mineralivm mexicanorvm historia ex Francisci Hernandez* (Rome: Ex Typographeio Vitalis Mascardi, 1651), p. 258, gives *eloxochitl* as an alternative (*quam alij* Eloxochitl, *seu* Florem Eloti, *alij verò* Cocauhquixochitl [coçauhqui?] *seu* Yexochitl pallidam, *vocant*"), a cold climate plant ("*provenit regionibus frigidis, & montosis locis*"). There is a confusion of terminology. Santamaría, *Diccionario de mejicanismos,* p. 470, identifies it (*elosúchil*) as *Magnolia dealbata* Succ. Emmart (*Badianus Manuscript,* p. 275) points out that, while according to Hernández it is a magnolia, in the *Badianus MS* the flower "appears to belong to the Compositae."

8. *Cacauaxochitl: Quararibea funebris* Llave, according to Santamaría, *Diccionario de mejicanismos,* p. 169 (*cacahuasúchil*). In Sahagún, Garibay ed., Vol. IV, p. 325, it is identified as *Lexarza funebris.* Emmart (*Badianus Manuscript,* p. 311 and Pl. 98) has *Theobroma angustifolium* DC, one of the important cacao plants.

flowers.[9] And they bore golden necklaces, necklaces with pendants, plaited neck bands.

And already Moctezuma met them there in Uitzillan. Thereupon he gave gifts to the commandant, the commander of soldiers; he gave him flowers, he bejeweled him with necklaces, he hung garlands about him, he covered him with flowers, he wreathed his head with flowers. Thereupon he had the golden necklaces laid before him — all the kinds of gifts of greeting, with which the meeting was concluded. On some he hung necklaces.

Then [Cortés] said to Moctezuma: "Is this not thou? Art thou not he? Art thou Moctezuma?"

Moctezuma replied: "Indeed yes; I am he."

Thereupon he arose; he arose to meet him face to face. He inclined his body deeply. He drew him close. He arose firmly.

Thus he besought him: he said to him: "O our lord, thou hast suffered fatigue, thou hast endured weariness. Thou hast come to arrive on earth. Thou hast come to govern thy city of Mexico; thou hast come to descend upon thy mat, upon thy seat, which for a moment I have watched for thee, which I have guarded for thee. For thy governors are departed — the rulers Itzcoatl, Moctezuma the Elder, Axayacatl, Tizoc, Auitzotl, who yet a very short time ago had come to stand guard for thee, who had come to govern the city of Mexico. Under their protection thy common folk came. Do they yet perchance know it in their absence? O that one of them might witness, might marvel at what to me now hath befallen, at what I see quite in the absence of our lords.[10] I by no means merely dream, I do not merely see in a dream, I do not see in my sleep; I do not merely dream that I see thee, that I look into thy face. I have been afflicted for some time. I have gazed at the unknown place whence thou hast come — from among the clouds, from among the mists. And so this. The rulers departed maintaining that thou wouldst come to visit thy city, that thou wouldst come to descend upon thy mat, upon thy seat. And now it hath been fulfilled; thou hast come; thou hast endured fatigue, thou hast endured weariness. Peace be with thee. Rest thyself. Visit thy palace. Rest thy body. May peace be with our lords."[11]

Auh ie vncan in vitzilla ontenamjc Motecuçomatzin, njman ie ic contlamamaca in iautachcauh, in intepachocauh iauqujzque, coxochimacac, concozcati in cozcatl, consuchicozcati, consuchiapan, conjcpacsuchiti: njman ie ic ixpan contequjlia in teucujtlacozcatl, in jzqujtlamãtli tenamjconj, tenamjctli in jca oiecauh, cequj cõcozcati:

Njmã qujoalilhuj in Motecuçoma. Cujx amo te? cujx amo ie te? ie te in timotecuçoma:

qujto in Motecuçoma, ca quemaca ca nehoatl:

njmã ie ic vel ommoquetza conjxnamjctimoquetza, connepechtequjlia, vel ixqujch caana, motlaquauhquetza:

injc contlatlauhti, qujlhuj. Totecujoe oticmjhiovilti, oticmociavilti, otlaltitech tommaxitico, oitech tommopachiviltico in Matzin, in motepetzin mexico, oipan tommovetzitico in mopetlatzin, in mocpaltzin, in oachitzinca njmjtzõnopielili, in onjmjtzonnotlapielili, ca oiaque in motechiuhcaoan in tlatoque: in Jtzcoatzin, in veve Motecuçoma, in Axaiaca, in Tiçocic, in Avitzotl, in oc uel achic mjtzommotlapielilico, in oqujpachoco in atl, in tepetl in Mexico: in incujtlapan, inteputzco in ovalietia in momaceoaltzin, cujx oc vallamati in jmonjca, in inteputzco, ma ceme iehoantin qujtztianj qujmaviçotianj, in nehoatl in axcan nopan omochiuh in ie njqujtta, in ça imonjca, inteputzco totecujovan camo çan njtemjquj, amo çã njcochitleoa, amo çan njccochitta, amo çan njctemjquj ca ie onjmjtznottili, mjxtzinco onjtlachix, ca ononnentlamatticatca in ie macujl in ie matlac, in vmpa nonjtztica, in quenamjcan in otimoqujxtico in mjxtitlan in aiauhtitlan: anca iehoatl inin qujteneuhtivi in tlatoq in ticmomachitiqujuh in matzin, in motepetzin: in jpã timovetzitiqujuh in mopetlatzin, in mocpaltzin in tioalmovicaz. Auh in axcan ca oneltic, otioalmovicac, oticmjhiovilti, oticmociavilti, ma tlaltitech ximaxiti, ma ximocevitzino, ma xoconmomachiti in motecpancaltzin, ma xicmocevili in monacaiotzin, ma tlaltitech maxitican in totecujovan.

---

9. Sahagún, Garibay ed., Vol. IV, p. 108: *"En grandes bateas han colocado flores de las finas: la flor del escudo, la del corazón; en medio se yergue la flor de buen aroma, y la amarilla fragante, la valiosa. Son guirnaldas, con travesaños para el pecho."*

10. *Ibid.: "Lo que yo veo ahora: yo el residuo, el superviviente de nuestros señores."*

11. A number of the allusions made here to Moctezuma's ancestry are explained in Alfonso Caso, "Instituciones indígenas precortesianas," *Memorias del Instituto Nacional Indigenista*, Vol. VI (1954), pp. 20–21.

And when Moctezuma's address which he directed to the Marquis was ended, Marina then interpreted it, she translated it to him. And when the Marquis had heard Moctezuma's words, he spoke to Marina;[12] he spoke to them in a barbarous tongue; he said in his barbarous tongue:

"Let Moctezuma put his heart at ease; let him not be frightened. We love him much. Now our hearts are indeed satisfied, for we know him, we hear him. For a long time we have wished to see him, to look upon his face. And this we have seen. Already we have come to his home in Mexico. At his leisure he will hear our words."

Thereupon [the Spaniards] grasped [Moctezuma] by the hand. Already they went leading him by it. They caressed him with their hands to make their love known to him.

And the Spaniards looked at him; they each looked at him thoroughly. They were continually active on their feet; they continually mounted, they continually dismounted in order to look at him.

And the rulers who had gone with him were, first, Cacamatzin, ruler of Texcoco; second, Tetlepanque-tzatzin, ruler of Tlacopan; third, the *tlacochcalcatl* Itzquauhtzin, ruler of Tlatilulco; fourth, Topante-moctzin, Moctezuma's storekeeper in Tlatilulco. These went. And still other noblemen of Tenochti-tlan were Atlixcatzin, the *tlacateccatl*; Tepeuatzin, the *tlacochcalcatl*; Quetzalaztatzin, the *tiçociauacatl*; To-tomotzin, Ecatenpatiltzin, Quappiatzin. When Moc-tezuma was made captive, they not only hid them-selves, took refuge, [but] they abandoned him in anger.

Auh in ontzonqujz in jtlatlatlauhtiliz Motecuçoma concaqujti in Marques: njman ic concaqujztili con-naoaittalhuj in Malintzin. Auh in ocõcac in Marques in jtlatol in motecuçoma: njman ie qujoalnaoatia in Malitzin qujnoalpopolotz: qujoalito in jpopoloch-copa.

Ma moiollali in Motecuçoma, macamo momauhti, ca cenca tictlaçotla, ca axcan uel pachiuj in toiollo, ca tiqujximati in ticcaquj, ca ie ixqujch cavitl in cenca tiqujttaznequj in jxco titlachiaznequj. Auh injn ca otiqujttaque, ie otioallaq̃ in jchan in Mexico, iujan qujcaqujz in totlatol:

njman ie ic imatitech conanque, ie ic qujvicatiuj-tze, qujtzotzona injc qujnextilia in intetlaçotlaliz.

Auh in Españoles qujitta, qujcecemjtta, icxitlan ompepeoa, ontletleco, oaltetemo injc qujtta.

Auh in tlatoque izqujntin in jtlan mantiaque. Inic ce, Cacamatzin, Tetzcucu tlatoanj. Injc vme, Tetle-pãquetzatzin: tlacuban tlatoanj. Injc ei, Itzquauh-tzin tlacochcalcatl: tlatilulco tlatoanj. Injc navi, To-pantemoctzin, tlatilulco itlatlatlalicauh catca, in Mo-tecuçoma in ommantiaque. Auh in oc cequjntin pipiltin tenochca in Atlixcatzin, tlacatecatl, in tepe-oatzin, tlacochcalcatl, Quetzalaztatzin, Ticociaoacatl, Totomotzin, hecatẽpatiltzin, Quappiatzin in nanoc Motecuçoma camo çã motlatique, mjnaxque, quj-tlauelcauhque.

12. The Aztec should read "Malintzin."

motecucalhuiçque, njman
aocac maquiz. Auh in onte
mjctico, njman ieic callacq
valmotzatzacutivetzque.
Auh in in muchiuh ietla
qualizpan: auh in ieiuhquj
njma ieic teiximacho, te
çaçaco: auh in iemuchintin
oçacoque in moteucalhuiçq:
njma ieic tatlatilo intetel
puchcali.

Capitulo. 23. de como Motecuço
ma yel gouernador del Tlatilulco
fueron echados muertos fuera de
la casa donde los españoles estaua
fortalecidos.

Despues delo arriba dicho, quatro dias
andados despues dela matança que
se hizo conel cu, hallaron los mexicanos
muertos a Motecuçoma, yal gouer
nador del Tlatilulco echados fuera de
delas casas reales cerca del muro dõ
de estaua vna piedra labrada como
gala pago que llamauã Teoayoc: y
des pues que conocieron los que los

Injc cempoalli vmei Capitulo
vncan mjtoa in quenjn Motecu
çoma, yoan ce vei pilli tlatilul
co mjcque: auh inin nacaio quj
vallazque igujtia oatoci gujtia
oatoc in cacalli in vncan catca
Españoles.

Auh ie iuh navilhujtl ne
teuteuhujloc in qujmontla
çaco in Motecuçoma, yoan
Itzquauhtzin, omjcque, até
co itvcaioan, Teoaioc: ca
vncan catca injxiptla atoll,
tetl in tlaxixintli, iuh qujn
aioll ipan mjxeuhtica in
tetl. Auh in oittoque, inca

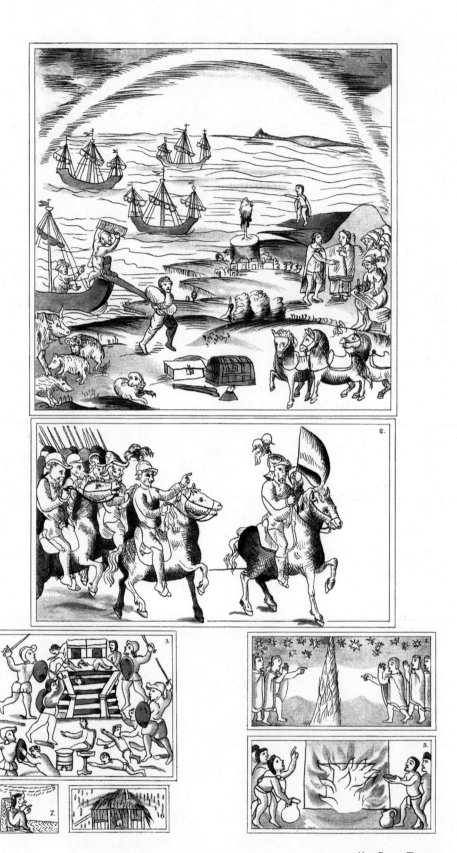

1. Landing of the Spaniards (preceding text). 2. Spaniards marching (preceding text). 3. Spaniards assaulting a temple in Mexico (Chapter 1). 4. First omen: the tongue of fire (Chapter 1). 5. Second omen: burning of Temple of Uitzilopochtli (Chapter 1). 6. Third omen: burning of Temple of Xiuhtecutli (Chapter 1). 7. Fourth omen: comet in three parts (Chapter 1).

8. Sixth omen: the weeping woman (Chapter 1). 9. Seventh omen: the ashen bird with a mirror (Chapter 1). 10. Eighth omen: two-headed men (Chapter 1). 11. Stewards present Spaniards' gift to Moctezuma (Chapter 2). 12. Moctezuma's messengers present gifts to Cortés (Chapter 5). 13. Spaniards bind Moctezuma's messengers (Chapter 5). 14. Spaniards fire guns and terrify the messengers (Chapter 5). 15. Spaniards give food to Moctezuma's messengers (Chapter 5). 16. Moctezuma's messengers return to the mainland (Chapter 6). 17. Captives are slain before Moctezuma's messengers (Chapter 6). 18. Spaniards in war array (Chapter 7). 19. Moctezuma hears description of the Spaniards (Chapter 7).

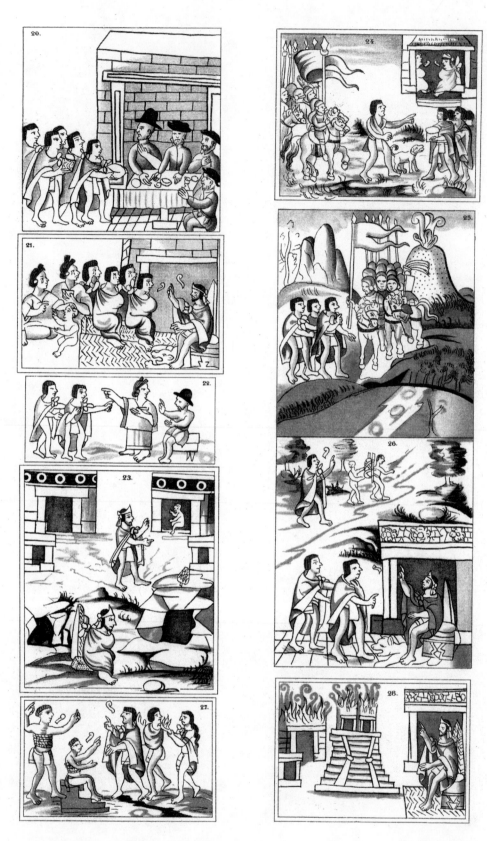

20. Moctezuma's messengers offer food to the Spaniards (Chapter 8). 21. Moctezuma and the Mexicans weep on hearing of the power of the Spaniards (Chapter 9). 22. Marina interprets for Cortés (Chapter 9). 23. Moctezuma debates whether to flee (Chapter 9). 24. Spaniards are welcomed in Tlaxcalla (Chapter 11). 25. Moctezuma's emissaries meet the Spaniards between Iztactepetl and Popocatepetl (Chapter 12). 26. Moctezuma's emissaries return to tell of the meeting with the Spaniards (Chapter 12). 27. Moctezuma's soothsayers meet the drunkard (Chapter 13). 28. Burning Mexican temples shown by the drunkard (Chapter 13).

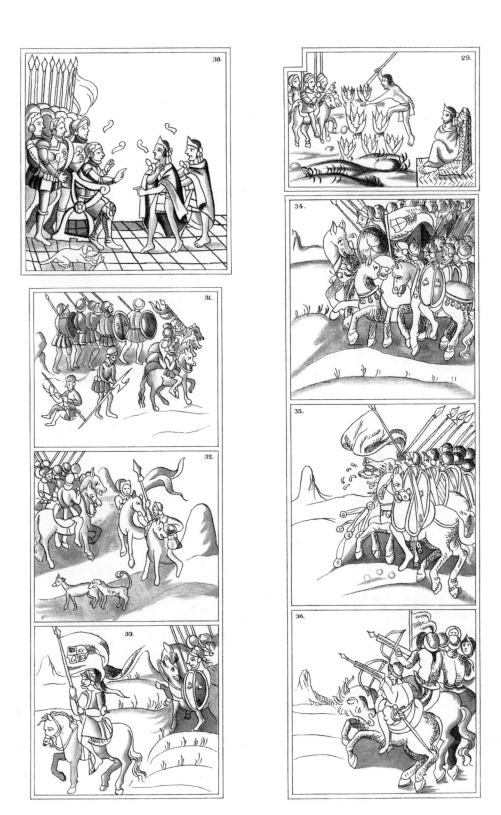

29. The road to Tenochtitlan is sown with maguey plants (Chapter 14). 30. Spaniards receive the submission of two of the Four Lords (Chapter 14). 31-36. Spaniards on the march from Itztapalapan to Tenochtitlan (Chapter 15).

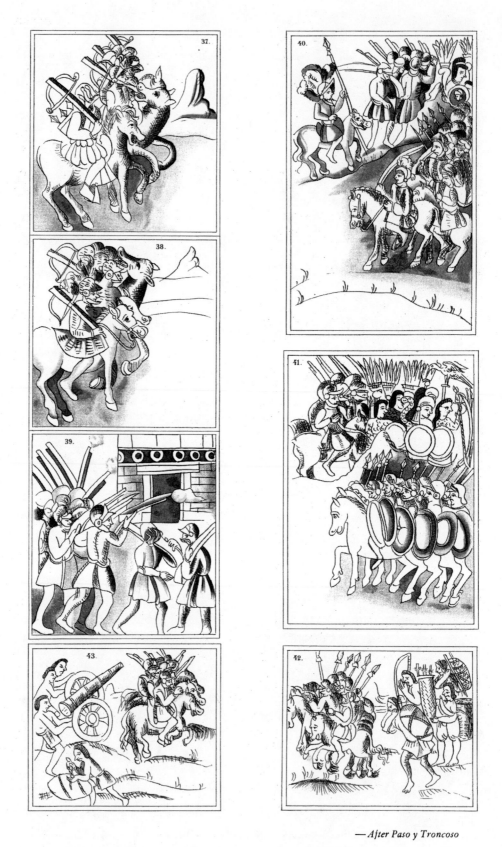

37-43. Spaniards on the march from Itztapalapan to Tenochtitlan (Chapter 15).

44. Marina interprets for the Spaniards when Moctezuma meets Cortés (Chapter 16). 45, 46. Spaniards take Moctezuma with them as they enter the great palace (Chapter 17). 47. Supplies demanded by the Spaniards (Chapter 17). 48. Moctezuma leads Cortés to the treasure (Chapter 17). 49, 50. Spaniards and allies loot the treasure house (Chapter 17). 51. Marina addresses Mexican noblemen (Chapter 18). 52. Mexicans leave supplies for the Spaniards (Chapter 18).

—After Paso y Troncoso

53. Tribute left for the Spaniards (Chapter 18). 54. Alvarado asks to see the Feast of Uitzilopochtli (Chapter 19). 55, 56. Spaniards see preparations for the Feast of Uitzilopochtli (Chapter 19). 57, 58. Preparation of the image of Uitzilopochtli (Chapter 19).

59-64. Preparation of the image of Uitzilopochtli (Chapter 19).

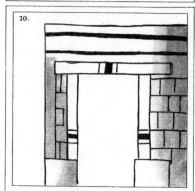

—*After Paso y Troncoso*

65. Preparation of the image of Uitzilopochtli (Chapter 19). 66-70. Massacre of participants in the Feast of Uitzilopochtli (Chapter 20). 71. The massacre is announced to the Mexicans (Chapter 20). 72. War breaks out between the Spaniards and the Mexicans (Chapter 21).

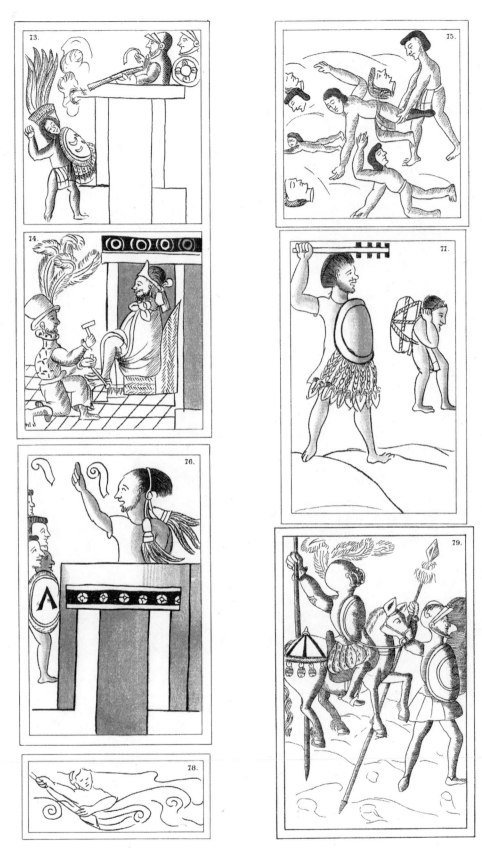

73, 75. War breaks out between the Spaniards and the Mexicans (Chapter 21). 74. Moctezuma is put in irons (Chapter 21). 76. Itzquauhtzin addresses the Mexicans (Chapter 21). 77. Mexicans are seen carrying furs into the palace (Chapter 21). 78. Ornamental design from Book XII. 79. Cortés arrives in Tenochtitlan with more Spaniards and allies (Chapter 22).

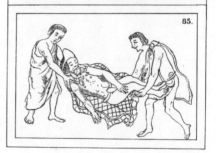

80-82. Cortés arrives in Tenochtitlan with more Spaniards and allies (Chapter 22). 83. Spaniards rout chieftains from the pyramid temple (Chapter 22). 84. Bodies of Moctezuma and Itzquauhtzin are cast out of the palace by the Spaniards (Chapter 23). 85. Moctezuma's body is carried away (Chapter 23).

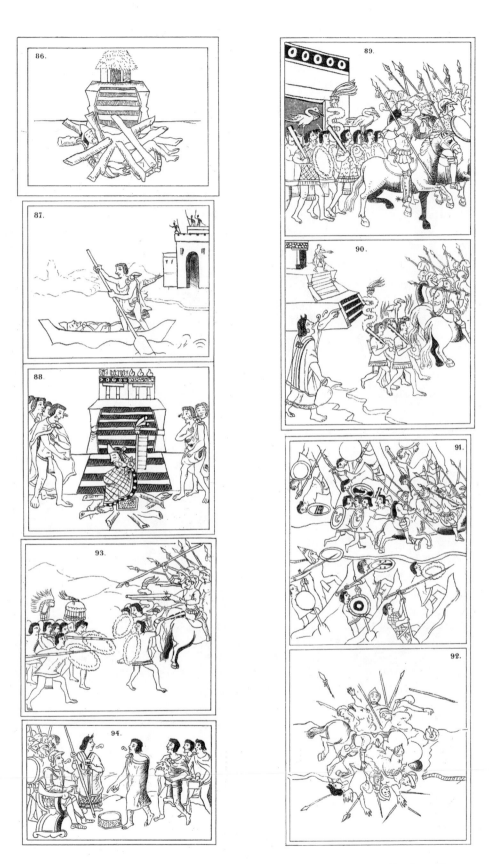

—After Paso y Troncoso

86. Burning of Moctezuma's body (Chapter 23). 87. Itzquauhtzin's body is carried away (Chapter 23). 88. Burning of Itzquauhtzin's body (Chapter 23). 89. Spaniards set forth from their quarters in Tenochtitlan (Chapter 24). 90. Spaniards are detected leaving (Chapter 24). 91-93. Flight from Tenochtitlan (Chapter 24). 94. People of Teocalhueyacan comfort the Spaniards (Chapter 25).

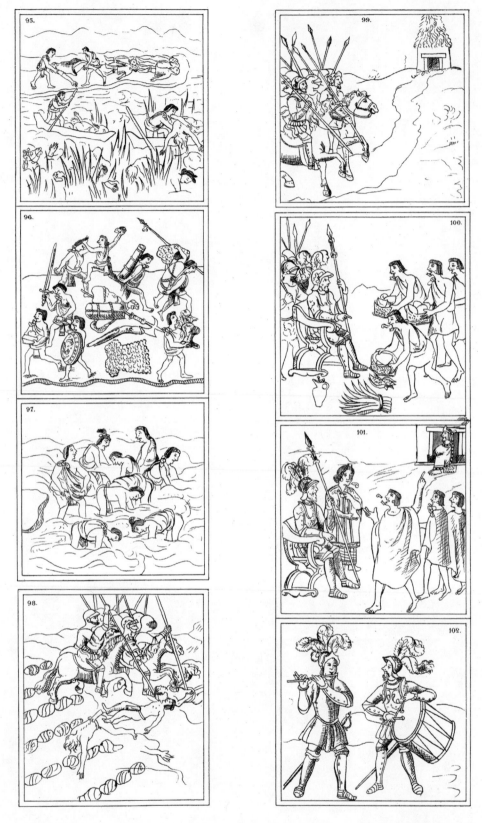

95-97. Mexicans recover bodies and loot from the Tolteca canal (Chapter 25). 98. Massacre at Cala-coayan (Chapter 25). 99. Spaniards climb up to Teocalhueyacan (Chapter 25). 100, 101. People of Teocalhueyacan welcome the Spaniards (Chapter 26). 102. Spaniards prepare to depart from Teocalhueya-can (Chapter 26).

103. Spaniards reach Tepotzotlan (Chapter 26). 104. Mexican warriors pursue the Spaniards (Chapter 26). 105. Spaniards reach Citlaltepec (Chapter 26). 106. Spaniards reach Xoloc (Chapter 26). 107. Spaniards reach Aztaquemecan (Chapter 26). 108. Mexicans on mountain-top watch for the departure of the Spaniards (Chapter 27). 109, 110. Battle at Mt. Tonan (Chapter 27).

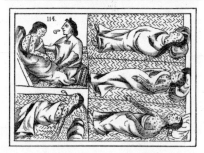

111. Burning of bodies of Mexicans slain in battle at Mt. Tonan (Chapter 27). 112, 113. Refurbishing of a temple in Tenochtitlan on the departure of the Spaniards (Chapter 28). 114. Smallpox plague (Chapter 29). 115-117. Return of the Spaniards to attack Tenochtitlan (Chapter 29). 118. Spanish brigantines (Chapter 30).

119. Spaniards attack Çoquiapan (Chapter 30). 120. Spaniards crumble the wall at Xolloco (Chapter 30). 121. Fighting at Xolloco (Chapter 30). 122. Spaniards pierce the wall at Uitzillan (Chapter 31). 123. Allies of the Spaniards fill the canals (Chapter 31). 124. Spanish horsemen ride in at Uitzillan (Chapter 31). 125. Spanish horseman spears a Tlatilulcan (Chapter 31). 126. Mexican warriors unhorse and kill the Spaniard (Chapter 31). 127. Shorn ones land from warboats (Chapter 31).

—*After Paso y Troncoso*

128. Spaniards are attacked on both sides (Chapter 31). 129. Mexican warriors toss the captured **cannon** into the water at Tetamaçolco (Chapter 31). 130. Mexicans flee from Tenochtitlan (Chapter 32). 131. Exploits of Tzilacatzin (Chapter 32). 132-134. Battle about Ayauhcaltitlan and Nonoalco (Chapter 32). 135-137. The warrior Tzilacatzin in three disguises (Chapter 32).

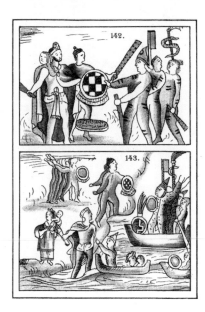

138, 139. Spaniards are fought off and withdraw (Chapter 32). 140. Warriors of Xochimilco, Itztapalapan, and Cuitlauac arrive to work treachery upon the Mexicans (Chapter 33). 141. Quauhtemoc and a nobleman (Chapter 33). 142-145. The treachery of those of Xochimilco, Itztapalapan, and Cuitlauac is prevented (Chapter 33).

—*After Paso y Troncoso*

146. Quauhtemoc and Mayeuatzin punish the traitors (Chapter 33). 147, 148. Spaniards arrive at Yauhtenco (Chapter 33, 34). 149-151. Mexicans disperse the Spaniards and capture some (Chapter 34). 152-155. Mexicans capture and sacrifice fifty-three Spaniards, some horses, and many allies (Chapter 35).

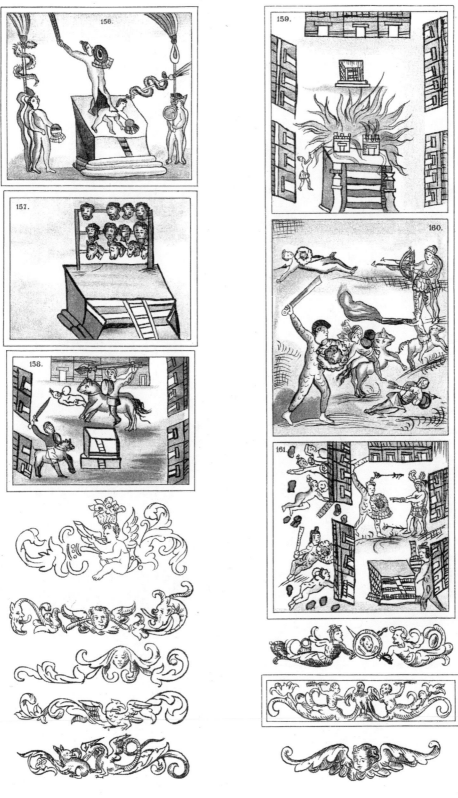

—After Paso y Troncoso

156, 157. Mexicans capture and sacrifice fifty-three Spaniards, some horses, and many allies (Chapter 35). 158. Spaniards enter the market place at Tlatilulco (Chapter 36). 159. Spaniards fire the temple at Tlatilulco (Chapter 36). 160, 161. Battle in the market place at Tlatilulco (Chapter 36).

Seventeenth Chapter, in which it is told how the Spaniards took Moctezuma with them when they went to enter the great palace, and what there happened.

And when they had gone to arrive in the palace, when they had gone to enter it, at once they firmly seized Moctezuma. They continually kept him closely under observation;[1] they never let him from their sight. With him was Itzquauhtzin.[2] But the others just came forth [unimpeded].

And when this had come to pass, then each of the guns shot off. As if in confusion there was going off to one side, there was scattering from one's sight, a jumping in all directions. It was as if one had lost one's breath; it was as if for the time there was stupefaction, as if one were affected by mushrooms, as if something unknown were shown one. Fear prevailed. It was as if everyone had swallowed his heart. Even before it had grown dark, there was terror, there was astonishment, there was apprehension, there was a stunning of the people.

And when it dawned, thereupon were proclaimed all the things which [the Spaniards] required: white tortillas, roasted turkey hens, eggs, fresh water, wood, firewood, charcoal, earthen bowls, polished vessels, water jars, large water pitchers, cooking vessels, all manner of clay articles. This had Moctezuma indeed commanded.

But when he summoned forth the noblemen, no longer did they obey him. They only grew angry. No longer did they come to him, no longer did they go to him. No longer was he heeded. But nevertheless he was not therefore neglected;[3] he was given all that he required — food, drink, and water [and] fodder for the deer.

And when [the Spaniards] were well settled, they thereupon inquired of Moctezuma as to all the city's treasure — the devices, the shields. Much did they im-

---

Injc caxtolli omume capitulo: vncan mjtoa in quenjn Españoles qujvicatiaque Motecuçoma injc calaqujto vei tecpã: yoan in tlein vmpa mochiuh.

Auh in oacito tecpan, in ocalaqujto: çan njman vel quitzizqujque, vel qujxpixtinenca, amo connjxcaoaia in Motecuçoma, in nehoan Itzquauhtzin: auh in oc cequjntin çan oalqujzque.

Auh in ie iuhquj: njman ie uevetz in in tlequjqujztli, iuhqujn tlayxneliuj, avic viloa, tlaixmoiaoa, tlachichitoca, iuhqujn tlacica, çan oqujuhqujn netequjpacholo, iuhqujn nenanacavilo, iuhqujn tlen mach onnettitilo, maujztli oonoc, iuhqujn mochi tlacatl qujtollo yiollo: çãnoc iuh onioac, nemamauhtilotoc neihiçavilotoc, necujcujtiuechotoc, necochmamauhtilotoc.

Auh in otlatvic, njman ie ic motzatzilia in jxqujch intech monequj, in iztac tlaxcalli, totollaleoatzalli, totoltetl, chipaoac atl, in quaujtl, in tlatlatilquaujtl, in tecolli, in apaztli, in petzcaxitl, in apilloli, in tzotzocolli, in tlatzoionjlcaxitl, in ie ixqujch in çoqujtlatqujtl: iehoatl uel tlanaoatica in Motecuçomatzin.

Auh in qujnoalnotzaia pipilti, aocmo qujtlacamatia, ça quallanj, aocmo iujc qujça, aocmo ivic qujça, aocmo iujc onuj, aocmo mocaquj: auh tel amo ic xiccaoalo, maco in jxqujch itech monequj in qualonj, in joalonj, ioan in atl, in maçatlaqlli.

Auh in no uel motlalique: njmã ie ic qujntemolia in Motecuçomatzin in jxqujch in jtetzõ in altepetl, in tlaujztli, in chimalli, cenca qujmatataqujlia, cẽca

---

1. Francisco Cervantes de Salazar, in *Crónica de Nueva España* (Mexico, D.F.: Talleres Gráficos del Museo Nacional de Arqueología y Etnografía, 1936), Vol. II, Chaps. XXVII *sqq.*, develops this narrative with much color and detail.

2. Governor of Tlatelolco (corresponding Spanish text).

3. Seler (*Einige Kapitel*, p. 495) reads the phrase *auh tel amo ic xiccaualo — Aber es wurde darum doch nicht versäumt*; in Sahagún, Garibay ed., Vol. IV, p. 111, the translation is: "*y, sin embargo, llevaban en bateas.*"

portune him; with great zeal they sought gold. And Moctezuma thereupon went leading the Spaniards. They went surrounding him, scattered about him; he went among them, he went in their lead; they went each holding him, each grasping him. And when they reached the storehouse, a place called Teocalco,[4] thereupon were brought forth all the brilliant things; the quetzal feather head fan, the devices, the shields, the golden discs, the devils' necklaces, the golden nose crescents, the golden leg bands,[5] the golden arm bands, the golden forehead bands.

Thereupon was detached the gold which was on the shields and which was on all the devices. And as all the gold was detached, at once they ignited, set fire to, applied fire to all the various precious things [which remained]. They all burned. And the gold the Spaniards formed into separate bars. And the green stone, as much as they saw to be good they took. But the rest of the green stone the Tlaxcallans just stole. And the Spaniards walked everywhere; they went everywhere taking to pieces the hiding places, storehouses, storage places. They took all, all that they saw which they saw to be good.

qujmaujztemoa in teucujtlatl. Auh in Motecuçomatzin: njman ie ic qujniacantiuh in Españoles, cololhujtiuj, qujtepeujtiuj, innepantla icatiuh, tlaiacac icatiuh, qujtzitzizqujtiuj, caantiuj. Auh in onacique in tlatlatilcali: itocaiocan, teucalco: njman ie ic oallaqujxtilo in jxqujch in petlacotl, in quetzalapanecaiutl, in tlaujztli, in chimalli, in teocujtlacomalli in incozquj diablome, teucujtlaiacametztli, in teocujtlacotzecoatl, in teocujtlamatemecatl, in teocujtlaixquaamatl:

njman ie ic tlaixcoleoalo in jtech chimalli in teucujtlatl: yoan in jtech in jxqujch tlaviztli: auh inic muchi omocoleuh in teucujtlatl, ie ic contlecavia, cõtlequechia, contlemjna in ixqujch nepapan tlaçotli muchi tlatlac. Auh in teucujtlatl qujxaxantecaque in Españoles: auh in chalchivitl in quexqujch qujqualittaque, qujcujque: auh in oc cequj chalchivitl, çan qujnamuxque in tlaxcalteca: yoan noviã nenque, qujxaqualotinenque in novian tlatlatican, tlatlatilcali, tlatlatiloian, muchi qujcujque in jxqujch in qujttaque, in qujqualittaque.

---

4. The Spanish text of Chaps. 16 and 17 refers to *casas reales*, presumably the location of the Teocalco.

5. Read *teocuitlacotzeuatl*.

Eighteenth Chapter, in which it is told how the Spaniards went to enter Moctezuma's princely home, and what happened there.

Thereupon they went to Moctezuma's own storehouse, where was kept Moctezuma's own property, a place called Totocalco.[1] It was as if they each worked tirelessly; each was content, each clapped the other on the back, each one's heart was brightened. And when they came to arrive, when they entered the storehouse, it was as if there was a dispersal; they quickly entered everywhere, as if they were lustful, greedy.[2] Thereupon was brought forth [Moctezuma's] own property, that which was indeed his personally, his very own lot, precious things all; the necklaces with pendants, the arm bands with tufts of quetzal feathers, the golden arm bands, and the bracelets, the golden bands with shells, to fasten at the ankle, and the turquoise diadem, the attribute of the ruler, and the turquoise nose rods, and the rest of his goods without number. They took it all. They possessed themselves of all, they appropriated all to themselves, they took all to themselves as their lot.

And when they had detached all the gold, when it had been detached, thereupon in the courtyard, in the middle of the courtyard, they brought together all the precious feathers. And when it had come to pass that all the gold was gathered together, thereupon Marina summoned hither, ordered summoned hither, all the noblemen. She went upon a roof terrace, upon a terrace parapet. She said: "Mexicans, come hither![3] The Spaniards have suffered great fatigue. Bring food here, fresh water, and all that is required. For they already suffer fatigue; they suffer weariness for it, they suffer fatigue for it; they are wearied, they are fatigued. Why do you not wish to come? It therefore appeareth that you are angered."

But the Mexicans dared not at all to go there. They were in great terror; they could not control themselves for fear; they were astounded. Fear prevailed; fear

Injc caxtolli omei capitulo: vncan mjtoa, in quenjn Españoles calaqujto in jpilchan Motecuçoma: auh in tlein vmpa muchiuh.

Niman ie ic vi in vel itlatlatiaia Motecuçoma in vmpa mopia in vel itech iaxca in motecuçoma: itoca iocan Totocalco iuhqujn mocecenquetza, iuhqujn yioiolipan, iuhqujn moquequetzotzona, iuhqujn iiztaia iniollo. Auh in onacito, in oncalacque tlatlatiloian, iuhqujn tlacecēmana, novian aactivetzi, iuhqujn mjhicultia, mjhicolia: njmã ie ic oallaqujxtilo in vel ixcoian yiaxca, in vel ineixcavil, in vel itonal, mochi tlaçotlanquj, in chaiaoac cozcatl, in machoncotl, in teucujtlamatemecatl, yoan in matzopetztli, teucujtlaicxitecuecuextli, yoan in xiuvitzolli tlatocatlatqujtl, yoã in iacaxivitl, yoan in jxqujch in oc cequj in jtlatquj in amo çan tlapoalli muchi qujcujque, moch intech compachoq̄ moch cōmotechtique, moch cōmotonaltique.

Auh in ocōcocoleuhque in jxqujch in teucujtlatl: in ontlacocoleoaloc, njman ie ic qujcentlalia itoalco, itoalnepantla in jxqujch in tlaçohivitl. Auh in ie iuhquj in omochi munechico in teucujtlatl. Njmã ie ic qujoalnotza, qujoalnenotzallanj in jxqujchtin in pipiltin in Malintzin: tlapanco oalmoquetz, atenanticpac: Quitoa. Mexica xioalhujan ca cenca ie tlaihiovia in Españoles: xiqualcujcã in tlaqualli, in chipaoac atl, yoan in jxqujch monequj, ca ie tlaihiovia, ie qujciavi, ie qujhiovia, ie mociavi, ie mjhiovia: tleica in amo anoallaznequj? ic neci ca anqualanj.

Auh in Mexica çã njmã aocmo motlapaloaia in ma onvian, cenca momauhtiaia, mauhcaçonequja mjhiçaviaia, cenca maviztli onoc, maviztli moteca, aocac

1. See Anderson and Dibble, *Book VIII*, p. 45.
2. Seler (*Einige Kapitel*, p. 496) translates thus: "*Man sah sie stolz aufgerichtet gehen, wie Narren (oder wie Tiere), gleichsam einander wegbeissend, hochzufrieden*"; Sahagún, Garibay ed., Vol. IV, p. 112:

"*eran como si hubiesen llegado al extremo. Por todas partes se metían, todo codiciaban para sí, estaban dominados de avidez.*"

3. *Xiqualcujcan*: read *xicualuican*.

was widespread.[4] No one dared do anything. It was as if a fierce beast were there; it was as the deep of night. Yet not because of this did they stop; not for this was there hesitation in leaving what [the Spaniards] required, but they left it in fear. They went only in great fear, they only ran in fear as they left it. And when they came to scatter it over the ground, there was running back; they shot back. There was panting, there was trembling.[5]

tlaxtlapaloa, ça iuhq'n tequanj vnca, ça iuhqujn tlalli mjctoc: tel amo ic mocaoa, amo ic netzotzonalo in concaoa in jxqujch intech monequj, ça in mauhcac in concaoaia, çan momamauhtitivi, ça onmomauhcatlaloa in ontlacaoa. Auh in ocontepeoato valnetlalolo, vallachichitoca, tlacica, tlaviviioca.

---

4. *Moteteca*: the word is blurred in the MS.

5. In Seler, *Einige Kapitel*, p. 497, this passage is rendered: *"Und nachdem sie es auf den Boden gelegt hatten, rannten sie zurück, stoben auseinander, ... zitternd (vor Furcht)."* A note on p. 494 compares *tla-* *cica* with *tlatlatzca* (see Alonso de Molina, *Vocabulario de la lengua mexicana*, ed. Julio Platzmann [Leipzig: B. G. Teubner, 1880]); in Sahagún, Garibay ed., Vol. IV, p. 113: *"Y cuando se habían dejado, no más se volvían atrás, se escabullían de prisa, se iban temblando."*

Nineteenth Chapter, in which it is told how the Spaniards commanded the Mexicans to observe the Feast of Uitzilopochtli. But this did not come to pass in the presence of the Captain, for it was when he went there to the coast when Pánfilo de Narváez came to arrive.

And afterwards [Pedro de Alvarado][1] thereupon inquired about the Feast of Uitzilopochtli: what sort of feast day it was. He wished to marvel at it, he wished to see what it was, how it was done. Thereupon Moctezuma commanded those of his governors who could enter. They brought forth the word.[2]

And when the word had come forth there from where Moctezuma was enclosed, thereupon the women who had fasted for a year ground up the amaranth, the fish amaranth,[3] there in the temple courtyard. The Spaniards came forth. They were elaborately attired in battle gear; they were arrayed for battle, arrayed as warriors. They came to [the women]: they came among them; they circled about them; they looked at each one, they looked into the faces of each of the grinding women. And when it had come to pass that they came looking at them, thereupon they entered the great palace. As was known, it was said that at that time they would have slain the men if many of us warriors had been assembled.

And when the Feast of Toxcatl had arrived, toward sundown they began to give man's form to [Uitzilopochtli's amaranth seed dough image]. They formed it like a man, they gave it the look of a man, they gave it the appearance of a man. And that of which they made its body was only amaranth seed dough, a dough of fish amaranth seed. They laid it out on a

Injc caxtolli onnavi capitulo: vncan mjtoa in quenjn Españoles, qujnnaoatique Mexica: injc qujchioazque injlhujuh vitzilobuchtli: auh inin amo ixpan muchiuh in Capitan: ca iquac in vmpa ia atenco injc acico Panphilo de narbayez.

Auh çatepan, njman ie ic qujtlanj in jilhujuh vitzilobuchtli, in quenamj ilhujuh, qujmaviçoznequj qujttaznequj, in quenamj, in quenjn muchioa: njmã ie ic tlanaoatia in Motecuçoma, in aqujque vel oconcalaquj itechiuhcaoan, qujoalqujxtiaia in tlatolli.

Auh in ovalqujz tlatolli in vmpa caltzacutica motecuçoma: njman ie ic qujteci in oauhtli chicalutl in cioa, mocexiuhçauhque, vncã in teuitoalco, oalqujzque in Españoles, cenca omocecencauhq̃ in jca iautlatqujtl, moiauchichiuhque, moqujchchichiuhque, intlan qujqujça, intzalan qujqujça, qujniaiavaloa, qujncecemjtta, imjxco tlatlachia in teci cioa. Auh in ie iuhquj in oqujmonjttaco, njmã ie ic calaquj in vei tecpan, iuh machiztic: qujlmach iquac temjctizqujа intla mjec tlacatl cenqujçani toqujchtin.

Auh in ie oacic ilhujtl in toxcatl, teutlacpa in qujpeoaltia in qujtlacatilia in jnacaio, qujtlacatlaliaia, qujtlacatlachieltiaia, qujtlacanextia. Auh inin qujnacaiotiaia çan tzoalli, ie in mjchioauhtzoalli, tlacopepechpan in qujtlaliaia, ie in vitzitzillacutl, yoã nacaztlacutl.

1. Cf. corresponding Spanish text. Garibay (Sahagún, Garibay ed., Vol. IV, p. 113) says that "*Luego pidieron (los mexicanos) la fiesta de Huitzilopochtli.*"

2. Cf. Charles E. Dibble, *Historia de la nación mexicana ... Códice de 1576* (Madrid: Ediciones José Porrúa Turanzas, 1963), pp. 54 *sqq.*,

where the narrative of the Conquest contains a different version.

3. *Chicalotl: chicallotl o espino*; "*cardo*," *Argemone mexicana* L. (Hernández, *Historia de las plantas*, Vol. III, pp. 803–5); *chicalote* (Santamaría, *Diccionario de mejicanismos*, pp. 372–73); common *Argemone* of Mexico (Emmart, *Badianus Manuscript*, p. 263).

framework of sticks; these were thorny sticks and sticks forming angles.[4]

And when it became a man in form, then they pasted his head with feather down and made his diagonally striped face painting, and [gave him] his serpent ear plug of glued turquoise [mosaic]. And from the serpent ear plug hung the golden ring of thorns, with toes — cut in the form of toes. And his nose rod was arrow[-shaped], of gold workmanship, beaten, and set with stones: a thin [plate] painted as if with stones. Also from it hung what was called the thorn ring, painted with diagonal stripes. Thus was it diagonally striped: there were [alternating] blue and yellow [bands]. And upon his head they stood his hummingbird disguise. Then there followed what was named *anecuyotl*, [a headdress] of featherwork, cylindrical, a little pointed, a little narrow at the base. Thereupon they set in place upon the back of his head a ball of yellow parrot feathers from which hung a child's lock of hair. And [he had] his cape of nettles,[5] colored black, in five places ornamented with feathers, with eagle down. It was wrapped about him. And below, he was wrapped in his cape with severed heads and bones. And above, he was wrapped in and [wore] his sleeveless jacket, painted like the *tlaquaquallo* [jacket]. There were there painted all severed heads, ears, hearts, entrails, livers, breasts, hands, feet. And [he had] his breech clout. Only his breech clout was very precious. And its workmanship was also of the *tlaquaquallo* design; it was so woven. But his large [breech clout][6] was only of paper; it was of white paper,[7] one fathom wide and twenty long, painted

Auh in ie utlacat, njmã qujquapotonja, yoan qujchioa, ixtlã tlatlaan, yoan icoanacochxivitl in tlaçalolli: auh in jcoanacoch itech pipilcac in vitznaoaiotl, teucujtlatl xoxopiltic, tlaxoxopiltectli, yoã yiacapilol, mjtl: Teucujtlatl in tlachiuhtli, tlatzotzontli, yoan tlateantli, tlacanaoalli, tlateicujlolli: no itech pilcaia moteneoa vitznaoaiutl, ixtlan tlatlaan: injc ixtlan tlatlaan, vncan icac texutli, yoan têcuxtli yoã icpac conquetza ivitzitzilnaoal: njmã contoqujlia, itoca anecuiutl, hivitl in tlachichioalli, mjmjltic, achitzin vitztic, achi tzimpitzaoac: njmã ie ic in tozpololli icuexcochtlan in contlalilia itech pilcac tzíuhcuexpalli, yoã itzitzicaztilma, tlatlilpalli: macujlcan in tlapotonjlli, quauhtlachcaiotica, qujmololotica, yoan in jtilma in tlanj qujmoquentia, tzotzontecomaio, oomjcallo: auh in panj qujmolpilia, yoan ixicul: injc tlacujlolli tlaquaquallo, ca much vncã icujliuhtoc in tzontecomatl, nacaztli, iollotli, cujtlaxculli eltapachtli, tochichi, macpalli, xocpalli, yoan imaxtli: çan in maxtlatl, vellaçotlanquj: auh in jtlamachio injc no tlaquaquallo injc tlaqujttli: auh in jvei[maxtli] çan amatl, iehoatl in quaoamatl, injc patlaoac cemmatl: auh injc viac cempoalli, injc tlacujlolli texoacaxilquj, auh in jquezpan qujmamanticatca iacatecpaio: in jezpan çan amatl catca, tlapalli injc tlacujlolli, injc tlaezicujlolli: iacatecpaio, çan no amatl in tlachioalli, çan no iuhquj injc tlacujlolli, tlaezicujlolli, yoan ichimal ietica otlatl in tlachioalli, otlachimalli, nauhcan tlapotonjlli, quauhtlachcaiotica, hivichachapanquj, moteneoa: Tevevelli, auh chimalpaio, çan no

---

4. Personal communication from Mgr. Angel María Garibay and Byron McAfee, Nov., 1954: "Y a este le hacían su cuerpo con bledos, con bledos de chicalote (Argemone mexicana, seg. Lehmann). En un armazón de varas lo ponían; es el armazón de Huitzil(opochtli), y el armazón de esquinas." These authorities explain: "Lo llama vitzillacotl o sea 'varas de Huitzil,' porque está formado de palos delgados y cortados de mezquite que es madera dura y ligera (mizquicuauitl in tlaxintli), y el nombre del dios está abreviado Huitzil 'precioso colibrí' que supone el elemento Opochtli el de la izquierda del mundo, que es el sur.— Nacaztlacotl lit. 'varas de oreja.' La palabra tlacotl, tlacotli significa una vara dura y resistente, como era la de los dardos. Se halla también en el anterior vocablo. Nacaztli es 'oreja, esquina,' y 'varas de esquina' supone que era el armadijo, o aparato una construcción de varas tajadas o acomodadas en forma de pirámide alargada y truncada. Sobre esta armazón se ponían los bledos o semillas de huauhtli, que eran precisamente de la planta dicha. Llamados michi huauhtli, 'bledos de pescado.'" Cf. also Anderson and Dibble, Book II, p. 68. In the present chapter, however, chicalotl appears to be a synonym for fish amaranth (michiuauhtli); see Charles E. Dibble and Arthur J. O. Anderson, trans., "Earthly Things," Florentine Codex, Book XI (Santa Fe: School of American Research and University of Utah, 1963; hereafter referred to as Dibble and Anderson, Book XI), p. 287.

5. Hernández (Historia de las plantas, Vol. II, pp. 390–91) trans-

lates tzitzicaztli as ortiga (Urtica sp.?); on pp. 388–90 he mentions seven kinds: four are Urtica sp.; others are Urtica dioica, var. angustifolia; Borraginácea Wigandia Kunthii Choisy ("quemadora," "ortiga"); and W. caracasana H. B. K. ("ortiga de tierra caliente"). Santamaría, Diccionario de mejicanismos, p. 378, writes of chichicaste: "Planta herbácea compuesta, semitrepadora, común en las zonas cálidas y templadas" (Eupatorium denticulatum). Also, "Planta urticácea, llamada también ortiga, mal hombre, mala mujer, quemador, chichicastillo, tlachinole, en Méjico." See also Maximino Martínez, Las plantas medicinales de México (Mexico, D.F.: Ediciones Botas, 1933), pp. 414–15 — chichicaxtli, Urera caracasana (Jacq.) Griseb.

6. In the MS, a blank follows jvei. Seler (Einige Kapitel, p. 500) has supplied –acaio. Reference to the description of this ceremony in Book II, however, suggests that the omission is –maxtli.

7. In Victor Wolfgang Von Hagen, The Aztec and Maya Paper Makers (New York: J. J. Augustin, 1944), p. 60, cuah-amatl is given as "coarse, thickly fibered paper, more difficult to fashion than the fig tree variety"; from bull's horn acacia (Acacia cornigera). On the other hand, a note in Sahagún, Robredo ed., Vol. V, p. 231, reads: "la materia suministrada por la capa de líber de algunos árboles del género ficus. Servía de papel para las pinturas o los libros, y de tela para hacer los adornos, vestidos y otros objetos que el culto de los dioses requería."

with a blue striped design. And as to his shoulders: he was carrying as a burden for the back [the blood banner] with the flint knife at the point [of the staff]. His blood banner was only of paperwork painted similarly, painted with [stripes of] blood. And the flint knife at the point was likewise only of paperwork, and also painted similarly, painted with [stripes of] blood. And he went with his shield of stout reedwork; it was a shield of stout reeds decorated in four places with feathers, with eagle down, with tufts of feathers. It was called *teueuelli*. And the shield banner was likewise painted like the blood banner. And he held his four arrows together with his shield. And his left arm band hung from his arm. It was arranged of [strips of] coyote fur, and from it was hanging paper cut in strips.

And when dawn broke, when it was already the feast day, when it was early morning, already those who had made vows to him uncovered his face. Before him they formed a row; they offered him incense; before him they laid, on all sides, gifts — fasting foods, rolls of amaranth seed dough. But when this was done, not now did they take him up, not now did they lift him up to Itepeyoc. And all the men, the young seasoned warriors, were each as if diligently engaged, as if content, in proceeding with the feast, in observing the feast, in order to make the Spaniards see it, to make them wonder at it, to show it to them.

There was hastening, there was running, there was going to the temple courtyard, in order that the winding dance be danced. And when the assembling had taken place, thereupon was the beginning; already began the singing, the winding dance. And those who had fasted twenty days and those who had fasted a year went facing the others; they detained the people [with] their pine staves. Whosoever tried to leave they menaced with the pine staves. But one who would [leave to] urinate took off his net cape and his forked heron feather ornament. And one who was completely disobedient, who did not consider himself rejected, who was impudent, they soundly beat his back therefor, they beat his thighs, they beat his shoulders; they thrust him outside, they put him out by force, they threw him face down; he went falling face down. He went out on his ear. No one in the hands [of those who kept order] answered back.

The elder brothers of Uitzilopochtli, those who had fasted a year, were very much looked upon with extreme fear; they were looked upon with terror; there

iuhquj in ezpanjtl injc tlacujlolli: yoan navi imjuh ic qujcentzitzquja in jchimal yoan iopochmacuex imacpilcac, coiotomjtl in tlavipantli, yoan itech pilcatica amatl tlaxoxotlalli.

Auh in otlatvic in ie ilhujuh ipan, in ioatzinco ie ic qujxtlapoa in jvic monetoltia, ixpan oncenpanti qujtlenamaqujlia, ixpan qujmana in izqujcan ventli in tlacatlaqualli, in tzoalilacatzolli. Auh in jquac in, aocmo qujtlecavique, aocmo cacoqujxtique in itepeioc: auh in ixqujch tlacatl in telpopochtequjoaque iuhqujn nececēquetzalo, iuhqujn in ioiolipā in jlhujtlazque, in ilhujtlamatizque, injc qujntlattitizque, qujntlamaviçoltizq̃, qujntlaixtlatizque, in Españoles:

tlatotoca, netlalolo, vmpa itztiova in teuitoalco, injc vmpa necocololoz. Auh in ocecenqujxoac: njmā ie ic peoalo, ie ic vmpeoa in cujco yoan necocololoz. Auh in mocenpoalçauhque, yoan yoan in mocexiuhçauhque nepan jxtinemj: in tetzaqua imoocoquauh, in aqujn qujçaznequj ic qujtlaieiecalhuja in ocoquavitl: auh in aqujn maxixaz qujtlalitiuh icuechi, yoan iaztaxel. Auh in aqujn çan njman atlatlacamati, in amo tetlaçaltoca in aquen tlatta, vel ic qujcujtlavitequj, qujmetzvitequj, caculhujtequj, caliticpa contopeoa, conchiccanaoa, conjxiquetza, mjhixiquetztiuh, nanacazitztiuh aiac temacnaoati:

cenca iehoā tlamamauhtiaia, tlamauhtiaia, cemjmacaxoa, cemjmacaxtincatca in jachvan vitzilobuchtli in mocexiuhçauhque. Auh in tlaiacatia in vevei

was complete dread; they were completely to be dreaded. And those at the head, the important personages, those who did great things — they nevertheless could pass; no one prevented them. But all the very young men, those with the lock of hair at the back of the head, with the back lock of hair, and with the jar-shaped hairdress, those who had taken a captive with others' help, the leaders, those called leaders of young men, who were unmarried, who had gone [to war] to take a captive, who had gone to take two captives, these they also detained. They said to them: "Go along there, O rogue! You are showing it to the people; it is not seen by us!"

tachcavan, in vevei chiva tel huel qujçaia, amo qujntzacujliaia: auh in ie ixqujch telputzintli, in cuexpaltzine in cuexpaltzitzineque, yoan in tzotzocoleque, in tepallamanj, in yiaque: in moteneoa in telpuchiaque, in ce ic nemj, in ce cacitinemj, in anoço vme cacitinemj no qujntzaquaia: qujmjlhujaia, vmpa xiviã on nocne, anqujteittitia, amo techitto.

Twentieth Chapter, in which it is told how the Spaniards[1] slew the Mexicans, destroyed them, when they celebrated the Feast of Uitzilopochtli, there where it is called Teoitualco.

And when this was happening, when already the feast was being observed, when already there was dancing, when already there was singing, when already there was song with dance, the singing resounded like waves breaking.

When it was already time, when the moment was opportune for the Spaniards to slay them, thereupon they came forth. They were arrayed for battle. They came everywhere to block each of the ways leading out [and] leading in — Quauhquiauac, Tecpantzinco, Acatl yiacapan, Tezcacoac.[2] And when they had blocked them, they also remained everywhere. No one could go out.

And when this had been done, thereupon they entered the temple courtyard to slay them. Those whose task it was to slay them went only afoot, each with his leather shield, some, each one, with his iron-studded shield, and each with his iron sword. Thereupon they surrounded the dancers. Thereupon they went among the drums. Then they struck the drummer's arms; they severed both his hands; then they struck his neck. Far off did his neck [and head] go to fall. Then they all pierced the people with iron lances and they struck them each with iron swords. Of some they slashed open their backs: then their entrails gushed out. Of some they cut their heads to pieces; they absolutely pulverized their heads; their heads were absolutely pulverized. And some they struck on the shoulder; they split openings, they broke openings in their bodies. Of some they struck repeatedly the shanks; of some they struck repeatedly the thighs; of some they struck the belly; then their entrails gushed forth. And when in vain one would run, he would only drag his intestines like something raw as he tried to escape. Nowhere could he go.[3] And

Injc cempoalli capitulo: vncã mjtoa in quenjn Espanoles qujnmjctique, qujmjxtlatique in Mexica, in qujlhujqujxtiliaia Vitzilobuchtli in vncã mjtoaia Teuitoalco.

Auh in ie iuhquj, in ie ilhujtlamacho, in ie netotilo in ie cujco, in ie cujcoanolo: in cujcatl, iuhqujn xaxamacatimanj.

In ie inmã, in otlainmantic injc temjctizque in Españoles: njman ie ic oalqujça omoiauchichiuhque, ocontzatzaquaco, in jzqujcampa qujxoaia, calacoaia, in quauhqujiaoac tecpantzinco, acatl yiacapan, Tezcacoac. Auh in ocõtzatzacque: no izqujcã momanque, aocac vel hoalqujça.

Auh in ie iuhquj, njmã ie ic calaquj in teuitoalco in temjctizque: in intequjuh in temjctique çan tlacxipãvia imeevachimal, cequj intotopchimal, yoan intetepuzmaquauh: njman ie ic qujniaoaloa in mjtotia, njmã ie ic vi in vevetitlan, njmã qujmavitecque in tlatzotzona oalcocoton vmexti in jmacpal çatepan qujquechvitecque veca vetzito in jquech: njmã ie muchintin texixili tepuztopiltica, yoan teviviteque tepuzmaquauhtica: cequjntin qujncujtlaço, njman valmotoxaoa in incujtlaxcol, cequjntin qujnquatzatzaianque, vel qujtzeltilique in intzontecon, vel itzeltix in intzõtecõ. Auh in cequjntin qujmaculhujtecque, oalcacamatlapan, oaltzatzaian in innacaio: cequjntin qujncotzvivitecque, cequjn qujnmetzvivitecque, cequjntin qujmjtivitecque, njmã moch oalmotoxaoa in incujtlaxcul. Auh in aca oc nen motlaloa in jcujtlaxcul ça qujvilana, iuhqujn xoxoqujova in momaqujxtiznequj, aoc campa vel huj: auh in aqujn qujçaznequj, vmpa qujoalhujtequj, qujvalxixili.

---

1. The tilde is omitted in the Nahuatl text.

2. These were, respectively, the south gate of the main temple square (see map) to the Itztapalapan road, the west gate to the Tlacopan road, and, probably, the north and east gates. See Caso, "Barrios antiguos," pp. 44–45.

3. Sahagún, Garibay ed., Vol. IV, p. 117: "Y había algunos que aun en vano corrían: iban arrastrando los intestinos y parecían enredarse los pies en ellos. Anhelosos de ponerse en salvo, no hallaban a dónde dirigirse."

him who tried to go out they there struck; they stabbed him.

But some climbed the wall; they were able to escape. Some entered the *calpulli* [buildings]; there they escaped. And some escaped [the Spaniards] among [the dead]; they got in among those really dead, only by feigning to be dead. They were able to escape. But if one took a breath, if they saw him, they stabbed him.

And the blood of the brave warriors ran like water; it was as if it lay slippery. And a foul odor rose and spread from the blood. And the intestines were as if dragged out. And the Spaniards went everywhere as they searched in the *calpulli* [buildings]. Everywhere they went making thrusts as they searched, in case someone had taken refuge. They went everywhere. They went taking to pieces all places in the *calpulli* [buildings] as they searched.

And when [the massacre] became known, thereupon there was shouting: "O brave warriors, O Mexicans, hasten here! Let there be arraying — the devices, the shields, the arrows! Come! Hasten here! Already they have died, they have perished, they have been annihilated, O Mexicans, O brave warriors!" Thereupon there was an outcry, already there was shouting, there was shrieking with hands striking the lips. Quickly there was a marshaling of forces; it was as if the brave warriors each were determined; they bore the arrows and the shields with them. Thereupon there was fighting. They shot at them with arrows with barbed points, with spears, and with tridents. And they cast at them barb-pointed arrows with broad, obsidian points. It was as if a mass of deep yellow reeds spread over the Spaniards.

Auh cequjntin, tepantli qujtlecavique, tel huel momaqujxtiq̄: cequjntin calpulco cacalacque vmpa momaqujxtique. Auh in cequjntin intlan momaq'xtique, intlan cacalacque in ovelmjcque, çan momjccanenequja, vel momaqujxtique: auh in aca oc mopoçaoa in conjtta, conjxili.

Auh in jmezço in tiacavan iuhqujn atl ic totocac, iuhqujn aalacatoc, yoan xoqujiac eoatoc in eztli. Auh in cujtlaxcolli iuhqujn tlavilanj. Auh in Españoles, novian nemj in tlatemoa in calpulco, novian ontlaxiltivi in tlatemoa, in açaca vmpa mjnaia, novia nenque, qujxaqualotinenque in izqujcan calpulco in tlatemoque.

Auh in omachoc, njman ie ic tzatzioa. Tiacavane mexicae vallatotoca, ma nechichioalo in tlaviztli, in chimalli, in mjtl, vallacivi, vallatotoca, ie mjquj in tiacaoan: ommjcque, onjxpoliuhque, ommjxtlatique: Mexicae tiacaoane. Njmã ie ic tlacavaca, ie ic tzatzioa, netenviteco, iciuhca valnechicaovac in tiacavan iuhqujn nececenquetzalo in mjtl in chimalli qujitquj. Nimã ie ic necalioa, qujmõmjna in jca tlatzontectli, in jca tlacochtli, yoan in mjnacachalli, yoan in tlatzontectli, itzpatlacio in contlaça: iuhqujn cozpul ommoteca in acatl, in impan Españoles.

Twenty-first Chapter, in which it is told how the war newly began when the Mexicans gave battle to the Spaniards here in Mexico.

And the Spaniards then enclosed themselves behind the stone [walls]. And the Spaniards also shot the Mexicans with iron arrows and fired the guns at them. And then they placed Moctezuma in irons.

And thereupon there was the bringing forth, the taking out, the identification of each of the brave warriors who had died. And their mothers, their fathers raised a cry of weeping; there was weeping for them; there was weeping. First they had taken them, each one, to their homes; then they took them forth to the temple courtyard; they brought them together. There they burned them together, in a place apart, where it is called Quauhxicalco.[1] But some burned only at the various young men's houses.

And when the sun was about to set, when there was still a little sun, thereupon Itzquauhtzin shouted forth; from the [palace] roof terrace he shouted forth. He said: "O Mexicans, O men of Tenochtitlan, O men of Tlatilulco, your ruler the *tlacatecutli* Moctezuma beseecheth you; he saith: 'Let the Mexicans hear! We are not the equals of [the Spaniards]![2] Let [the battle] be abandoned! Let the arrow, the shield be held back! Unfortunate are the miserable old man, the miserable old woman, the vassals, the one not yet of understanding, the one who toddleth back and forth, who crawleth, who lieth placed in the cradle, who lieth placed on the [cradle] board, who yet knoweth nothing! 'For this reason doth your ruler say: 'We are not their equals; let there be a cessation [of war].' They have put him in irons, they have placed irons on his feet!"

And when he had gone to say this, thereupon the Mexicans raised a clamor. They chid him. Already they flew into a great fury. They were angry. One of them was much inflamed with rage. He said to him: "What doth Moctezuma say, O rogue? [Art thou]

Injc cempoalli oce capitulo: vncan mjtoa iancujcan peuh iauiotl, injc qujmjcalque Mexica in Españoles in njcan mexico.

Auh in iehoantin Españoles: njman valmotepetlatzatzacque. Auh in Españoles no qujnvalmjna in Mexica in jca tepuzmjtl, yoan ic qujnvalmotla in tlequjqujztli. Auh njman tepuztli contlatlalilique in Motecuçoma:

auh in jxqujchtin tiacavan in omjcque: njmã ie ic tequjxtilo, teçaçaco, teiiximacho. Auh in tenanvan in tetaoan tlachoqujztleoa techoqujlilo, nechoqujlilo, oc inchachan qujnvicaca, çatepan qujnoalhujcaque in teuitvalco, qujncentlalique: vmpa qujncentlatique, cecnj in jtocaiocan: Quauhxicalco. Auh in cequjntin tlatlaque çan tetelpuchcali.

Auh in ie oncalaqujz tonatiuh, in oc achiton tonatiuh: njman ie ic valtzatzi in Jtzquauhtzin, tlapanco valtzatzi: qujoalito. Mexicae, Tenuchcae, Tlatilulcae, amechtlatlauhti in amotlatocauh, in Tlacatecutli in Motecuçoma: qujoalitoa. Ma qujcaqujcan in Mexica, ca amo titenamjcvan, ma motlacavaltican, ma momana in mjtl in chimalli, motolinja in jcnoveve, in jcnoilama in cujtlapilli, in atlapalli in aiamo qujmati in moquequetza, in movilana, in coçultentoc, in vapaltentoc, in aiamo qujmomachitia: ipampa conjtoa in amotlatocauh. Camo titenamjcvan, ma netlacaoaltilo, ca ocontepuziotique, tepuztli icxic ocontlatlalilique:

Auh in oconjto in, njmã ie ic conchachalatza, conaoa, çan ie ilhujce tlavelcuj in Mexica qualanj, ce ilhujce poçonj: conjlhuja. Tlein qujoalitoa Motecuçoma nocne? amo ce yioqujchoan? Nimã ie ic tlacaoaca, niman ic maantimoquetz in tlacaoaca:

---

1. Four places named Quauhxicalco, in the temple square, are mentioned in Anderson and Dibble, *Book II*, pp. 168, 170, 171.

2. Corresponding Spanish text: "*porq̃ estos hombres son muy fuertes mas que nosotros.*"

not one of his warriors?"[3] Thereupon there was an outcry; then there arose an increasing outcry. Thereupon arrows fell upon the roof terrace. But the Spaniards sheltered Moctezuma and Itzquauhtzin under their shields lest the Mexicans pierce them with the arrows.

For this reason were the Mexicans very angry: because [the Spaniards] had completely annihilated the brave warriors; without warning them they had slain them by treachery.[4]

Not because of weakness did the Mexicans abandon going about surrounding the palace. They watched various places where perchance one might secretly enter, where perchance one might secretly take in tortillas. Thus was competely cut off all that might be given [them]; no one at all could leave [them] anything. It was as if they withered their entrails.

And if any in vain should inform, should warn [them], should gain [their] favor who secretly might give them a little food, if they were seen, if they were espied, right there they slew them; there they did away with them. Perhaps they struck them on the back of the head or they stoned them.

Some Mexicans were once seen carrying in rabbit skins. These let fall the information that through them some had secretly entered. Therefore it was strictly commanded that every road be well guarded, well watched, and that at every canal there be good care taken, that it be well observed. And those who had taken in the rabbit skins were servants, messengers of the stewards of Ayotzintepec and of Chinantla.[5] Right there they breathed their last; their work ended. At the canal they struck each one on the back of the head with wooden staves.[6] Those of Tenochtitlan had really contended against one another and quite wrongfully had seized the servants. They had said: "This is he!" Then they had slain him. And if they saw someone with a fine crystal lip rod, then they quickly seized him; they slew him. They said: "This one also goeth entering; he giveth food to Moctezuma." And if they saw someone who had tied on himself the maguey fiber cape[7] of a servant, also they

njmã ie ic onvetzi in mjtl in tlapanco. Auh in Motecuçomatzin yoan Itzquauhtzi, qujnchimalcaltia in Españoles in ma qujnmjnti in Mexica.

Inic cenca qualanque in Mexica: iehica ca vel qujmjxtlatique in tiacaoan in ainnemachpan in qujnpoiomjctique,

in amo ivivi ic concauhque qujiaoalotinemj in tepancalli: tlatlapia in açaca onjchtacacalaquj, in açaca conjchtacacalaquja tlaxcalli, çan njman ic ommotzacu in jxqujch in omacoia, çan njmã aocac tle concaoaia: iuhqujn qujncujtlaoatzque.

Auh in aqujque oc nen xonexcaia, tlamatzoaia, motlamaceviaia, in ichtacatzin cõmacaia in tlaqualtzintli: intla oittoque, intla oittaloque, njman vncã qujnmjctia, vncan qujntlatlatia, aço qujncuexcochvitequj, anoço qujntetepachoa.

Cequjntin mexica ceppa ittaloque, qujcalaqujaia totomjtl: iehoantin tlanexotlaque, inca cequjntin oncalaquj ichtaca, ic cenca netlaquauhnaoatiloc injc vellapieloz, vel mopiaz in jzquj vtli yoan in jzquj acalutli, vel necujtlaviloa vel ixpialoia. Auh in qujcalaqujaia totomjtl tequjtque intlaivalhoã in calpixque aiutzintepecatl yoan chinantecatl: njman vncan ihiotl qujz, njmã vncã intequjuh vetz, acaloco in qujmõcuexcochvivitecque, vitzantica, çan monetechvia in tenuchca, yoan çan jliviz in qujntzitzquja in tequjtque, qujtoaia. Ca iehoatl in: njmã ic conmjctia. Auh intla aca conjttaia ichopilotenteuh: njman qujcujtivetzi, conmjctia: qujtoa, ca no iehoatl in oncalactinemj in contlatlamaca in Motecuçoma: yoan intla aca qujtta, qujmolpilia tequitcaaiatl, no qujcujtivetzi, qujtoa: ca no iehoatl in tlapalpul, in tetzauhtlatolli qujtqujtinemj, cõcalaquja, in conjtta motecuçoma.

---

3. *Ibid.:* "*Que dize el puto de Motecuçoma? Y tu vellaco con el, no cesaremos de la guerra.*" *Nocne:* literally, "my friend." In Sahagún, Garibay ed., Vol. IV, p. 119, the passage reads: "*Cuando hubo acabado de hablar Itzcoatl* [sic] *le hicieron una gran grita, le dijeron oprobios. Se enojaron en extremo los mexicanos, rabiosos se llenaron de cólera y le dijeron:*

"*¿Qué es lo que dice ese ruin de Motecuhzoma? ¡Ya no somos sus vasallos!*"

4. For *qujnpoiomjctique* read *qujnixpopoiomjctique*.
5. Corresponding Spanish text: "*los serujdores o pajes de Motecuçoma.*"
6. *Vitzantica:* read *vitzoctica.*
7. Corresponding Spanish text: "*trayan mantas delcadas que llamã ayatl.*"

quickly seized him. They said: "This one also is a wretch who goeth bearing words of scandal. He taketh them in to Moctezuma; he seeth him."

And he who in vain tried to escape besought them; he said to them: "What do you do, O Mexicans? It is not I." They answered him: "It is also thou, O rogue. Art thou not a servant?" At once they there slew him. They only observed each of the people, they went careful of the people. Only that was their concern, their work; the Mexicans only observed each person. Many they punished for imagined [evil]. They slew them treacherously; they punished them not for their own misdoing.

And still other servants hid themselves, took refuge. No more were they to be seen; no more did they show themselves to one; no more did they come forth to one. They were greatly terrified; they could not control themselves for fear. They each lived in refuge, so that they would not fall into the people's hands.

And when they laid siege to the Spaniards, for only seven days did they fight them. And they were shut in for twenty-three days. And for as many days the canals were each dredged, widened, deepened, made precipitous. Everywhere the canals were made dangerous, were made difficult. And on each of the roads, there was the erection of ramparts; ramparts were erected; there was the erection of ramparts. The passages between houses were made dangerous.

And as this took place[8] —

Auh in oc nen momaqujxtiznequj, in qujntlatlauhtia quimjlhuja. Tle amai mexicae, camono nehoatl: conjlhuja, ca no tehoatl nocne, amo titequjtquj: njman ic vncan cõmjctia ça teixpipia, ça motecujtlavitinemj, ça imjx intequjuh, ça tepipia in mexica: ca mjequjntin in tlapictli qujtzacutiaque in jxpopoiomjctiloque in amo vel intlatlacul qujtzacutiaque.

Auh in oc cequjnti tequjtque motlatique, mjnaxque, aocmo moteittitiaia, aocmo motenextiliaia, aocmo tevic qujçaia, cenca momauhtiaia, mauhcaçonequja, mjinaxtinenca, injc amo temac vetzizque.

Auh in jquac oqujncaltzacque in Españoles: çan chicomjlhujtl in qujncalicalque. Auh in caltzacuticatca cempoalilhujtl omei: auh izqujlhujtl in, in acalotli motatatacac, mopapatlauh, movevecatlano, motetepexiq̃tz novian movicantlali, moovitili in acalotli: Auh in vtli ipã, netetenantiloc, tenamjtl motetecac, netetenantlaliloc, mooviujcantlali in caltzalãtli:

auh in ie iuhquj.

8. Chap. 21 may end with an interruption completed in the beginning of Chap. 22. Garibay K. (*Historia de la literatura náhuatl* [Mexico, D.F.: Editorial Porrua, 1954], Vol. II, p. 252), however, identifies the break as one of several lacunae. See also the ending of Chap. 33.

Twenty-second Chapter, in which it is told how it came to be known that the Captain Don Hernando Cortés already came as he was returning to Mexico.

— it came to be known that the Captain was already coming from Tepeyacac.[1] As he came setting forth, he brought with him many Spaniards and very many Tlaxcallans and Cempoallans — very many; indeed a great number; indeed great numbers; an abundance, a superabundance. They not only were coming, they were coming to war; they came provided with devices; they came arrayed for war, each one with his shield, his obsidian-bladed sword, his hand staff which he came shouldering. They came stirring up columns of dust. Their faces were indeed covered with dust, ashen with dust; they were indeed all covered with dust, indeed each cloaked in dust, all pure dust. They were indeed fast runners; speedily did they run; greatly did they hasten. They went each one shouting. They said: "Hurry along, O Tlaxcallans, O Cempoallans!"

And the Mexicans determined among themselves that thereafter they would not be seen; they would only hide themselves, they would take refuge. It was as if the earth were stretched out dead. No one spoke aloud. Yet they remained watching out of door openings, and gaps in walls, and holes which in some measure they had pierced through walls so that there they could look out. Only those with [houses] by the roadside, those which lay along the road, could do so. But those who lay among houses could not do so. If the Spaniards had seen how many brave warriors were in some places, assembled together, they would have known in their hearts that the Mexicans would undertake, would begin the outbreak of the battle.

And when things were thus, when [Cortés] went to enter the palace, thereupon they shot off the guns.[2]

And when this was done, thereupon [the Mexicans] came forth; they coped with the fighting. Thereupon there were war cries; thereupon the battle

Injc cempoalli omume capitulo: vncã mjtoa in quenjn machiztico in ie vitz capitan don hernãdo Cortes injc oalmocuepaia mexico.

In omachiztico in ie vitz in Capitan tepeiacacpa in qujçaco, mjequjntin in qujnoalhujcac in Españoles yoan cenca mjequjntin in tlaxcalteca yoã in cempoalteca vel mjequjntin vel ixachin, vel ixachintin, vel tonac, vel tonaque: amo çan iuh vallaque, valiauiaque, valmotlaviztitiaque, valmoiauchichiuhtiaque, inchichimal, inmamaquauh, inmamavitzoc quiquequequechotivitze, teuhtli qujoalq̄tztiaque, omach iixtlaliuhque omach yixtenexiuhque, omach moca tlalloaque, omach teteuhqujmjliuhque, ça moca tlaltin, omach cocotztlaloaq̃, cenca oalmotlaloa, cenca oalhujcinj, motzatzatzilitivi: qujtotivi, vallatotoca tlaxcaltecae, cempoaltecae.

Auh in Mexica monaoatique, injc amo qujn mottitizque, çã motlatizque, mjnaiazque, iuhqujn tlalli mjctimotecac, aocac naoati, tel hoallachielotoc in tlatzacujlcamac, yoan tepancamac, yoan tlacoiocco achi qujcocoionjque in tepantli, injc vmpa ontlachie: çan iehoan in otenoaque, in otentli qujtocatoque in juh qujchiuhque: auh in calnepantla onoque amo iuh qujchiuhque. Auh intla qujmjttanj in cana quexqujchtin manj, tepeuhtimanj, in tiacaoan, ca iniol iuh tlamatizqujia in Españoles, ca in mexica iehoan qujpeoaltia, iehoan qujtzintia, iehoan inpeoal in iauiotl.

Auh in ie iuhquj in ocalaqujto vei tecpan: njman ie ic qujtlatlaça in tlequjqujztli:

auh in ie iuhquj, njmã ie ic oalqujça qujoalixtia in mjcalizque: njmã ie ic tlacaoaca, ie ic necalioa, njmã ie ic muchioa in iauiotl, njman ie ic tlaiecolo

---

1. Tepeyacac: presumably not the site north of Tenochtitlan, but one between it and Tlaxcalla.

2. Corresponding Spanish text: "començaron a soltar todos los tiros en alegria de los que aujan llegado, y para atemorizar a los contrarios."

was joined; thereupon there was fighting. Arrows, stones fell upon the Spaniards.[3]

But the Spaniards shot iron bolts and guns. Many men were pierced by arrows and shot by guns. The crossbowman aimed the bolt well; well did he aim the bolt at the one whom he would shoot. And the iron bolt as it went, seemed to go humming, seemed to go hissing; it sped with a great rush. And not to no purpose did the bolt fly. All struck men; all pierced men through. And the guns were well trained upon the people; well did they aim at them. And when the shots fell, they went to the ground, there was covering of the ground as if a mattress were stretched out.[4] Without one's noticing, it came upon one; without one's knowing it, it slew one; as many as they overtook, so many indeed died[5] when they struck their vital parts, perhaps their foreheads, or the back of their heads, or on their hearts, or their chests, or their bellies, or indeed their abdomens. But if they struck only on their thighs or their shoulders, they did not then therefore die, they were not therefore in danger, rather they recovered. And when the Mexicans saw how the gun[shots] and the iron bolts struck, they just went to one side; it was as if they went to the side; there was a going to the side; they were very watchful; they were very careful.

And after there had been fighting for four days, the brave warriors climbed up — the select, the chosen ones, those who possessed deyices, those in whose faces was war — they all climbed up to the top of the [pyramid] temple. They took up two beams and many cylindrical oak logs, called the god's wood. What they took up they would cast down [upon the foe].

And thereupon the Spaniards climbed up the [pyramid] temple. The Spaniards[6] went marching in order, in files. The arquebusiers went leading them. Very slowly did they climb. They did not stop. They went firing the arquebuses; they went shooting them. Second went the crossbowmen, those who used the crossbows. Third went the swordsmen. Fourth went the lancers, the halberdiers.

But to no purpose did the brave warriors mass themselves to cast the wood, the thick oak logs, upon the Spaniards. These only warded them off with their shields; [the wood] was completely ineffective. And

onvetzi in mjtl, in tetl,

Auh in iehoãtin Españoles: qujoallaça in tepuzmjtl, yoan in tlequjqujztli, mjec tlacatl mjnaloc yoan tlequjqujzviloc: in tlatepuztlavitolhujanj, vel qujxcatzitta in mjtl, vel ipan qujtlachialtia in mjtl in aqujn qujmjnaz: auh in tepuzmjtl injc iauh iuhqujn qujqujnacatiuh, iuhqujn çoçolocatiuh, cenca çolonj: auh atle çan nen qujça in mjtl, moch temjna, mochi nalqujça in teitic: yoan in tlequjqujztli, vel tepan qujiacatia, vel tepan contlachialtia. Auh in jquac vetzi, vellaltitech viloa, vellaltitech nepacholo, iuhqujn pepechtli neteco, amo tenemachpan in tepã iauh, amo qujteimachitia in temjctia, in quezquj ipan iauh vel izquj mjquj: in jquac imovican vetzi, in aço imjxquac, in anoço incuexcochtlan, anoço iniollopan, anoço imelchiqujpan, anoço imjtipan, in anoço vel inxillan: auh intla çan īmetzpan, anoço imacolpan vetzi, amo njmã ic mjquj, amo ic oviti, çan tel vmpati. Auh in oqujttaq̃ mexica in juh vetzi tlequjqujztli yoan in tepuzmjtl, ça avic vivi, iuhqujn ixtlapalhujuj, tlatlaxtlapaloa cenca vel motlachielia, vel mjmati.

Auh in ie iuh navilhujtl necalioa: in tiacaoan tlecoque, iehoan in tlatzonanti, in tlapepenti, in tlaviceque, in jmjxco ca iauiotl, muchintin tlecoque in jcpac teucalli, vme vepantli qujtlecavica, yoan mjec in aoaquavitl, mjmjmjltic, itoca, teuquavitl in qujtlecavique, in impan qujoallaçazquja.

Auh njmã ie ic tleco in Españoles qujtlecavia in teucalli, tlatlamãtitivi, cuecuentitivi in Espanoles: tlaiacantivi in matlequjqujceque, cencã tlamach in tleco, amo mamana, qujtlaztivi in matlequjqujztli, ic tlamotlativi, tlaõcaiotitivi, in tepuztlavitoloanj, in tlatepuzmjvianj, tlaiecaiotia in tepuzmaquaveque, in tlanauhcaiotitivi, tepuztopileque, tzinacãtopileque.

Auh in tiacaoan oc nen valmomamanaia in qujoallaça quavitl, in tomaoac aoaquavitl in impã Españoles: çan qujchimaltopeoa, çan njman aoc tle onievat. Auh in opanvetzito in Españoles: njmã ie ic

3. The tilde is omitted in the Nahuatl text.

4. Garibay, in Sahagún, Garibay ed., Vol. IV, p. 122: *"cuando caia su tiro, iba a dar hasta la tierra, en la tierra se clavaba, cual si se hubiera extendido una cama sobre el suelo."*

5. Corresponding Spanish text: *"tirauan los españoles todos sus tierras [tiros?] muy certeros que nũca hereauan tiro que no matase con el."*

6. The tilde is omitted in the Nahuatl text.

when the Spaniards had climbed the heights, they thereupon repeatedly struck them, pierced them, stabbed them. And the brave warriors thereupon threw themselves to the landings of the [pyramid] temple;[7] like black ants they threw themselves down. And the Spaniards[8] hurled from the temple every one of all the brave warriors who had climbed up. They hurled down indeed all of them; not one escaped. And after they had come killing them, thereupon they went in [the palace] and quickly shut themselves in.

And all this took place during the hour of eating.

And when this had come to pass, thereupon [the dead] were made known, taken forth. And when all who had been hurled from the temple had been taken forth, then there was their burning at the various young men's houses.[9]

tevivitequj, yoan texixili, tetzotzopitza. Auh in tiacaoã njman ie ic valmotepeoa in jtlamamatlaioc teucalli, iuhqujn tlilazcatl valmotepeoa. Auh in Españoles vel mochintin qujnteucalhujque in jxqujchtin tlecoca in tiiacaoan, vel mochinti moteucalhujque, njman aocac maqujz. Auh in ontemjctico, njman ie ic callacq̃ valmotzatzacutivetzque.

Auh inin muchiuh ie tlaqualizpan:
auh in ie iuhquj njmã ie ic teiximacho, teçaçaco: auh in ie muchintin oçacoque in moteucalhujq̃, njmã ie ic tetlatilo in tetelpuchcali.

---

7. See Pl. 83.

8. The tilde is omitted in the Nahuatl text.

9. Corresponding Spanish text: "Y *llegando a lo alto del cu, comē-çarõ a herir y matar a los que estauan arriba, y muchos dellos se des-* *perauã por el cu abaxo, finalmente todos murieron los que aujan subido al cu tornaronse los españoles a su fuerte y barrearonse muy bien. Los mexicanos enterraron a los que alli murieron porque toda era gente principal y de mucha cuēta en la guerra.*"

Twenty-third Chapter, in which it is told how Moctezuma and a great nobleman of Tlatilulco died and [the Spaniards] cast their bodies out before the gate — before the gate of the house in which the Spaniards were.

And four days after they had been hurled from the [pyramid] temple, [the Spaniards] came to cast away [the bodies of] Moctezuma and Itzquauhtzin, who had died,[1] at the water's edge at a place called Teoayoc. For at that place there was the image of a turtle carved of stone;[2] the stone had an appearance like that of a turtle.

And when they were seen, when they were known to be Moctezuma and Itzquauhtzin, then they quickly took up Moctezuma in their arms. They carried him there to a place called Copulco.[3] Thereupon they placed him on a pile of wood; thereupon they kindled it, they set fire to it. Thereupon the fire crackled, seeming to flare up, to send up many tongues of flame; many tongues of flame, many sprigs of flame

Injc cempoalli vmei Capitulo vncan mjtoa in quenjn Motecuçoma, yoan ce vei pilli tlatilulco mjcque: auh in innacaio qujvallazque iqujiaoaioc iqujiaoaioc in calli in vncan catca Españoles.

Auh ie iuh navilhujtl neteucalhujloc in qujmontlaçaco in Motecuçoma, yoan Itzquauhtzin, omjcque, atēco itocaiocan, Teoaioc: ca vncan catca in jxiptla aiotl, tetl in tlaxixintli, iuhqujn aiotl ipan mjxeuhtica in tetl.

Auh in oittoque, in oiximachoque in ca ie Motecuçomatzin, yoan Itzquauhtzin: in Motecuçomatzin njman qujoalnapalotiqujzque, qujoalhujcaque in vncan itocaiocan Copulco: njman ie ic qujjquaquauhtlapachoa, njman ie ic contlemjna, contlequechia: njman ie ic cuecuetlaca in tletl, iuhqujn tetecujca, iuhqujn nenenepiloa tlecueçalutl, iuhqujn tlemjmjiavatl moquequetza, in tlenenepilli: auh in jnacaio

---

1. Rafael García Granados points out, in a personal communication, that "concerning the death of Moctezuma various versions exist, but all of them may be included in two large groups: those emanating from the natives and those emanating from the Spaniards. The former maintain that Moctezuma was killed by the Spaniards, and the latter that his death was due to being struck by a rock as he tried to calm his subjects. Among the reports of indigenous origin we consider the opinions of Durán, *Hist. de las Indias de Nueva España*, II, 50 — '... le hallaron muerto con una cadena a los pies y con cinco puñaladas en el pecho'; Alva Ixtlilxochitl, *Décima Tercia Relación de la venida de los Españoles*, p. 12 — '... en donde dicen que uno de ellos le tiró una pedrada de lo cual murió, aunque dicen sus vasallos que los mismos españoles lo mataron, y por las partes bajas le metieron la espada'; Acosta, *Hist. de las Indias*, p. 588 — 'Al rey Moctezuma hallaron los mexicanos muerto, y pasado, según dicen, de puñaladas; y es su opinión que aquella noche le mataron los españoles con otros principales'; *Códice Ramírez*, p. 199 — "... dicen que le dieron una pedrada, mas aunque se la dieron no le podían hacer ningún mal porque había ya más de cinco horas que estaba muerto, y no faltó quien dijo que porque no le vieron la herida le habían metido una espada por la parte baja'; Orozco y Berra, *Hist. Ant. y de la Conquista*, IV, 436 — 'Sea cual fuere el tino con que hemos discurrido, lo cierto fué que Cortés mandó dar garrote a los reyes y señores que en su poder estaban'; Sahagún, [Robredo ed.], III, 51 — 'hallaron los mexicanos muertos a Moctezuma y al Gobernador de Tlatilulco — echados fuera de las casas reales....' Reports of Spanish origin are given by Díaz del Castillo, *Hist. Verdadera*, II, 83 — '... y le dieron tres pedradas, una en la cabeza, otra en un brazo y otra en una pierna, y puesto que le rogaban se curase y comiese y le decían sobre ello palabras, no quiso, antes cuando no nos catamos vinieron a decir que era muerto'; López de Gómara, *Hist. de la Nueva España*, I, 301 — 'que de una [pedrada] que le acertó en las sienes le derribaron y mataron sus propios vasallos'; Cortés, *Cartas de Rel.*, I, 233 — '... le dieron una pedrada los suyos en la cabeza, tan grande, que de allí a tres días murió'; Váz-

quez de Tapia, p. 39 — '... tanto que no le dieran con una piedra, tirada con honda, enmedio de la frente, que luego se sintió mortal'; Aguilar, [*Relación breve*], p. 77 — '... entre otras piedras que venían desmandadas, una redonda como una pelota, la cual dió a Moctezuma estando entre los dos metido, entre las sienes y cayó'; *ibid.*, p. 78 — 'Moctezuma herido en la cabeza, dió el alma a cuya era ... y en el aposento donde él estaba había otros muy grandes señores detenidos con él, a los cuales el dicho Cortés con parecer de los capitanes mandó matar, sin dejar ninguno.' Besides these, we have the opinion of Clavijero, which we consider the most reasonable (*Hist. Ant. de México*, II, 211) — 'Los historiadores mexicanos atribuyen su muerte a los españoles y los españoles a los mexicanos. — Yo no puedo creer que los españoles se decidiesen a quitar la vida a un rey a quien debían tantos bienes y de cuya muerte sólo podían aguardar grandes males.' Muñoz Camargo, *Hist. de Tlaxcala*, p. 234, says that he died baptizado and that his godfathers were Cortés and Alvarado." Chimalpahin (*Annales*, p. 191 — *quimictique Españoles y Moteucçomatzin quiquechmatillotehuaque*, the Spaniards killed Moctezuma; they strangled him) agrees with the source used by Orozco y Berra.

2. The corresponding Spanish text has, for *ayotl, galapago* — fresh water tortoise. According to Ignacio Alcocer, *Apuntes sobre la antigua México-Tenochtitlan* (Tacubaya, D.F.: Instituto Panamericano de Geografía e Historia, 1935), p. 86, it was where now is "*la esquina de Escalerillas con Tacuba.*"

3. Corresponding Spanish text: *un oratorio.* The version of this report in Dibble, *Historia de la nación mexicana*, pp. 56–60, differs considerably from that of the *Florentine Codex*.
Caso ("Barrios antiguos," pp. 30–31) identifies Copulco (Copolco) with a *barrio* adjacent to Tlatilulco, bounded now N. by Calle de Mosqueta; E., Gabriel Leyva; S., Moctezuma; and W., Lerdo (formerly a canal).

seemed to arise. And Moctezuma's body seemed to lie sizzling, and it smelled foul as it burned.

And as it burned, only with fury, no longer with much of the people's good will, some chid him; they said: "This blockhead! He terrorized the world; there was dread in the world, there was terror before him in the world, there was astonishment. This man! If anyone offended him only a little, he at once disposed of him. Many he punished for imagined [faults] which were not real, which were only a fabrication of words."[4] And still many who chid him groaned, cried out, shook their heads in disapproval.

But Itzquauhtzin they went off with in a boat; they went carrying him off in a boat. Thus they came to arrive here in Tlatilulco. They had great pity, they felt great compassion in their hearts. One's tears flowed.[5] There was no one who chid him, there was no one who scorned him. They said: "The personage, the *tlacochcalcatl* Itzquauhtzin, suffered fatigue. He suffered fatigue, he was unfortunate along with Moctezuma. How much fatigue he suffered on our account when we came there, when we continued, all the time that Moctezuma was [alive]!"[6] Thereupon they arrayed him; they arrayed him in the palace flag and the other paper goods, and they made offerings to him.[7] And thereupon they took him in order to go to burn him in the temple courtyard at the place called Quauhxicalco. With great honors his body burned.

And for four days there was fighting. And for seven days were the Spaniards shut in the house. And when the seven days had passed, they again went forth, going to look, each one going to look. They went to arrive there at Maçatzintamalco.[8] They went to gather stalks of green maize; the maize was just maturing. Just like enemies they went gathering the fodder. They went in great haste; they did no more than go to arrive [there], when they quickly reentered the building. And at the time that they set forth, the sun was high; [on their return] the sun was setting.

Motecuçoma, iuhqujn tzotzoiocatoc, yoan tzoiaia injc tlatla.

Auh injc tlatlac, çan tlavelpan, aocmo cenca teiollocopa: cequj caoa: qujtoa. Inin tlapalpul: cemanaoac in otlamamauhtiaia, cemanaoac in ooalimacaxoia, cemanaoac in oivic valnemamauhtiloia, valneiçaviloia: in iehoatl in, in aqujn çã tepitzin, injc qujiolitlacoaia, njman contlatlatiaia, mjec in tlapictli oqujtzacujlti in amo nelli in çan tlatolchichioalli: yoan oc mjectin in caoaia, qujqujnacaia, ôoiovaia, moquaquacuecuechoaia.

Auh in Itzquauhtzin conacalhujto, acaltica conanato in jnacaio, injc caxitico njcan tlatilulco, cenca motlaocultique, cenca icnoioac in iniollo, teixaioviton, aiac ma cavaia, aiac in ma qujtelchioa: qujtoaia. Oqujhiovi in tlacatl, in tlacuchcalcatl in Itzquauhtzin, ca ivan otlaihiovi, yõ omotolinj in Motecuçoma, quexqujch oqujhiovi in topampa in vmpa otivallaque, otioalitztiaque in ixqujch cavitl in ocatca in Motecuçoma: njman ie ic qujchichioa in tecpanjtl, yoan oc cequj amatlatqujtl ic qujchichiuhque: yoan njman ic qujvicaque in qujtlatito in teuitvalco, itocaiocan quauhxicalco: cenca tlamaviztililiztica injc tlatlac in jnacaio.

Auh iuh navilhujtl necalioac, ça on chicomjlhujtique in caltzacuticatca in Españoles. Auh in oacic chicomjlhujtl: oc valqujzque ommotlachielito, ommotlatlachielito, vmpa onacito in maçatzintamalco: concujto ovatl, valxiloiotia, çan coniaucujto in toqujzvatl, cenca çan onjciuhtivia, çan tequjtl onacito: njma ic valcalactivetzque: auh in onqujzca ie vmmotzcaloa, ie vncalaquj in tonatiuh.

4. Corresponding Spanish text: *"algunos dezian mal de Motecuçoma porque auja sido muy cruel."*

5. Corresponding Spanish text: *"los del tlatilulco llorauan mucho a su gouernador porque era muy bien quisto."*

6. Sahagún, Garibay ed., Vol. IV, p. 124: "*¡Cuántas tribulaciones soportó por nosotros! ¡Al punto que hemos venido! ¡Que cosas hemos visto! ¡Todo el tiempo que estuvo en ser Motecuhzoma . . .!*"

7. See Pl. 88.

8. "*Entre Popotla y Chapultepec,*" according to R. H. Barlow,

"Anales de la conquista de Tlatelolco en 1473 y en 1521," *Tlatelolco a través de los tiempos,* Vol. V (1945), p. 40, n. 7; it is also noted that "Ixtlilxóchitl (2:397) lo coloca en 'el salto de Alvarado.'" The *Anales de Tlatelolco,* ed. Heinrich Berlin (Mexico, D.F.: Antigua Librería Robredo, 1948), p. 65 (§ 312), mentions the place in connection with Nonoalco.

In this paragraph, as in many others, is to be noted a great similarity between Sahagún's translation and the *Anales de Tlatelolco* (§§ 302, 303) (personal communication, Rafael García Granados).

Twenty-fourth Chapter, in which it is told how the Spaniards and the Tlaxcallans set out, fled from Mexico by night.

And when night had fallen, when midnight arrived, thereupon the Spaniards came forth. They were crowded together. And there were all the Tlaxcallans. The Spaniards went ahead and the Tlaxcallans went following behind, went covering the rear; it was as if they went becoming their walls, their ramparts. [The Spaniards] went carrying a wooden platform; they went placing it over the canal; on it they went across.[1]

At the time there was a drizzle, there was fine sprinkle, there was a gentle shower of rain. They were yet able to cross the canals of Tecpantzinco, of Tzapotlan, of Atenchicalco. But as they went to arrive at Mixcoatechialtitlan,[2] at the fourth canal, there they were seen; already they were going forth. It was a woman fetching water who saw them. She thereupon shouted; she said: "Mexicans! Come, all of you! Already they go forth! Your foes already go forth secretly!" Then also a man on top of the [pyramid] temple of Uitzilopochtli also shouted. His cries well overspread the people; everyone heard him. He said: "O brave warriors, O Mexicans! Your foes already go forth! Let there be hastening of the shield-boats and on the road!"

And when it was heard, thereupon there was an outcry; thereupon there was the breaking forth of the shield-boatmen. They hastened; they poled vigorously; boats struck, went striking each other, reaching Mictlantonco macuilcuitlapilco.[3] And the shield-boats from two sides pressed upon them; they joined them — the shield-boats of those of Tenochtitlan and the shield-boats of those of Tlatilulco. And some went

Injc cempoalli onnavi Capitulo: vncan mjtoa in quenjn Españoles yoan in tlaxcalteca qujzque, choloque in mexico ioaltica.

Auh in ovaliovac in oacic ioalnepantla, njmã ie ic qujça in Españoles: ommotenque, yoan in ie ixqujch tlaxcaltecatl: in españoles iacattivi, auh in tlaxcalteca tlatoqujlitivi, tlatzinpachotivi, iuhqujnma intenanoan, intzacujlhoan muchiuhtivi, qujvicatiaque quauhtlapechtli contecatiaque in acaloco in jpan ompanotiaque:

in jquac in aoachqujauhtimanj, aoachtzetzeliuhtimanj, aoachpixauhtimanj, oc cequj in vel companavique acalotli Tecpantzinco, Tzaputla Atenchicalco. Auh in oacito mjxcoa mjxcoatechialtitlã injc nauhcan acaloco: ie vncan ittoque, in ie qujça: ce atlacujc civatl, in qujmjttac: njman ie ic tzatzi: qujto. Mexica, xioalnenemjcan, ie qujça, ie navalqujça in amoiaovan: njmã no ce tlacatl tzatzic in jcpac vitzilobuchtli vel tepan motecac in jtzatziliz, ixqujch tlacatl qujcac: qujto. Tiacavane, mexicae, ie onqujça in amoiauoan, vallatotoca in acalchimalli, yoan in vtli ipan.

Auh in ocacoc: njmã ie ic tlacaoaca: njmã ie ic tlatzomonj in acalchimaleque, totoca, tequjtlaneloa, macalhujtequj, macalhujtectivi, tlamattivi mjctlantonco, macujlcujtlapilco: auh in acalchimalli, necoc in impan valmonamjc, in impan valmopic, in tenuchca imacalchimal, yoã in tlatilulca imacalchimal: yoan cequjntin icxipã iaque, nonoalco tlamelauhque, tlacupampa itztiaque, qujniacatzacujlizquja:

---

1. The Aztec would permit reading "bridges" and "canals." According to all other sources, they carried only one wooden bridge, which was mired in the first canal (that is, at Tecpantzinco, before the present site of the Post Office) and could not be used for the rest of the canals (personal communication, Rafael García Granados).

2. Mixcoa is repeated in the Nahuatl text.

These places were all at canals near the main temple square, on the road to Tlacopan. Caso ("Barrios antiguos," pp. 16–17) says of Tecpantzinco that it may have been the canal of S. Juan de Letrán. Of Tzapotlan, Atenchicalco, and Mixcoatechialtitlan he states that they were

probably included between S. Juan de Letrán and Zarco. As for Tzapotlan, "indudablemente estaba en el barrio de Tzapotlan.... Seguramente en 1519 pertenecía a este barrio una buena parte de lo que hoy es la Alameda."

3. The corresponding Spanish text refers to "vn lugar que se llamaua mjctlantonco, macujlcujtlapilco"; Caso ("Barrios antiguos," p. 21) mentions a Macuiltlapilco, bounded N. by Ave. del Taller; E., Antonio Torres; S., Chabacano; and W., San Antonio Abad. In Sahagún, Garibay ed., Vol. IV, p. 125, the passage mentioning it reads: "se dirigen hacia Mictlantonco, hacia Macuiltlapilco."

on foot. They went direct to Nonoalco; they proceeded to Tlacopan. [There] they would stop the rout.

Thereupon the shield-boatmen cast the barbed spears on the Spaniards. From both sides, on both sides the barbed spears fell. But the Spaniards also shot arrows at the Mexicans; they shot iron bolts and guns. There were deaths on both sides. The Spaniards and the Tlaxcallans were shot with arrows; the Mexicans were shot with arrows. And the Spaniards, when they reached Tlaltecayoacan, there at the Tolteca canal,[4] there seemed to fall into a chasm; they filled the chasm. All fell in there. The Tlaxcallan, the man from Tliliuhquitepec, and the Spaniards, and the horses, [and] some women dropped there. The canal was completely filled with them, completely crammed with them. And those who came at the very last, those came forth, crossed over only on men, only on bodies.

And when they had gone to reach Petlacalco,[5] where there was still another canal, quite unobtrusively, quite softly, quite slowly, only with great caution they set forth upon the wooden platform. There they went to mend themselves, there they restored themselves, there they recovered their manhood.

And when they had gone to reach Popotlan,[6] it was dawn, it was day. Already they went taking courage; already they went recognized from afar.[7] And thereupon the Mexicans went roaring at them, they went surrounding them, took after them; they went taking numbers of the Tlaxcallans, and the Spaniards they went slaying. And also were slain Mexicans and Tlatilulcans. There were deaths on both sides. They drove [the Spaniards] to Tlacopan; they pursued them. And when they went driving them to Tiliuhcan, to Xocotl ihiouican, there at Xoxocotla,[8] there Chimalpopoca, Moctezuma's son, died in battle. They came upon him lying pierced by a barbed spear and lying wounded. There similarly died Tlaltecatzin, a Tepaneca lord who was guiding them, who went pointing out [the way] to them, making them avoid

njmā ie ic contlaça in acalchimalleque in tlatzontectli in impā in Españoles: necoccampa necoc in valhuetzi in tlatzontectli. Auh in iehoantin Españoles, no qujnvalmjna in Mexica, qujvallaça in tepuzmjtl, yoan in tlequjqujztli necoc mjcoa: mjnalo in Españoles, yoan tlaxcalteca: mjnalo in Mexica. Auh in Españoles in oacique in tlaltecaioacan in vncan in tulteca acaloco: vncan iuhqujn motepexivique, motepexitenque, mochintin vncā onvetzque, ommotepeuhque in tlaxcaltecatl, in Tliliuhqujtepecatl, yoan in Españoles, yoā in cavallome, cequj cioa: vel ic ten in acalotli, vel ic tzoneuh. Auh in ça tlatzacutiaque, ça tlacapan, ça nacapan in onqujzque, in vmpanoque.

Auh in oacito petlacalco, in oc ce vncan icaca acalutli, çan jvian, çan matca, çan tlamach, çan tlamatzin in onqujzque, in jpan quauhtlapechtli, vncan patito, vncan imjhio qujcujque, vncā moqujchquetzque.

Auh in oacito popotlan, otlatvic, otlanez, ie oqujcheuhtivi, ie veca motlamatilitivi. Auh njmā ie ic qujmjcaoatztivi, qujmololhujtivi, intech icativi in Mexica, qujmaantivi in tlaxcalteca yoā in Españoles mjctivi: auh no mjctilo in Mexica in tlatilulca, necoc mjcoatiuh, tlacupan qujnqujxtique in qujntoca. Auh in oqujnqujxtito Tiliuhcan, xocotlihiovican, vncan in xoxocotla, vncan in iaumjc in chimalpupuca, in jpiltzin Motecuçoma: in jpan qujçato mjntoc, tlatzōtectica, yoan vivitectoc, çā ie no vncan in mjc, Tlaltecatzin, tepanecatl tecutli in qujniacanaia, in qujntlaixtlatitivia, qujmotlaxilitivia, qujmotequjlitivia, qujmoquechilitivia in Españoles:

4. Caso, "Barrios antiguos," p. 17: *"estaba por Sn. Fernando y la Ermita de los Mártires o de Sn. Hipólito"* (citing Dn. Fernando Ramírez).

5. *Ibid.*: the last canal before the Spaniards reached Popotlan. It may have been between Buenavista and Ramón Guzmán.

6. See map. Caso (*ibid.*), citing Romero de Terreros in Carlos Sigüenza y Góngora, *Relaciones Históricas* (Mexico, D.F., 1954), p. 111

and n. 3, suggests that it may be *"donde actualmente es el Panteón Inglés."*

7. Seler, *Einige Kapitel*, p. 517, reads *ie veca motlama[n]tilitivi,* *"da stellten sie sich in Reihen auf."* In Sahagún, Garibay ed., Vol. IV, p. 126, it is *"a los lejos tenían combate."*

8. Bustamante, *Aparicion*, p. 122: *"el camino que va ácia Tlacuba."*

[the wrong way], undertaking things for them, cautioning them.[9]

Thereupon they crossed the Tepçolatl (a small river). They forded it, they forded the water there at Tepçolac.[10] Then they climbed up to Acueco.[11] They went to rest themselves at Otoncalpulco,[12] [where] about the courtyard lay wooden barriers, wooden palisades. There they rested themselves, each one rested himself, and there they restored themselves. They restored themselves; there they went to mend. There those of Teocalhueyacan[13] came to meet them, to guide them.

njmã ie ic companavique in Tepçolatl (ce atoiatontli) vmpanoque, onapanoque, in vncan tepçolac, njmã ic ontlecoque in acueco, ommotlalito otoncalpulco, quauhtenaniotoc, quauhtenametoc in itvalli: vncã mocevique, mocecevique, yoã vncan ihiio cujque, imjhio qujcujque, vncan patito, vncã qujnnamjqujco in teucalhujacan in valteiacan.

9. In *ibid.* the account is that "*murieron dos hijos de Moctheuzoma, el uno se llamaba* Chimalpupuca *y el otro* Tlaltecatzi, *los cuales iban guiando á los españoles.*"

10. Tepçolatl: a stream near Otoncalpulco (*ibid.*).

11. *Ibid.*: "*una cuesta que se llama* Acueco."

12. Corresponding Spanish text: Otonteocalco; Bustamante, *Aparicion*, p. 122: "*ahora se llama* Santa María de los Remedios."

13. Teocalhueyacan is the usual spelling.

Twenty-fifth Chapter, in which it is told how the people of Teocalhueyacan peacefully, quietly came to meet the Spaniards and gave them food when they fled from Mexico.

Tlacatecutli was the [common] name, Otoncoatl the lordly name of the one who led [the natives]. He came there to leave food. White tortillas, turkey hens, roast turkey hens, stewed turkey hens, eggs, and some live turkey hens, and some tuna cactus fruit he laid out before the Captain.

They said: "You have suffered fatigue. Our lords the gods have become weary; let them rest; may peace be with them; may they restore themselves."

Then Marina answered them; she said: "My governors, the Captain saith: 'Whence have they come? Where is their home?'" They then said to her: "Let our lord hear. We come from his house there in Teocalhueyacan. We are the people of Teocalhueyacan." Then Marina said: "It is well. They have shown us favor. There we shall go tomorrow. There we shall sleep."[1]

*　　　*　　　*

And then, just as the dawn broke, as day appeared, [the bodies] were removed; all the Tlaxcallans, the Cempoallans, and the Spaniards who had fallen into the chasm at the Tolteca canal, and at Petlacalco, or at Mictlantonco were removed. In boats they were removed. On the white rushes, among the white rushes, on the reeds, in the midst of the reeds they went to thrust each of them, to impale each of them. They just went thrusting each one. And they went to cast out each of the women. Each one went naked; they were yellow[-skinned]. Anointed yellow, painted yellow were the women. They stripped all of them, each of them; they despoiled each of them; they removed all from them; they left them lying bare.

But each of the Spaniards they laid out apart. They arranged them in separate rows. Their bodies were

Injc cempoalli ommacujlli capitulo, vncā mjtoa in quenjn Teucalhujacantlaca, ivian, iocuxca qujnamjqujco in Españoles yoan qujnmacaque in tlaqualli, in jquac choloque mexico.

Tlacatecutli itoca, otoncoatl in jpiltoca, in valteiacā, in vncan qujcavaco tlaqualli, iztac tlaxcalli, totolin, totollalevatzalli, totollaapoçonjlli, totoltetl, yoa cequjn ioioli in tutultin, yoan cequj nochtli contecaque ixpan in capitan:

qujtoque. Oanqujmjhioviltique, oqujmociaviltique in totecujovan in teteu, ma mocevitzinocan, ma tlaltitech maxitican, ma mjhiocujtican:

njmā qujnoalnāqujli in Malintzin: qujto. Notechiuhcavan, qujmjtalhuja in Capitan: campa vallaque, campa inchan: njmā qujlhujque. Ma qujmocaqujti in totecujo: ca vmpa tivallaque in jchantzinco in Teucalhujacan, ca titeucalhujaque: njmā qujoalito in Malintzin. Ca ie qualli otechmocnelilique, vmpa tiazque in muztla, vmpa ticuchizque.

*　　　*　　　*

Auh njmā vel iquac in otlatlavizcalli ieoac, in otlatlalchipaoac in teçacoc, in çacoque in ie ixqujch Tlaxcaltecatl, in cempoaltecatl, yoan in Españoles, in motepexivique in tulteca acaloco, yoan in petlacalcu, anoço mjctlantonco: acaltica in teçaçacoc, aztapilla, aztapiltitlan, tulla, tulitic in qujmamaiavito, qujmōtzotzopontitlaçato, inca vmmamaiavito, yoan in cioa qujntlatlaçato, pepetlauhtivi, cuztique, coztalanpopul, coztemjloltique in cioa, muchintin qujnpepetlauhq̄ qujntlacujcujlique, qujntlatepevilique, qujnpetztoccauhque.

Auh in Espanoles nonqua qujntetenque, qujnvivipanque, ie on tolcellome, ie ō meztallome, ie on

1. In Sahagún, Garibay ed., Vol. IV, p. 128, Garibay considers the ensuing section to be an alteration of an earlier text. Sahagún's corresponding Spanish text, however, follows the Nahuatl. The section might better be considered as parenthetical and characteristic of Aztec literary style. See the chapters on goldwork and featherwork in Arthur J. O. Anderson and Charles E. Dibble, trans., "The Merchants," *Florentine Codex, Book IX* (Santa Fe: School of American Research and University of Utah, 1952), for comparison.

like white reed shoots, like white maguey shoots, like white maize stalks, like the white reed shoot. And they removed each of the deer which bore men upon their backs, called horses.

And all of their goods, with which, with burdens on their backs, they had gone arrayed, all of it was taken, all of it was taken as if merited. He who came upon something quickly took it, took it to himself, put it upon his back, took it to his home. And, at the very time that there were the various deaths, all of whatever sort which one had gone away from, abandoning it in fear, and many of the war goods, were there taken; the lombard guns, the arquebuses. And some things lay strewn there; gunpowder, iron swords, iron lances, halberds, iron bolts, iron arrows were strewn there. And also were taken there as if merited the iron helmets, the iron corselets, the chain mail corselets, the leather shields, the iron shields,[2] the wooden shields. And there were taken as if merited the gold in bars, the golden discs, and the gold dust, and golden necklaces with pendants.

And when all the things had been taken, thereupon there was dispersal in the water, there was continual searching for things. Some searched with their hands, some searched with their feet.

And as for their going forth, it was those who had gone ahead who had been able to go forth. But those who had only been last, those were the ones who fell into the chasm, who fell into the water. All died. Indeed, what was like a mountain of men was laid down. They lay pressed against one another; they just killed one another; they smothered.

*   *   *

And while this was going on, there at Acueco [the Spaniards] slept; it was still deep night, yet well toward dawn, when they arose, when they arrayed themselves, when they arrayed themselves for battle, when each one put on his battle gear. Thereupon they got up, they moved, they put themselves in order. And the Mexicans went roaring at them, yelling at them. Not yet did they come up to them; they only remained facing them from afar, they only went dealing with them from there. And when [the Spaniards] reached a place apart, a place called Calacoayan, on top of a rounded hill, on a small elevation, there where there were ridges of rocks,[3] there [the Spaniards]

acaxilome ie on tolcellutl innacaio, yoan qujnçaçacaque in mamaça in temamanj intoca cavallome.

Auh in jxqujch in intlatquj in tlamamalchichiuhtiuh muchi namoieloc, muchi maceoaloc, in aqujn çaço tlein ipan oqujçato qujcujtivetzi, qujmotechtia, qujmomamaltia qujtquj in jchan, yoan vel ipan nemjmjctiloc in jxqujch in çaço tlein oqujmauhcacauhtiqujzque yoan mjec in iautlatqujtl in vncan namoieloc in tomaoac tlequjqujztli in matlequjqujztli, yoan cequj vncan tepeoac, vncan tepeuh in tlequjqujztlalli, in tepuzmaquavitl, in tepuztopilli in tzinacantopilli, in tepuztlavitolli, in tepuzmitl: yoã no vncan maceoaloc in tepuzquacalalatli, in tepuzvipilli, in tepuzmatlavipilli, in eoachimalli, in tepuchimalli, in quauhchimalli: yoan vncan momaceuh in teucujtlatl in tlaxantectli, yoan teucujtlacomalli, yoan teucujtlatl tlaxaqualolli, yoan in chaiaoac cozcatl teucujtlaio.

Auh in ie ixqujch in otlanamoieloc, njmã ie ic onnetepeoalo in atlan, netlatetemolilo, cequjntin tlamatemoa, cequjntin tlacxitemoa.

Auh injc qujzque in iacattiaque, ie vel qujzque: auh in ça tlatzacutiaque, iehoantin in motepexivique in matlanvique, mochintin mjcque vel iuhquj tlacatepetl motlali monenepanotoque, çan monetechmjctique, mjhiomjctiã:

*   *   *

auh in ie iuhquj in vncã acueco, in oncochque, oc veca iovan oc vellavizcalpan in meuhã, in mochichiuhque, in moiauchichiuhque, in õmaaqujque in iautlatqujtl: njman ie ic oneoa, onolinj, õmotema. Auh in mexica qujmjcavatztivi qujmoiovitivi, aocmo intech onaci, ça vecapa qujmjtztivi ça qujnvecapavitivi, ça qujnnachcapavitivi. Auh in onacique cecnj, itocaiocan calacoaian, tlamjmjlolticpac, tlacpactonco, in vncã tecuecuentla, vncã õtemjctitiqujzque ontexixilque, amo qujmjmachitique in vncan tlaca, in calacoaiantlaca, amo innemachpan in mjctiloque, intech motlavelqujxtique, intech mellelqujxtique. Auh in ontemjctique: nimã ie ic ontemo in tlanj, connamj-

---

2. *Tepuchimalli*: read *tepuzchimalli*.

3. See Pl. 98.

quickly slew the people, they speared them. The people of Calacoayan did not provoke them; without notice were they slain. [The Spaniards] vented their wrath upon them, they took their pleasure with them. And when they had slain them, thereupon they came down; they came to the flat land, the small plain, called Tiçapan. Thereupon they climbed up to Teocalhueyacan.

quj in tlalpechtli, in jxtlaoatontli: itoca, Tiçapan: njman ie ic ontleco Teucalhujacan.

Twenty-sixth Chapter, in which it is told how the Spaniards went to reach Teocalhueyacan, and how the people there joyfully received them.

When they entered Teocalhueyacan, they went to settle themselves in the various buildings of the Otomí *calpulli.* In good time they came to arrive — it was not yet indeed noon.

And when [the Spaniards] arrived, all was at hand, all was arranged, all the food, the turkey hens, etc. Great contentment did they offer [the Spaniards]. Quite peacefully did they go among them; they gave them all, all that they asked them for; fodder for the deer, water, grains of maize, ears of green maize, ears of raw maize, ears of cooked green maize, tortillas of green maize, cooked ears of tender maize, roasted ears of green maize, tamales of green maize, and gourds cut into pieces. They kept lavishing, they kept pressing these upon them; they befriended them, they became friends with them.

And the Tliliuhquitepecans who came there had come to mingle with the Teocalhueyacan people because the Tliliuhquitepecans were relatives, kin of the Teocalhueyacan people.[1] Teocalhueyacan was the native land, the birthplace, the foundation place, the seat of the Tliliuhquitepecans.

There they consulted among themselves, there they agreed, there they determined in their discourses, they were as one, they established as procedure in their consultation that they would meet with, that they would beseech the Captain, the god, and all the gods. "[The Spaniards] have come to reach their humble home here at Teocalhueyacan. Here we beseech, we greet them, we who are vassals, who are men of Teocalhueyacan, who are Tliliuhquitepecans. And may our lord hear. Moctezuma and the Mexican have much afflicted us, much wearied us. To our very noses have they brought affliction. They have imposed all tribute on us. And this man is our lord, our ruler. And if

Injc cempoalli onchiquacen capitulo, vncan mjtoa in quenjn Españoles acito Teucalhujacan: auh in quenjn qujnpaccacelique vmpa tlaca.

In teucalhujacan oncalacq̄ onmocacaltemato in otōcalpulco, çan cuel in onacito, aiamo vel nepantla tonatiuh:

auh in onacique, ça temac: moch mocencauh in jxqujch qualonj in totoli. &c. cenca qujnpapaqujltique, çan ivian intlan oncalacque, ixqujch qujnmacaia in jxqujch qujmjtlanjliaia, in maçatlaqualli, in atl, in tlaolli, in elotl, in eloxoxouhquj, in elopaoaxtli, in elotlaxcalli, in xilopaoaxtli, in eloixcalli, in elotamalli: yoan in aiotlatlapanalli, qujntlanenectiaia, qujntlanenequjltiaia, qujmōmocnjuhtique, onmocnjuhtlaque.

Auh in tliliuhqujtepeca, vncā vallaque, qujmōneloco in teucalhujaque: iehica ca in tliliuhqujtepeca incotonca ioan invaniolque in teucalhujaq̄ in tliliuhqujtepeca, inqujzcā iniolcan, inquechtetzon yionocan in teucalhujacan, vncā qujzticate,

vncā mononotzque vncan qujcemjtoque, vncā qujcentlalique in intlatol, qujnepanvique, contlamāvique in innenonotzal, injc qujnamjcque, injc qujtlatlauhtique in capitan in teutl, yoan in ie mochintin teteu, ca omaxitico in inchantzinco in njcā teucalhujacan, ca njcan tictotlatlauhtilia, tictociauhquechilia in timaceoalhoā, in titeucalhujaque, yoan in Tliliuhqujtepeca: yoan ma qujmocaqujti in totecujo. Ca in motecuçoma yoā in mexicatl, ca cenca otechtolinj, otechtlaciavilti, vel toiacacpa oqujqujxti in netolinjliztli: ca ixqujch inin techtequjtia in tlacalaqujli: auh inin ca totecujo ca totlatocatzin. Auh intla techmocavilitiqujça ca tlacatl in mexicatl, vel-

---

1. Corresponding Spanish text: *"y ellos tenjan los otomjes de tlaxcaltecas que se escaparon de la guerra conozieronse con los de Teucalujacan porque eran todos parientes y desde* [sic] *pueblo de Teucalujacan anjan ydo a poblar a Tlaxcalla."* The connection is shown in Pedro Carrasco Pizana, *Los otomies* (Mexico, D.F.: Instituto de Historia, 1950), p. 281, Fig. 29.

[the gods] hasten to abandon us — for inhuman is the Mexican, very perverse — if they will hasten to abandon us, if they will tarry somewhere in coming, in returning, the Mexican will have slain us, will have destroyed us. For indeed he is greatly perverse; indeed he surpasses in perverseness."

And when Marina had informed the Captain of the discourse, he then said to them: "Let them not worry. I shall not tarry somewhere, I shall come quickly, I shall come to find them quickly. Here judgment will be made, here will be the place of judgment. The Mexican will be destroyed. Do not be grieved."

And when the people of Teocalhueyacan thus heard, each one was contented; each one was proud because of it; they were arrogant because of it. Behold, because of it they rose up, because of it they thought well of themselves, they thought themselves worthy of favor. It was as if they were much more satisfied, it was as if they were much more proud; it was as if there they were convinced; they took it to themselves; they thought it already to be fact. And finally, when they had slept, it was yet deep night when the flutes were already blown, when they blew the flutes, the wooden flutes,[2] and drums were beaten, war drums were beaten.

Already there was arising; the Spaniards arose. There was arraying. And when this was done, there was leaving, there was the filling of the road. They went crowding the road. Then they went to reach Tepotzotlan. It was indeed early, still in good time, that they went to settle themselves. Only a little did they follow [the road]. And the people of Tepotzotlan then broke; they moved; they ran; they entered the forest. Some climbed the mountain, some [descended into] the gorge; they only left [all] in the Spaniards'[3] hands. No one dealt with them, because very great had been their victory. [The people of Tepotzotlan] therefore took flight, fled. Only their bodies did they save. And all their goods they scattered in haste, they merely abandoned in haste. [The Spaniards] entered the palace; they filled the courtyard. There they slept; they were together, they grouped together, they crowded together. For they went only in fear; they went fearing.

laveliloc, intla techmocavilitiqujçaz, intla movecavitiz, in oalmovicaz in valmocueptzinoz, aotechtlamjque, aotechpopoloque in Mexicatl: ca vel huei tlaveliloc, ca vel qujmaxilti injc tlaueliloc.

Auh in ocõcaqujti in Malintzin in tlatolli in capitan: njmã qujnoalhuj. Macamo motequjpachocã camo njvecaoaz, iciuhca njoallaz, iciuhca njqujnmatiqujuh, njcan tlatoloz, njcan tlatoloian iez, popoliviz in Mexicatl, macamo amechiolitlacocan.

Auh in oiuh qujcaque in teucalhujaque cenca papacque, ic aatlamatque, ic cuecuenotque, iz ic moquetzque, ic moiehoatocaque, qujmolhujltocaque, ilhujz iuhqujn mocacã ilhujz iuhqujn aatlamati, iuhqujn vncã motlatlalia iniollo monelchiuhque, ie om ma nelli iuh momatque. Auh inic iuhquj in ocuchque oc veca iovan in ie tlapitzalo, in qujpitza quauhtlapitzalli, quavilacapitztli, yoan tlatzotzonalo, iautlatzotzonalo:

ie ic neeoalo, meeva in Españoles, nechichivalo: Auh in ie iuhquj, ie ic oneoalo neutemalo, pepexocatiuh in vtli: njmã ic onacito in teputzutla, aia vel quẽman oc qualcan in ommotlalito, çan achi qujtocatiaque: auh in teputzoteca njman ic tzomonque olinque, ic choloque, quauhtla calacque: cequjntin tepetl qujtlecavique: cequjntin atlauhtli, çan inpan macauh in Espanoles, aiac inca muchiuh: iehica ca cenca vei in intepololiz, ipampa mochololtique, mocholtique: çan ixqujch in innacaio qujmaqujxtique: auh in ixqujch in intlatquj qujtepeuhtiqujzque, çan iuh tlacauhtiqujzque: tecpan in oncalacque, ommotepancaltemato, vncã cochque, çan cenietivi, çan cemololiuhtivi, çan centepeuhtivi: iehica ca çan mauhcavi, çan momauhtitivi.

---

2. *Quauhtlapitzalli, quavilacapitztli*: cf. Eduard Seler, *Gesammelte Abhandlungen*, Vol. II, pp. 677, 679; Alvaro Tezozomoc, *Histoire du Mexique*, trans., H. Ternaux-Compans (Paris: P. Jannet, 1853), Vol. I, p. 121.

3. *Espanoles*: the tilde is omitted in the Nahuatl text.

And when dawn broke, when it was already rather early, thereupon each one ate; they ate their breakfast. When they had breakfasted, when they had eaten their breakfast, then they departed. Already they followed the road. [The Mexicans] roared at them. Only at a distance, only from a distance, only at a distance did they follow them, did they roar at them. And if besides any [Mexicans] dared go among them as if to interrogate them, [the Spaniards] speared them.[4] It came to an end for those they speared. No longer did they move; there was no one who saved the speared one.

Then they went to arrive, went to establish themselves in Citlaltepec. They were only made place for; the common folk did not wait for them.[5] And the brave warriors, the people there, those who had homes, no longer showed themselves; they only hid themselves; they took refuge behind something, perhaps a rock cactus,[6] perhaps a maguey, perhaps a pile of earth or a crag. For [the Spaniards] were not to be resisted. — There also they slept.

And when dawn broke, [when] it was already rather early, already warm, already pleasant, thereupon each one ate. Thereupon once again they started; they moved to Xoloc. In just the same way they left it in [the Spaniards'] hands. No longer did one, not even one, disclose himself, await them. Each house was vacant; no one came forth toward them. They had hidden themselves above, on top of Mt. Xoloc. From everywhere there was watching that nowhere were [the Spaniards] hidden on the high plains, in gullies, or in abysses. Already they dreaded [the Spaniards]; they were terrified of them lest they not be forewarned of their foes, lest unaware they might spring upon them.

And when dawn broke, when already they were about to go, when already they were about to set forth, when already they were about to move, thereupon each one ate. Already they started. On each side of the road went marching the deer, those which bore men upon their backs, called horses. And all who bore burdens on their backs went marching within [the files]; they went surrounded.[7] And when they

Auh in otlatvic, in ie achi qualcã: njman ie ic tlatlaqua, qujqua in inneuhca: in ommoneuhcaiotique, in oconquaque in inneuhca: njmã ic oneuhque, ie ic vtlatoca, qujmjcavatza, ça veca, ça vecapa, ça qujnvalhuecapavia, in qujnvalicavatza. Auh intla ça acame motlapaloa in intech onaci, iuhqujn aqujm õtlatoltia in q'nvalixili, çan ic cenvi in qujmjxili, aocmo valmocuecuetzoa aocac qujça, aocac qujqujxtia in qujxili:

njmã ic onacito in citlaltepec, ommotecato, çã no tlalcaviloque, amo qujnmochieltique in maceoalti. Auh in tiacaoan, in vncã tlaca, in chaneque, aocmo valmjxmana, ça motlatia, itla qujmotoctia, aço tenopalli, aço metl, aço tlaltepevalli, anoço texcalli: iehica ca amo ixnamjqujztin, no vncã cochque.

Auh in otlatvic, ie achi qualcan, ie tlatotonjc, in ie tlaiamanja: njman ie ic tlatlaqua, njman ie ic no ceppa vmpeoa, ommjquanja xoloc: çan ie no ivi, inpan macauh, aocac in ma nel ça çeton, qujnmochielti, vel cacactivetz in calli, aiac in ma ivic qujz: tlacpac in motlatique, icpac in tepetl xoloc: noviampa vallachielo, acã motlatique tlapechian, tlacomulco, anoço atlauhco, ie qujmacacia, ie qujnmauhtia, in ma amo qujmjmachititi in iniauvan, in maca innemachpan inpã valcholoti.

Auh in otlatvic in ie iazque, in ie oneoazque, in ie onolinjzque: njman ie ic tlatlaqua: ie ic vmpeoa, necoc omac onotivi, in mamaça in intemamacaoan, intoca cavallome: auh in ixqujch tlamama çan tlatic onotivi, ololiuhtivi. Auh in ontlanque in vi: nec contlequechia, contlemjna, contlecavia in otonteucalli, yoan in jxqujch teucalli, in incal tlatlacateculo, nec tlatla, cuecuetlaca: in tlecueçallutl, in tlenene-

4. Corresponding Spanish text: *"y por el camjno donde yuan: yuan tras ellos: los mexicanos dãdoles grita y si alguno se acercaua a los españoles, luego le matauã."* Cf. also Sahagún, Garibay ed., Vol. IV, p. 55, and Seler, *Einige Kapitel,* p. 524.

5. According to Siméon, *Dictionnaire de la langue nahuatl,* p. 82, *chialtia* with *nicno* implies that the foe is awaited with courage.

6. *Tenopalli: Epiphyllum* sp. (Martín del Campo, "Las cactáceas entre los mexica," p. 31).

7. Corresponding Spanish text: *"yuan por el camjno, en dos rencles, los de cauallo: y todos los de a pie, y los que lleuauã cargas, yuan en medio de los de cauallo."*

brought their going to an end, then they ignited, burned, set fire to the Otomí temples and to all the temples, the houses of the devils. Then they burned; they each crackled. The blaze, the tongues of flame, the sheet of fire spread rising in smoke. The smoke spread out; the smoke was overspread. And as they went marching off, the common folk went roaring at them, only from a distance.

Then they went to settle themselves at Aztaquemecan, at the foot, at the base of Mt. Aztaquemecan. They settled themselves there at the base, at a place called Çacamulco. Also above there was a rounded hill. There also there stood an Otomí temple. There they went to put themselves in the houses. Likewise was it left in their hands. No more did the common folk go to come among them; only the houses everywhere lay silent; the houses each remained clear.

pilli, in tlecocomochtli poctlevatoc, poctli mantoc, poctli moteca. Auh in jquac ie iativi, qujmjcavatztivi in maceoaltin, çan vecapa:

njman ic ommotlalito in Aztaquemecan: icxitlan itzintlã in iehoatl tepetl Aztaquemecã, in vncan motlalique tlatzintlan: itocaiocan çacamulco, no tlacpac, ololtontli in tepetl: no vncan icac otonteucalli, oncan in õmocaltemato, çan no impan macauh aocmo impan acito in maceoaltin, çan novian cactoc in calli, cacactivetz in calli.

Twenty-seventh Chapter, in which it is told how the Mexicans came to reach the Spaniards in order to follow them at the rear.

Also at this very time the Mexicans came arriving that they might intercept [the Spaniards]. The Mexicans went to establish themselves at the base of the mountain called Tonan. And when dawn broke, the Spaniards[1] then attired themselves; each one ate; likewise the Mexicans attired themselves. Each one ate, each one drank. They drank pinole mixed in water.[2] Some climbed to the top [of the mountain]. They spied, they observed, they lay looking for the time when the Spaniards would arise, would move. What was in their sight was the obligation of those who were watching.

And when this was done, when the Spaniards[3] already moved, already followed the road, thereupon the spies shouted out; they spoke out: "O Mexicans, your foes already go! Let us attire ourselves, let us each attire ourselves! Let us move together, let us go together! No one is to be left!" And when they heard this, then there was running, there was running hither and thither, there was pursuit.

And when the Spaniards looked toward them, they awaited their foes; therefore they checked themselves so that they might contend against them. They indeed pondered how they would be able to succeed against them. And when this happened, [the Mexicans] fell upon them, they threw themselves upon them so that all speedily would be enclosed within them. Then there was repeated spearing, striking down of the men. There indeed died Mexicans [and] Tlatilulcans. They had just gone to give themselves, to cast themselves into the hands of [the Spaniards]; they only followed after death. There were only a few who escaped their hands, who did not die. And those who remained at a distance, those who remained going at a distance, did not die. And when the Spaniards had slain them, when their ire abated, thereupon they went. All who bore burdens upon their backs went to

Injc cempoalli on chicume capitulo vncan mjtoa in quenjn Mexica intech acito in Españoles injc qujnteputztocaia.

No vel iquac in onacito Mexica in qujniacatzacujlizquja: in ommotecato mexica itzintlan tepetl itoca Tona. Auh in otlatvic nec mocencaoa in Espanoles tlatlaqua: no ivi mexica mocecencaoa tlatlaqua, aatli, pinolatl qujy: cequjntin tlacpac tlecoque, iautlachixque, iautlapixque, qujmonjtztoque in quēmā oneoazque, in quenman onolinjzque in Españoles: vel imjx intequjuh in ontlachixticate.

Auh in ie iuhquj in ie olinj in ie utlatoca in Espanoles: njman ie ic valtzatzi in iautlachixque: qujvalitoa. Mexicae ie iauh in amoiaouh, ticcencaoa, ticcecencaoa, ticemolinj, ticenvi, aiac mocauhtiaz. Auh in oqujcacque nec netlalolo, tlaixqujqujça, tlatotoca.

Auh in oqujnvalittaque in Españoles: qujnvalmochialtique, ic oalmomanque in qujnnamjqujzque, vel qujnnemjlia in quenjn vel qujnchivazque. Auh in ie iuhquj nec qujnxopiloa, qujncujtlaxeloa in quexqujch calitic momantiqujz, nec texixilioa, tetzotzopitzalo, vel vncan tonacamjcque in mexica in tlatilulca, çan qujmōmomacato, inmac ommotlaçato, çā conmotoqujlique in mjqujztli, ça quezqujn in tematitlampa qujz in amo mjc: auh in veca manca, in tevecapaviti manca amo mjcque. Auh in ontemjctique in imellel onqujz in Españoles: njman ie ic vi, qujnteputzvitivi in jxqujchtin tlamama. Ca aocac qujnmati in campa cochque in jquac: vncan in in valmocuepato, in qujmonjcxicaoato, qujmonteputzcaoato in Españoles.

1. *Espanoles*: the tilde is omitted in the Nahuatl text.

2. Santamaría (*Diccionario de mejicanismos*, p. 854) says that it is now a drink of ground maize mixed in water with cacao, sugar, cinna-mon, and *achiote* (*achiotl — Bixa orellana* L.).

3. See footnote 1 *supra*.

be the last. There was no one who knew of them, where they slept at that time. There was where [the Mexicans] went turning back, leaving the Spaniards' footsteps, leaving them behind.

And when this was done, thereupon were identified each of the brave warriors who had died, who had been speared. There they burned all of them. And they collected, gathered their charred remains, their bones, heaped them up, then buried them — buried them in the ground.

And these are all the days since the Spaniards came to enter Mexico upon the day-count One Wind and the year-count One Reed, [when] yet next day would be the tenth of Quecholli. And when they had passed the day Two House, at that time indeed it was the tenth of Quecholli. And when the end of Quecholli arrived, on the very day, thereupon Panquetzaliztli followed after it: twenty days.[4] Then Tititl followed after it: also twenty days. Then Izcalli, the ending,[5] followed after it: also twenty days. Then at that time were set in five days called Nemontemi. And when the five days ended, then began Atl caualo or Quauitl eua. There the year was taken hold of;[6] there began the new year: also a score. Then Tlacaxipeualiztli followed after it: also a score. Then Toçoztontli followed after it: also a score. Then Uei toçoztli followed after it: also a score. Then Toxcatl followed after it: also twenty days. There perished the brave warriors, when they were cut to pieces, when there was the slaying of Mexicans. Then Etzalqualiztli followed after it: also twenty days. Then Tecuilhuitontli followed after it. There was when they went forth, the very day upon which the Spaniards went forth, when they disappeared by night without one's knowledge; it was not in one's heart that they would go forth by night. And when are added together all the days attained, they are two hundred and thirty-five. And they had been our friends one hundred and ninety-five days. And they had been our foes forty days.

And when the Spaniards had thus gone, it was thus thought that they had gone forever, had departed forever; nevermore would they return, nevermore would they make their return. Then once again were arrayed, were ornamented the devils' houses. Each one was swept; the rubbish in each was picked up; the dirt in each was removed.

Auh in ie iuhquj: njmã ie ic teiiximacho in tiacaoan in omjcque, in oxixilioaque, vncan qujntlatique in jxqujchtin: auh in intecullo qujpepena, in jmomjo qujnenechicoaia, coololoaia, çatepã contocaia, contlaltocaia.

Auh in izqujlhujtico in Mexico inic calaqujco in Españoles: ipã ce hecatl in cemjlhujtlapoalli: auh in xiuhtonalli ce acatl, oc muztla tlamatlactiz Quecholli: auh in cemjlhujtique vme calli: vel iquac in tlamatlacti quecholli: auh in oacic, tlamj quecholli in vel ilhujtl: njman ie ic qujoaltoqujlia in Panquetzaliztli, cempoalilhujtl: njmã qujvaltoqujlia Tititl no cempoalilhujtl: njman qujvaltoqujlia Jzcalli tlamj, no cempoalilhujtl: njmã iquac valmotlalia macujlilhujtl moteneoa Nemontemj: auh in ontzonqujz macujlilhujtl: njmã ic vmpeoa in Atl cavalo, anoço quavitl eoa, vncã xiuhqujtzqujlo, vncan peoa in iancujc xivitl, no cempoalli: njmã qujoaltoqujlia tlacaxipeoaliztli no cempoalli: njman qujvaltoqujlia Toçoztontli, no cempoalli: njman qujvaltoqujlia vei toçoztli, no cempoalli: njman qujvaltoqujlia Toxcatl no cempoalilhujtl: ie vncan ixpoliuhque Tiacaoan in xaxamacaque, in mexica in mjcoac: njmã qujvaltoqujlia Etzalqualiztli, no cempoalilhujtl: njman qujvaltoqujlia Tecujlhujtontli, ie vncan in qujzque, vel ipan in ilhujtl in qujzque in Españoles, in moioalpoloque, amo tenemachpan, amo iuh catca teiollo inic qujzque ioaltica. Auh injc mocempoa in jzqujlhujtique matlacpoalli oçe, on caxtolli: auh in tocnjoan catca chicunapoalilhujtl on caxtolli. Auh in toiaovan catca vmpoalilhujtl:

Auh in oiuh iaque in Españoles: iuh nemachoc in ca oiccen iaque, in ca iccen oiaque, aocmo cepa valmocuepazque, aocmo ceppa imjloch qujchioazque: njman ie no ceppa ic tlachichivalo, tlacencavalo in diablome inchan: tlatlachpanoc, tlacujcujvac, moqujqujxti in tlalli.

4. The Aztec text skips Atemoztli.

5. Cf. Anderson and Dibble, *Book II*, p. 154. Seler (*Einige Kapitel*, p. 527) translates the passage thus: "*Darauf folgt Izcalli, das Schlussfest, ebenfalls zwanzig Tage.*"

6. Cf. Arthur J. O. Anderson and Charles E. Dibble, trans., "The Sun, Moon and Stars, and the Binding of the Years," *Florentine Codex*, *Book VII* (Santa Fe: School of American Research and University of Utah, 1953), p. 25; Sahagún, Garibay ed., Vol. II, p. 269.

Twenty-eighth Chapter, in which it is told how they celebrated a great feast day when the Spaniards had gone forth from here in Mexico.

And when Uei tecuilhuitl arrived, still once again the Mexicans celebrated the feast day there on the twentieth day.[1] All the images, the representations of the devils they again attired, each one; they clothed them, they ornamented each with precious feathers, they hung each with necklaces, they put turquoise mosaic masks on each one. And they clothed each one in godly garments — the quetzal feather garment, the yellow parrot feather garment, the eagle feather garment. And those goods which were required the great noblemen guarded.

Then Tlaxochimaco followed after it; they also passed twenty days. Then Xocotl uetzi followed after it; they also passed twenty days. And with Ochpaniztli they passed the fourth score. Teotl eco: with it they passed the fifth score. Tepeilhuitl: they passed the sixth score. Quecholli: with it they passed the seventh score. Here they would have passed the year if nothing had happened, if [the Spaniards] had not gone.[2] Panquetzaliztli: they passed the eighth score. Atemoztli: they passed the ninth score. Tititl: they passed the tenth score. Izcalli, the ending: with it, eleven score. Here happened the Nemontemi: five days. Atl caualo: twelve score. Tlacaxipeualiztli: thirteen score. Toçoztontli: fourteen score. Uei toçoztli:[3] with it, seventeen score. Tecuilhuitontli: with it, eighteen score. There a year had passed since [the Spaniards] had died, at the Tolteca canal.

And when once again they came drawing near, when once again we saw them, the one year was in its eleventh score, in Izcalli. They came drawing near from Quauhtitlan. They went to establish themselves in Tlacopan. They spent only seven days; then they went, they spent two score [days]. And once again they came drawing near; they only came forth quickly. They went toward Quauhtitlan. Their only

Injc cempoalli on chicuei capitulo: vncan mjtoa in quenjn Mexica vei ilhujtl qujchiuhq̄ in jquac oqujzque Españoles vncan mexico.

Auh in oacic vei tecuilhujtl: oc ceppa, ie no ceppa ilhujqujxtique in Mexica, vncā cempoaltica. Jn ixqujch in jmjxiptlavan, in impatilloan in diablome, ie no ceppa qujncecencauhque, qujntlaquentique, qujnquequetzallotique, qujncocozcatique, qujmonaaqujque xiuhxaiacatl, yoan qujnquequentia in teuquemjtl, in quetzalquemjtl, in tozquemjtl, quauhquemjtl. Auh inin tlatqujtl in monec, qujpiaia in vevei pipiltin:

njman qujoaltoqujlia in Tlasuchimaco, no cempoaltique: njmā qujvaltoqujlia in xocotl vetzi, no cempoaltique. Auh in Ochpanjztli ic nappoaltique. Teutl eco: ic macujlpoaltique. Tepeilhujtl chiquacempoaltique. Quechulli ic chicōpoaltique: vncan cexiuhtizqujaia y, intlacatle muchivanj, intlacamo ianj. Panquetzaliztli, chicuepoaltique. Atemuztli, chicunappoaltique. Tititl matlacpoaltique. Jzcalli tlamj, ic matlacpoalli oce: njcan in muchioa in Nemontemj, macujlilhujtl. Atl cavalo, matlacpoalli omume, anoço Quavitl eoa. Tlacaxipeoaliztli, matlacpoalli omei. Toçoztontli matlacpoalli onnavi. Vei toçoztli, ic caxtolpoalli omume. Tecujlhujtontli, ic caxtolpoalli omei: vncan cexiuhtico y, injc mjcque tulteca acaloco.

Auh in ie no ceppa qujçaco, in ie no ceppa tiqujmjttaque ce xivitl, ipā matlacpoalli oce, ipan in Jzcalli: quauhtitlan in qujçaco, ommotlalico in Tlacuban çan onchicomjlhujtico: njman iaque vmpoaltito. Auh ie no ceppa qujçaco, çan qujztiqujzque quauhtitlampa itztiaque: çan tequjtl ontemjctitiqujzque in tlaliztacapan yiztacalla: tlatilulca in mjcque, achi vel centzontli in mjc.

---

1. So the Aztec reads (*cempoaltica*: see Molina, *Vocabulario de la lengua mexicana*) *cexiuhtica* [fol. 18*v*], *ompoaltica* [fol. 76*v*]. Doubtless the twentieth day is meant, to conform with custom in observance of feast days (personal communication, Rafael García Granados).

2. Sahagún, Garibay ed., Vol. IV, p. 135: "*Allí hubiera hecho un año de que nada había sucedido, si no hubieran ido*"; Seler, *Einige Kapi-*

tel, pp. 529–30: "*In diesem Monat würden sie ein Jahr hinter sich haben, wo nichts geschah, wo sie sich nicht von der Stelle rührten (d. h. ein Jahr nach der Ankunft der Spanier)*."

3. The fifteenth and sixteenth months are omitted in the Nahuatl text.

accomplishment was that they were to slay people in Tlaliztacapan, in Iztacalla. Tlatilulcans died;[4] about four hundred died.

And when they had discussed one completely, when there had been a consultation about us, it was also after two [more] score [days], in Toxcatl. Already it was indeed the second year after the brave warriors had died in the temple courtyard, during Toxcatl.[5]

Auh in tecentlatalhuj, in ie topan nenonotzaloc, no vmpoaltica ipan toxcatl: ie vel ic oxivitl in tiacaoan mjcque in teuitvalco, in Toxcatica./.

4. This passage is paralleled in *Anales de Tlatelolco*, ed. Berlin, pp. 64–65, §§ 306–7: "*Después partió [Cortés] yendo otra vez a Citlaltépec. Se va a Tlacopan y se viene a meter en el palacio.... Pelean 7 días contra nosotros únicamente allá, en Tlacopan. Y nuevamente retrocedió él, a quien siguieron. De allá salieron y se establecieron en Tetzcoco. Transcurridos 80 (días) regresó aun otra vez y se fue a Uaztépec y a Quauhnáuac. De allá pasó a Xochimilco. Allá pereció gente Tlatelolca. De allá partió por segunda vez y marchó sobre Tlalliztacapan. Allá pereció gente Tlatelolca.*"

5. Cf. *ibid.*, p. 65, §§ 309–11.

Twenty-ninth Chapter, in which it is told how there came a plague,[1] of which the natives died. Its name was smallpox. It was at the time that the Spaniards set forth from Mexico.

But before the Spaniards had risen against us, first there came to be prevalent a great sickness, a plague. It was in Tepeilhuitl that it originated, that there spread over the people a great destruction of men. Some it indeed covered [with pustules]; they were spread everywhere, on one's face, on one's head, on one's breast, etc. There was indeed perishing; many indeed died of it. No longer could they walk; they only lay in their abodes, in their beds. No longer could they move, no longer could they bestir themselves, no longer could they raise themselves, no longer could they stretch themselves out on their sides, no longer could they stretch themselves out face down, no longer could they stretch themselves out on their backs. And when they bestirred themselves, much did they cry out. There was much perishing. Like a covering, covering-like, were the pustules. Indeed many people died of them, and many just died of hunger. There was death from hunger; there was no one to take care of another; there was no one to attend to another.

And on some, each pustule was placed on them only far apart; they did not cause much suffering, neither did many die of them. And many people were harmed by them on their faces; their faces were roughened. Of some, the eyes were injured; they were blinded.

At this time this plague prevailed indeed sixty days — sixty day-signs — when it ended, when it diminished; when it was realized, when there was reviving, the plague was already going toward Chalco.[2] And many were crippled by it; however, they were not entirely crippled. It came to be prevalent in Teotl eco, and it went diminishing in Panquetzaliztli. At that time the Mexicans, the brave warriors were able to recover from the pestilence.[3]

Injc cempoalli on chicunavi capitulo: vncan mjtoa in quenjn valla Totomonjztli, injc mjcque njcã tlaca: in jtoca vei çavatl, in jquac oqujzque Españoles in Mexico.

Auh in aiamo totechmoquetza in Españoles: achtopa momanaco vei cocoliztli, totomonaliztli, ipan tepeilhujtl in tzintic, in tetechmotecac vevei tepopul: cequj vel pepechtic, novian in motecac in teixco, in teicpac, in teelpan, &c. vellaixpolo, vel mjequjntin ic mjcque, aoc vel nenemja, ça onoca in jmonoian in incuchian, aoc vel molinjaia, aoc vel mocuechinjaia, aoc vel mocuecuetzoaia, aoc vel monacacicteca, aoc vel mjxtlapachtecaia, aoc vel maquetztitecaia. Auh in jquac mocuechinjaia, cenca tzatzia: cenca tlaixpolo, in pepechtic, in pepechiuhquj in çaoatl, vel mjec tlacatl, ic momjqujli, yoã mjequjntin çan apizmjcque, apizmjcoac, aocac motecujtlaviaia, aocac teca muchivaia.

Auh in cequjntin çan veveca in intech motlali in çavatl, amo cenca qujmjhioti, amo no mjequjntin ic mjcque: yoã mjec tlacatl ic itlacauh in jxaiac, ichachaquachiuhque, iacachachaquachiuhque, cequjtin yixcueponque, ixpopoiotque:

iquac in manca inin totomonjliztli, vel epoalilhujtl, epoaltonal in qujz in cuetlan, in neemachoc, in iolioac: ie chalcopa vatztia in totomonjliztli, yoã mjec injc cocototzauh: amo tel iccen cocototzauh. In momanaco Teutl eco: auh in cuetlanjto ipan in Panquetzaliztli: vncan vel caxavaque in Mexica, in tiacaoan.

---

1. Corresponding Spanish text: *pestilencia.* Seler (*Einige Kapitel,* p. 531) has smallpox for this term, and "great rash" for *vei çavatl.* Chimalpahin (*Annales,* p. 192, n. 5) has smallpox for *totomonaliztli.* The term is spelled *totomonjztli* in the Codex.

2. Probably either *valitztia* or *vetztia* should be read.

3. Cf., however, Seler, *Einige Kapitel,* p. 532. See also *caxaua* in Molina, *Vocabulario de la lengua mexicana,* fol. 13r.

And when this had happened, then the Spaniards came. They moved there from Texcoco; they went to set forth by way of Quauhtitlan; they came to settle themselves at Tlacopan. There the responsibilities were then divided; there, there was a division. Pedro de Alvarado's responsibility became the road coming to Tlatilulco. And the Marquis went to settle himself in Coyoacan, and it became the Marquis's responsibility, as well as the road coming from Acachinanco[4] to Tenochtitlan. The Marquis knew that the man of Tenochtitlan was a great warrior.

And in Nextlatilco, or Ilyacac, there indeed war first began. There [the Spaniards] quickly came to reach Nonoalco.[5] The brave warriors came following after them. None of the Mexicans died. Then the Spaniards turned their backs. The brave warriors waged war in boats; the shield-boatmen shot arrows at them. Their arrows rained upon the Spaniards. They entered [Nonoalco]. And the Marquis thereupon threw [the Spaniards] toward those of Tenochtitlan; he followed along the Acachinanco road. Many times he fought, and the Mexicans contended against him.

Auh in ie iuhquj: njmã ie vitze, valolinj in Españoles in vmpa Tetzcoco: quauhtitlampa in qujçato ommotlalico Tlacuban: nec vncan motequjmaca, vncã moxeloa: in Pedro de Aluarado, itequjppã muchiuh in vtli vallaticac tlatilulco. Auh in Marques coioacan motlalito: auh itequjuh muchiuh in marques: auh in vtli in acachinanco vallaticac tenuchtitlan, in moma marques ca vei oqujchtli in tenuchcatl vei tiacauh:

auh in nextlatilco, anoço iliacac, vel vmpa achto iaupevaco, njman acitiuetzico in nonoalco in qujnvaltocaque tiacavan, aiaac mjc in Mexica: njman ic moteputztique in Españoles. In tiacavan in acaltica tlaecoa, in acalchimaleque qujmõmjna: in immjuh, ontzetzelivi in impan Españoles: njman ic calaque. Auh in Marques njman ie ic qujvallaça in invicpa tenuchca qujvaltoca in vtli in acachinãco: mjecpa valmicalia, auh connamjquj in Mexica.

4. A location in the lake, which can now be fixed as to the east of the Calzada de S. Antonio Abad and south of the Calzada de Fr. Servando Teresa de Mier (personal communication, Rafael García Granados).

5. Nextlatilco and Iliacac are parts of the *barrio* of Nonoalco, which is described as an *"isleta al norte de la Calzada de Tacuba,"* an area today approximately bounded N. by Calle de la Emigración and Manuel González; E., irregular line approximating Guerrero; S., approximately Luna and Plaza de Abasolo; and W., Olivo (Caso, "Barrios antiguos," p. 41).

Thirtieth Chapter, in which it is told how the Spaniards fashioned their boats there in Texcoco in order to come to conquer Mexico here.

And when their twelve boats had come from Texcoco, for the time being all were assembled there at Acachinanco. Then the Marquis moved to Acachinanco. Thereupon he went searching out where the boats could enter; where the canals were straight, if perchance they were deep, if perchance they were not deep, so that they would not be grounded. But the canals were very winding, very recurved; they could not get them in there.

They got two boats in there; they forced them through the road which is coming straight from Xoloco. And for the first time they consulted together; they resolved that they would put all the Mexicans to the spear. This they resolved. Then they put themselves in order. They carried guns. The large cotton banner went leading them. They were in no way excited, they were not troubled; they went beating the drums and blowing [trumpets] and wooden flutes.

And the two boats came quite silently. Only along one side did the boats hold themselves. But on the other side no boat came, because there was a group of houses. Then they came apace; they came giving battle. There were deaths on both sides; captives were taken on both sides. And when the people of Tenochtitlan who dwelt in Çoquipan saw this, they then fled; in fear they fled. The babies were taken off along with the other people.[1] They just went into the water; all into the water went the common folk. There arose a cry of weeping. And those who had boats filled the boats with their babies. They poled them; they poled vigorously. Nothing else did they take with them; in fear they only hastily abandoned their poor goods; they only hastily scattered them there. But our foes went looting the things. They went taking whatsoever they came upon. Whatsoever they lit upon they took. They took with them perhaps capes, perhaps

Injc cempoalli ommatlactli capitulo vncan mjtoa in quenjn Españoles qujxinque imacal vmpa tetzcocu injc tepevaco njcan mexico.

Auh in ovalla imacal tetzcocu matlactetl omume, çan oc much vmpa mocenten in acachinanco, njman vncã valmjquanj in Marques in acachinanco: njmã ie ic qujtlatemolitinemj in campa vel calaqujz acalli, in campa ie melavaticac acalotli, in aço vecatlan, in acanoço vecatlan injc amo cana macanaz: auh in acalotli in cocoltic, in cuecuelpachtic, amo vel vncan qujcalaqujque,

vntetl in acalli in concalaqujque, concujtlaviltequjltique in vtli xolloco vallamelauhticac: auh ceppa qujcentlatalhujque, qujcemjtoque, injc qujncentlaxilizque mexica in qujncentlatalhujzque: nec motecpana, qujvica in tlequjqujztli qujniacantivitz in quachpanjtl, çan njman amo mamana, amo momocivia, tlatzotzontivitze, yoan tlapitztivitze yoan quavilacapitztli.

Auh in vntetl acalli, çan jvian onotivitz, çan cectlapal in vallonotia in acalli: auh in oc cectlapal atle valla in acalli, iehica ca calla, nec iativitze, necalivativitz, necoc mjcoa, necoc tlamalo. Auh in oqujttaque in tenuchca in çoqujpan onoque: nec motlaloa, momauhcatlaloa, tetlan tlaano in pipiltzitzinti, çan atlan in vi, cematl mantiuh in macevalli, tlachoqujztleva. Auh in acaleque qujmacaltenque in impilhoantzitzin, qujntlanelhuja, qujntequjtlanelhuja, aoc tle ma itla conmocujlique, çã moch conmauhcacauhtiqujzque, in intlatqujtzin, çan much vmpa contepeuhtiqujzque. Auh in toiaovan tlanamoxtivi, qujcujtivi in tlein ipan oqujçato, in tlein oqujpantito qujcuj, qujmotqujlia in aço tilmatli, in aço quachtli, in anoço tlaviztli, in anoço teponaztli in anoço vevetl.

---

1. Sahagún, Garibay ed., Vol. IV, p. 138: "Son llevados los niñitos al lado de otras personas." Seler, Einige Kapitel, p. 534: "die kleinen Kinder werden zu andern Leuten gebracht."

large cotton capes, or devices, or two-toned drums, or ground drums.

And the Tlatilulcans fought there in Çoquipan[2] in shield-boats. And at Xoloco [the Spaniards] came to arrive there where the wall lay; it lay in the middle cutting off the road. They fired at it with their big guns. It did not crumble when [the shot] fell for the first time; but at the second, it crumbled, and at the third at last it indeed went to the ground, and at the fourth the wall indeed went to the ground forever.

And the two boats went to contend against the shield-boatmen.[3] There was fighting in the water. And the guns went filling the prow of each boat. And there where [Mexican] boats lay thick, there where they lay massed, there they fired. Many men thus died. Then each [boat] quickly lifted its prow, quickly went sideways, quickly sank. Likewise the iron bolts: whomever they could take aim upon no longer escaped; he then died; he there breathed his last. But when the Mexicans could see, when they could judge how the gun[shots], the bolts would fall, no one followed a direct course. They went only from one side to the other; they went across; they only went a zig-zag course.

And also when they saw that the big gun[shot] was already about to fall, there was going to the ground, there was stretching out on the ground, there was crouching. And the brave warriors each quickly entered among the houses. The road became clear; the wide road lay as if clear.

And then [the Spaniards] came to reach Uitzillan.[4] There, there lay still another wall. And many [Mexicans] lay crouched by it; they lay hidden at the wall. For a short time [the Spaniards'] boats were grounded there; they struck [the ground]. There for a short time they waited while they prepared the guns.

Auh in tlatilulca vmpa tlaiecoque in çoqujpan, acalchimaltica: auh in xolloco in oacico in vncan tenamjtl onoca, in onepãtla in qujtzacutoca vtli: in tlequjqujztli vei, ic qujmotlaq̄, aiamo xitin in iancujcan vetz, auh injc vppa, xitin: auh injc expa, iequene vel tlaltitech ia: auh injc nappa iequene vel iccen tlaltitech ia in tenamjtl.

Auh in ontetl acalli qujnnamjctiuh in acalchimaleque, necaliva in atlan. Auh in tlequjqujztli imacaliacac tetentiuh: auh in vnca tetzavatoc acalli, in vncan tecpichauhtoc: vmpa inpan contlaça mjec tlacatl ic mjc: njman aaquetztivetzi, nenecujliuhtivetzi, papachiuhtivetzi: çan ie no ivi in tepuzmjtl in aqujn vel qujmottilia, aocmo qujça, njman mjquj, vncan qujhiovia. Auh in ovel qujttaque Mexica, in ovel qujnemjliq̄ in juh vetzi tlequjqujztli, yoã in tepuzmjtl, aocac motlamelauhcaquetza, ça avic vivi, tlatlaxtlapaloa, ça ixtlapalhujvi.

Auh in jquac ie no qujtta in ie vetziz in vei tlequjqujztli, tlaltech viloa, tlaltech neteco, nepacholo. Auh in tiacavan cacalactivetzque in caltzalan chipavatimoquetz in vtli, in vchpantli, ça iuhqujn chipacpul icac.

Auh njman onacico in vitzillan, in oc ce vncã onoc tenamjtl: auh mjequjntin itlan mopachotoca, qujmotoctitoca in tenamjtl: achitonca vncan ommacã, ontzotzon in jmacal, vncan achitonca onvecavaque in oqujc conchichiuhque tlequjqujztli.

---

2. *Barrio*, also known as S. Pablo Teopan, Çoquipan, or Xochimilca, an area now bounded N. by Calle de Guatemala and Miguel Negrete; E., Calzada de Balbuena; S., Calzada del Chabacano and Calle de Morelos; and W., Calzada de S. Antonio Abad (Caso, "Barrios antiguos," p. 18).

3. See Pl. 120.
4. Near the Church of S. Pablo (corresponding Spanish text). Caso ("Barrios antiguos," p. 35) links it to Atliceuhyan, and says that it has been "*mencionado bajo la advocación de Sta. Ana.*"

Thirty-first Chapter, in which it is told how the Spaniards came with the brigantines. They pursued those who were in boats. When they went contending against them, they then drew near to them. They came to reach all the houses.[1]

And when they had prepared [each of the guns], thereupon they shot at the wall. And the wall then broke to pieces; it broke through at the back. And the second time [the shot] fell, the wall then went to the ground. It was thrown down in various places; it was broken open; it was perforated. Then likewise it was as if the road was clear. And the brave warriors who lay by the wall at once dispersed. There was flight, there was escaping in fear.

And all the various people (allies of the Spaniards) quickly went filling each canal. Then they quickly leveled them with stones, with adobes and some logs. Thus they stopped up the water[ways].

And when this was done, when the canals were stopped up, thereupon the horse[men] passed over, perhaps ten of them. They came winding, wheeling, twisting, turning about. Once again a group of horse-[men] ran by; they went following after [the others]. And some Tlatilulcans who had quickly entered the palace which had been Moctezuma's home, then emerged in fear; they had come to contend against the horse[men]. One of these came spearing a Tlatilulcan, but when he had come spearing him, [the Tlatilulcan] could still grasp his iron lance. Then his friends went to take it from [the rider's] hands. They threw him down upon his back; they overcame him. And when he came falling to the ground, then they repeatedly struck him; they struck him repeatedly on the back of the head. There he died.

Thereupon the Spaniards made the determination to move together. Then they came to reach Quauhquiyauac. And they went taking with them the lombard gun [and] the equipment which went with it.

Injc cempoalli ommatlactli oce capitulo: vncan mjtoa in quenjn Españoles ic valietiaque in vergantines, qujnvaltocaque in acaltica nenca in qujnnamjqujto: njmã ic valqujzque itech acico in jxqujch calli.

Auh in oconchichiuhque: njmã ie ic qujvalmotla in tenamjtl: auh in tenamjtl, njmã tzatzaian, cujtlaxeliuh. Auh injc vppa vetz: njmã tlaltitech ia in tenamjtl, vevelocac, vmpet, oncoion: njman no iuhqujn chipacpul moquetz vtli. Auh in tiacavã in tenantitlan onoca, njmã ic valxitinque, valnetlalolo, nemauhcaqujxtilo.

Auh in jxqujch nepapan tlacatl: njman iciuhca contetentivi in acalotli, njman iciuhca conjxmana tetica, xantica yoan cequj quavitl injc tlaatzopque.

Auh in ie iuhquj, in ommatzop acalotli: njman ie ic valeoa in cavallome, aço matlacteme, ontlaiavaloco, ontlamalacachoco, ommocovitzoco, ommotevilacachoco: ie no ceppa centlamantli valevaque in cavallome, qujnvalcujtlapãvitiaque. Auh cequjntin tlatilulca calactivetzque in tecpan catca in jchan motecuçoma: njman ic valmauhcaqujçaia, qujmonmonamjctico in cavallostin: ce qujxilico in tlatilulca. Auh in oqujxilico, oc vel can in jtepuztopil: njman qujmacujlito in jcnjvan, icujtlapan qujoalmaiauhque, qujvaltzineuhque: auh in otlalpan vetzico mec qujvivitequj, concuexcochvivitecque, oncan ommjc.

Niman ie ic qujoalcentlaça, oalcemolinj in Españoles: njmã ic onacico in quauhqujiavac. Auh in tomaoac tlequjqujztli qujvicativi, intlatquj ietiuh, contecaque in quauhqujiavac. (Auh injc moteneoa

1. Corresponding Spanish text: "de como los de los vergantines, aujendo oxeado las canoas: que los salieron por la laguna: llegaron a tierra junto a las casas." Sahagún, Garibay ed., Vol. IV, p. 139: "Allí se dice como los españoles vinieron trayendo los bergantines. Vinieron siguiendo a los que andaban en barcas. Cuando llegaron cerca de ellos, luego se dejaron ir en su contra, se acercaron a todas las casas." Seler, Einige Kapitel, pp. 535–36: "Im einunddreissigsten Kapitel wird erzählt, wie die Spanier in den Brigantinen kamen, die in den Booten (Kämpfenden) verfolgten, sie aufsuchten (sie bekämpften), wie sie dann kamen, in die unmittelbare Nähe der gesamten Häusermassen kamen."

They put it down at Quauhquiyauac [the Eagle Gate]. (And hence was it called the Eagle Gate: there stood an eagle carved of stone, as tall as a man's height is tall; and flanking it was an ocelot on one side, and on the [other] side a wolf,[2] likewise carved of stone. [)] And when this was done, the great brave warriors hid themselves in vain behind the stone columns. And there were two rows of stone columns, eight altogether. And on the roof terrace of the Coacalli[3] the brave warriors lay crowded. They were crowded on the roof terrace. There was none of the brave warriors who ventured beyond.

And the Spaniards moved not at all. And when they fired the gun, it became very dark; smoke was spread. And among those who had been hiding behind the stone columns there was flight; and all those who had lain upon the roof terraces threw themselves down from there; there was flight far away. Then [the Spaniards] carried the gun up; they came to lay it upon the round stone of gladiatorial sacrifice. And at the summit of [the pyramid temple of] Uitzilopochtli [the priests] watched in vain. They struck the two-toned drums; as if excessively they struck the two-toned drums. And then two Spaniards climbed up. They went striking each one [of the priests]. And when they had gone to strike each of them, they cast them down, they threw them out.

And the shorn ones, all the brave warriors who were fighting in boats, all came forth; they came forth on dry land. And those who poled were the young boys; only they brought the boats. And when this was done, the brave warriors then took note of the spaces between the houses. There was indeed shouting; they said: "O brave warriors, hasten here!"

And when this was done, when the Spaniards saw that they were already near them, that they already pursued them,[4] they then crouched down, they turned their backs, they indeed ran, they fled. On both sides there was shooting with arrows, with barbed arrows, and on both sides stones were cast. Afterwards [Mexican warriors] went to mend, to restore themselves at Xoloco. There they went to stop; thereupon there was turning back. And the Spaniards then turned. They

quauhqujiaoac, ca vncan icaca in quauhtli, tetl in tlaxixintli, vel cennequetzalli injc quauhtic, inic vecapan: auh qujtzatzacutimanj, in centlapal icaca ocelutl: auh in centlapal icaia cujtlachtli, çanno tetl in tlaxintli. Auh in ie iuhquj in vevei tiacavan, oc nē qujmototoctiticaca in tetlaquetzalli: auh in tetlaquetzalli ompantli, nepan chicuej. Auh in coacalli itlapāioc, no tetentoque in tiacavan, motlatlapantenque aocac ixtlapal iauh in tiiacavan.

Auh in Españoles çā njman amo mamana: auh in oqujtlazque tlequjqujztli cenca tlaiovac, poctli motecac. Auh in qujmotoctitimanca in tetlaquetzalli, netlaloloc yoan in jxqujchtin tlapanco onoca valmotepeuhque veca netlaloloc, nec qujvallecavia in tlequjqujztli contecaco temalacatitlan: auh in jcpac vitzilobuchtli, oc nē tlapiaia, qujvitequja in teponaztli, iuhqujn ontetemj qujvitequj teponaztli: auh njmā ic ontlecoque vmentin Españoles, vmpa qujmonvivitequjto: auh in oqujmonvivitequjto in ca valmaiauhque, qujnvalchicanauhque:

auh in quaquachictin in jxqujchtin in tiacavan in acaltica tlaiecoaia, muchintin valqujzque, vallalvacaqujzque: auh in tetlanelhuja in telpopotzitzinti, çan iehoātin in qujvalhujvicaque in acalli. Auh in ie iuhquj in tiaiacavan, nec qujmottilia in caltzalantli vellatotoca, vel netzatzililo: qujtoa. Tiacavane, ma vallatotoca:

auh in ie iuhquj, in oqujttaque in Españoles in ie impan monamjquj in ie qujntotona, njmā ic mocototztztlalique, moteputztique, vel totoca, motlaloa necoccampa in valmjnaloia in tlatzontectica, yoan necoccampa in valtepacholo, qujn vmpa xolloco patito, imjhio qujcujto, vmpa valmomanato: njman ie ic valnecuepalo. Auh in iehoantin Españoles, njman ic no mocuepa motlalito in acachinanco: auh in tlequjqujztli vncan qujcauhtiqujzque in temala-

---

2. *Cuitlachtli*, "*vn oso*" in the corresponding Spanish text. See Dibble and Anderson, *Book XI*, where it is described (p. 5) and illustrated (Pl. 6). We there identify it as *Ursus horriaeus*, grizzly bear; *Euarctos machetes*; or *Ursus americanus machetes* (Elliott), black bear. Cf. also Molina, *Vocabulario de la lengua mexicana*, fol. 26, where the term is translated as *lobo* (wolf).

3. Corresponding Spanish text: "*mucha otra gente estaua encima de la casa que estaua armada sobre las coluñas.*" The Coacalli is described in Book VIII of the *Florentine Codex*.

4. *Qujntotona*: probably *qujntotoca* is meant.

went to establish themselves in Acachinanco. But in their haste they left the gun upon the round stone of gladiatorial sacrifice. The brave warriors then seized it, forced it forward, went to drop it in the water. They went pulling it to Tetamaçolco.[5]

catitlan: njman conanque in tiacavan, qujtototza qujmaiavito atlan, tetamaçolco qujtztiltitiaque.

_____

5. Corresponding Spanish text: "*en vna agua profunda que llamauā Tetamaçulco, que esta cabe el monte que se llama Tepetzinco, donde estan los baños.*"

Thirty-second Chapter, in which it is told how the Mexicans in fear went forth from their city here when they dreaded the Spaniards.

And when this had occurred, the people of Tenochtitlan entered here into Tlatilulco. There was raised a cry of weeping; there was raised a shout. Many were the tears of the beloved women. And as for us men, each one took his woman; one or another carried his child upon his shoulders. When they were abandoning their city, it lasted an entire day. But the Tlatilulcans again already went there to Tenochtitlan to fight.

And when this was done, Pedro Alvarado already was to move against Iliacac, which is toward Nonoalco. There was nothing he could do. It was as if he had come to arise against a stone, because the Tlatilulcans exerted themselves powerfully. On both sides there was fighting on the road, and on the water in shield-boats. When Alvarado continued to tire himself, he then turned back; he went to establish himself in Tlacopan. But only[1] two days later, when the first two boats, which [the Mexicans] repulsed, came, thereupon all assembled; they went to establish themselves near the houses of Nonoalco. Thereupon they came forth on dry land, on the dry ground. Thereupon they followed the narrow road which was among the houses; they reached the very center.

And when the Spaniards came forth there, all was clear. No man of the common folk came forth. But Tzilacatzin, a brave warrior, very courageous, then cast three of his stones which he carried — very large, huge stones; round, each one: wall stones, these, or white stones. One of them went in his hand, two went upon his shield. Thereupon he pursued the Spaniards, he went scattering them, dispersing them into

Injc cempoalli ommatlactli omume capitulo: vncan mjtoa in quenjn Mexica valmauhcaqujzque in vncan imaltepeuh ipan in qujmjmacazque Españoles.

Auh in jquac in, in tenuchca valcalacque in njcan tlatilulco, tlachoqujztleoa, tlatzatziztleoa, ixachi in jmjxaio cioatzitzinti: auh in toqujchtin qujnvivicatze in incicivaoã in aca qujquechpanoa in jpiltzin: njmã iquac in qujcauhque in jmaltepeuh ça cemjlhujtl. Auh in tlatilulca ie ne vmpa itztivi in tenuchtitlan in mjcalizque.

Auh in ie iuhquj in Pedro aluarado: ie ne vmpa qujvallaz in iliacac, in jvicpa nonoalco, aiatle vel qujchiuhque, iuhqujn tetitech onevaco: iehica ca in tlatilulca cenca mochicauhque, necoc in tlaiecoloc, vtli ipan, yoan atlan in acalchimaltica: in omoxixiuhtlati in aluarado, njmã ic mocuep, motlalito in tlacuban: auh çan jviptlaioc in qujvalcentlazque in acalli in acachto valla, can oc ontetl: auh çatepã muchi cẽquiça in caltenco nonoalco ommotemato: njman ie ic oalqujça in tlalhoacapã, in tlalhoacpan: njma ie ic qujvaltoca opitzactli, in calla icac, qujvaliollotia.

Auh in vncan valqujzque Españoles ocactivetz, aocac tlacatl oqujz in maçevalli. Auh in tzilacatzin vei tiacauh cenca oqujchtli: njmã ic qujvallaz, etetl in qujtquj iteuh, vevei tepopul mamalacachtic ie in tenaiocatetl, anoço iztac tetl, centetl imac ietiuh, vntetl ichimaltitlan ietiuh, njman ie ic qujntoca qujmontepevato atlan, qujmõtoxavato in Españoles, ça atlan in oniaque, vel aaietixque in ontetemoque

1. *Can*: read *çan*.

the water. They went only into the water. Each became well soaked as he descended [into the water].[2]

And this Tzilacatzin as a brave warrior was an Otomí [in rank], because of the Otomí hairdress; for he despised his foes, though they were Spaniards. He altogether despised them. There was indeed complete terror. Our foes, when they saw Tzilacatzin, then crouched. And much did they seek to slay him; perchance they would pierce him with an iron bolt or they would shoot him with a gun. But Tzilacatzin only disguised himself so that he would not be known. At times he put on a device, he hung his lip pendants and each of his golden ear plugs, and he put on his necklace of white shells. Only his head went uncovered, whereby it was evident that he was an Otomí [warrior]. And sometimes [he had] only his padded cotton armor shirt [and] the thin little [band] with which his forehead was bound. And sometimes in order to disguise himself he put on a feather headdress with a wig, with [two] eagle feather pendants which went tied at the back of his head. This [was the array] of one who cast men into the fire.[3] As one who cast men into the fire did he go acting; he went imitating one who cast men into the fire. Each of his golden arm bands went, on both sides; they went on both arms. And the golden arm bands glistened.[4] And also on each leg went leather leg bands, golden leather leg bands. They were quite brilliant.

And then next day again, once more, their boats came setting forth; they came to ground them at Nonoalco, at Ayauhcaltitlan.[5] And then also came setting forth those who went afoot and all the Tlaxcallans and Otomí. The Spaniards came indeed in force to overcome [the Mexicans]. And when they came to reach Nonoalco, thereupon there was combat, there was fighting; there indeed developed combat, battle. On both sides there were deaths. All of their foes were shot with arrows; also all the Mexicans. On both sides equally were there wounds. Thus all day, thus all night was there fighting.

There were only two great brave warriors who turned not their faces away, who altogether despised those who were their foes, who did not value their

(Auh inin Tzilacatzin otomjtl catca injc tiacauh, ipampa in tlaotonxintli, iehica amo imjxco tlachiaia in iniaovan in manel Españoles, amo tle impan qujmjttaia, vel tlacenmamauhtiaia: in jquac in qujttaia in Tzilacatzin, njman mocototztlaliaia in toiaovan: auh cenca qujtemoaia, injc qujmjctizque, in aço qujtepuzmjvizque, in anoço qujtlequjqujzvizque. Auh in Tzilacatzin, çã mjxpoloa injc amo iximachoz: in quenman tlaviztli in ommaqujaia, itenpilol compiloaia, yoan iteteucujtlanacoch yoã conmocozcatia in jcozquj chipoli, çan tlapouhtiuh in jtzontecon, neztiuh injc otomjtl: auh in quẽmanjan çanjo in ichcavipil canactontli injc ommoquaqujmjloa, auh in q̃manjan injc mjxpoloa cõmaqujaia ihujtzoncalli, quatzone quauhtlalpilonj icuexcochtlampa tentiuh, ic tlalpitiuh iehoatl injc tetlepantlaxoia, iuhqujn tetlepantlazquj ipã qujztiuh, qujntlaieiecalhujtiuh in tetlepantlazque iteteucujtlamatemecauh necoccampa in ietiuh yiocanjxti ietiuh in jmac: auh in teucujtlamatemecatl cuecuenio auh no ie in jcxic ieietiuh, cotzeoatl, teucujtlacotzeoatl çan petlanquj)

Auh njmã imuztlaioc in ie no cuel ceppa qujçaco in jmacal conacanaco nonoalco, aiauhcaltitlã: auh njman no qujçaco in tlacxipanvia yoan in ie ixqujch tlaxcaltecatl yoan otomjtl, vel tonac in qujntepevitivitze in Españoles. Auh in oacico nonoalco: njmã ie ic tlaiecolo, necaliva, vel motetemman in tlaiecoliztli in iauiotl, necoc in mjcoaia ixqujch mjnaloa in iniaovan, no ixqujch in mexicatl, necoc ivi, necocolo, iuh cemjlhujtl, iuh ioac in necalioac.

Çan vmen in vevei tiacaoã in amo mjtzacujlianj, in atle inpan qujmitta in iniaovã catca, in amo qujtlaçotlaia in innacaio. Jnjc ce tlacatl itoca Tzaiectzin.

---

2. Corresponding Spanish text: "y salieron otros tras, el hizieron retraer a los españoles. Y boluieron al agua, hazia donde tenjan los vergantines." Seler, Einige Kapitel, p. 540: "Danach verfolgt er sie, jagt sie auf das Wasser, zerstreut die Spanier, zum Wasser gingen sie (wieder) im Wasser, wurden schwer beladen (die Bergantinen), zu denen sie hinabstiegen." See Pl. 131.

3. See Anderson and Dibble, Book II, Chap. 29. Cf. also Seler's discussion of Otontecuhtli in Gesammelte Abhandlungen, Vol. II, p. 1039.

4. Cuecuenio: read cuecueio.

5. A part of Nonoalco (Caso, "Barrios antiguos," p. 41).

bodies. The name of the first man was Tzoyectzin. The name of the second was Temoctzin. And the name of the third was the aforementioned Tzilacatzin.[6]

And when the Spaniards were tired, when they could do nothing against, when they could not break the Mexicans, they then went. They entered [their quarters]. They were indeed afflicted. Their allies went following behind them.

Jnjc vme itoca, Temoctzin: auh ic teeca in omoteneuh in Tzilacatzin.

Auh in omoxiuhtlatique in Españoles, in avel qujnchioa, in avel qujnpetla in Mexica: njman ic iaque, calacque, vel imellel acic, qujncujtlapanvitivi in intlavilanalhoan.

---

6. Read *ic yei itoca*.

Thirty-third Chapter, in which it is told how the people of the floating gardens, the Xochimilcans, the Cuitlauacans, those of Itztapalapan, and still others came so that they might help the Mexicans.

And once it came to pass that the people of Xochimilco, of Cuitlauac, of Mizquic, of Colhuacan, of Mexicaltzinco, of Itztapalapan sent messengers. They came to consult with Quauhtemoc and still others who were lords, who were brave warriors. They came saying to them: "O my beloved noblemen, with a little we have come to help the city. Perhaps it is possible that thus we have come satisfying the words of the rulers who yet keep watch there. In truth, the rulers dwell here. The eagle warriors, the ocelot warriors have come, have come assembled in boats. It is said that now they will expel our foe."

And when this was done, when [the messengers] had said their say, when [the Mexicans] had consulted over the matter, thereupon they answered them: "It is well. You have shown favor. You have suffered fatigue. You have wearied yourselves. Help the city; let it be attempted."[1]

Thereupon they presented them, they gave them devices, shields, and they gave each chocolate. To each one they gave a broad gourd of chocolate. Thereupon they said to them: "Courage! Let it be attempted, O brave warriors! Our foe is already come." Thereupon the messengers, those who dwelt there, those of Cuitlauac, went, [the Mexicans] escorted them [to the battle].[2] And when they went, then there grew a roar extending everywhere on the road. Thereupon there was fighting.

But the Xochimilcans thereupon roared, hurled themselves upon the boats. They by no means helped us; they only thereupon robbed the people; they robbed the beloved women and the small children and the beloved old women. Then they slew some there; there they breathed their last. But still others they did not slay; they only tranquilly lowered them into the boats.

Injc cempoalli ommatlactli omei capitulo vncan mjtoa in quenjn chinanpaneca in Suchmjlca, cujtlavaca, yoan in Jtztapalapaneca, yoan oc cequjntin vallaque in qujnpalevizquja mexica

Auh ceppa muchiuh in iehoantin suchmjlca, cujtlaoaca mjzqujca, colhoaque, Mexicatzincatl, Jtztapalapanecatl, vallaivaque, qujnonotzaco in quauhtemoctzin, yoã in oc cequjntin in tlatoque, in tiacavan: qujmjlhujco. Nopiltzintzine ca achitzin ic ticpalevico in atl, in tepetl, aço velitiz ca çan ic ixtlavico in intlatol in tlatoque, in oc vmpa tlapia, ca nel njcan onoque in tlatoque, ca ovallaque, ocenqujçaco in quauhtli ocelutl in acaltica: ca qujl axcã qujcentlaçaz in toiaouh.

Auh in ie iuhquj in oconjtoque in intlatol, in ontlanonotzque njman ie ic qujmjlhuja. Ca ie qualli, oanmotlacnelilique oanqujmjhioviltique, oanqujmociaviltique ma xicmopalevilican in altepetl, ma tlaieiecavi:

njman ie ic qujntlauhtia, qujnmaca in tlaviztli, in chimalli, yoan qujncacacavatique, cecen xicalpechtli in qujnmacaque cacaoatl: njmã ie ic qujmjlhuja. tlacueleoatl, tla tlaieiecavi tiacaoane, ca ie vitze in toiaovan, njma ie ic vi in titlanti in vmpa onoque in cujtlavaca in qujnvalhujcaque. Auh in oiaque njman ic maantimoquetz in tlacavaca in jzqujcan vtlica: njman ie ic necalioa.

Auh in iehoantin in, in Suchmjlca njman ie ic no icavaca, yoan macalhujtequj: amo ma techpalevique, çan njmã ie ic tenamoia, qujnnamoxque in cioatzitzinti, yoan in pipiltzitzinti, yoan in jlamatzitzin njman cequjntin vncan q'nmjctique vncan ihiotl qujz. Auh in oc cequjntin amo qujnmjctique, çan ivian acalco qujmontemovique.

---

1. Garibay (Sahagún, Garibay ed., Vol. IV, p. 144) appears to derive his meaning of *tlaieiecavi* from *yecoa* or *tlayecoa*: *"Que haya en ella combate."*

2. Corresponding Spanish text: *"y luego los pusieron en el lugar donde aujan de pelear. Y puestos en sus lugares todos començaron a pelear."*

And when they were so doing this, [when] already they had treacherously harmed the people, then the seasoned warriors shouted; they said: "O Mexicans, why do the wretches do this? Let there be pursuit!" Thereupon there was a roar. [The Mexicans] pursued them in boats.

And the boats which lay at Nonoalco were all taken there together; all went from there in order for there to be pursuit.[3] Then they went to close the Xochimilcans in. Thereupon they slew them; they speared them, they struck them repeatedly. But some they only took captive. And indeed all died there, indeed they were annihilated there. And all whom [the Xochimilcans] had taken captive they left there, all of them. None of the beloved women were taken away.

And when this thus befell, then the Spaniards settled themselves down.

And as the Xochimilcans had conceived, so would they have done; they would just thus have destroyed us by treachery. And all whom [the Mexicans] took captive of the Xochimilcans, Cuitlauacans, etc., they thereupon took, they forced, there to Yacacolco, where [the Church of] Santa Ana[4] now is. There were Quauhtemoc and Mayeuatzin, ruler of Cuitlauac. (He was here at the time that war was made.)

And when the arrival [of the captives] had taken place, they massed greeting Mayeuatzin. They said to him: "O my beloved younger brother, fare thee well." And Mayeuatzin replied to them: "You vagabonds! Did I perchance summon each of you? What have you done?" And Quauhtemoc then said to Mayeuatzin: "O my beloved younger brother, perform thy office." And Mayeuatzin thereupon offered up [some of] them as sacrifices. He slew four of his vassals. Quauhtemoc also slew four.

And later it was commanded that whosoever was included among the captives be slain everywhere in the temples of the devils. Everywhere the captives were sacrificed.[5]

And later the Mexicans were angry because of this. They said: "The Xochimilcan is near us here; he lieth mingled with us. He already hath made his home

Auh in ie iuh qujchioa inin ie tenaoalpoloa: njman ic tzatzique in tequjvaque, qujtoque. Mexicae tlein ic qujchioa in, tlaveliloque? ma vallatotoca: njman ie ic tlacavaca, qujntoca acaltica.

Auh in nonovalco in onoca in jxqujch acalli: njmā ic muchi vmpa mocemjtqujc, much vmpa ia inic tlantoca: njmā ic qujntzacujlico in Suchmjlca: njman ie ic temjctia, texixili, tevivitequj. Auh cequjntin çan qujmacique: auh vel muchintin, vncā mjcque, vel oncan mjxtlatique. Auh in jxqujchtin in qujmacique, çā muchtin vncan qujncauhq̄ aiac vicoc in cioatzitzinti.

Auh in jquac ie iuh muchioa in, njman ic mocototztlalique in Españoles.

Auh in juh qujmolhujca, in juh qujchivazquja xochmjlca, çan ic technaoalpolozquja: auh in jxqujchtin qujmacique in suchimjlca: in Cujtlavaca. &c. njman ie ic qujnvica, qujntototza in vmpa Jacaculco, in axcan ie sant Ana: vmpa icaca in Quauhtemoctzi, yoan in Maiehoatzin, cujtlaoac tlatoanj (ca njcan ipan muchiuh in iauiotl).

Auh in oaxivaque contlapalotimanj in Maiehoatzin: conjlhuja. Nicauhtzine, moiolicatzin: auh in maiehoatzin, qujnvalilhuja. Jn antlapalpopul cujx namechcujcujtlavi, tle oamaxque. Auh in quauhtemoctzin njman qujoalilhuj in Maiehoatzin. Nicauhtzine ma ximotlacotili: auh in Maiehoatzin: njman ie ic tlamjctia, navi in cōmjcti in jmaceoalhoan: no navi in conmjcti in Quauhtemoctzin.

Auh in çatepan in ac onaaquj in mamalti, oallanavatiloc injc mjctilozque novian in inteteupan tlatlacateculo, vel novian tepan jxque in mamalti.

Auh çatepā ie ic qualanj in Mexica: qujtoque. Ca njcan totlan onoc, technelotoc in suchimjlcatl in ie njcan chanchiva, amo nel vmpa contlalia in jtlatol.

---

3. *Tlantoca*: read *tlatoca*.

4. Corresponding Spanish text: "*en el Tlatilulco.*" A *barrio*, "*sede del gobierno de Cuauhtémoc, donde actualmente se encuentra el templo de Santa Ana en la calle del Peralvillo,*" according to R. H. Barlow ("Una pintura de la conquista en el templo de Santiago," *Tlatelolco a través de los tiempos*, Vol. VI [1945], p. 58). Caso ("Barrios antiguos,"

p. 35) identifies it as a *tlaxilacalli* or neighborhood in the *barrio* of Sta. Ana Atenantitech, in the southern part of Tlatilulco.

5. Garibay (Sahagún, Garibay ed., Vol. IV, p. 145) translates: "*y en seguida a los que habían cogido cautivos se dispuso que los mataran. Por todas partes en los templos de los ídolos, por todas partes, fueron sacrificados los cautivos.*"

here. Doth he not indeed lay his message over there [with the foe]? But we shall just abandon them. They will each just perish." And after this, when the sentence was indeed pronounced, thereupon the beloved women, the beloved old women, and young men already maturing were freed. All of [the rest] were slain, each one. There was no one who was spared, for it was as if they went bearing false witness against them, went doing them undeserved harm when those of Xochimilco and Cuitlauac came as if to help us.

And then after some days two boats came drawing in there to Yauhtenco.[6] The Spaniards came doing only this. It was in the early dawn that they came drawing in. There was no [other] man; for the time they came doing only this. And when this was done, when they had beached their boats, thereupon they came out on dry land. And when they had come out on dry land, thereupon they came giving battle, firing guns, shooting crossbows.

And the brave warriors crouched low at the walls and remained each hidden [among] houses or walls. And where there was to be breaking forth was indeed the object of attention, the charge of the sentinel. And when it was already a good time, when it was already the moment, he thereupon shouted; he said: "O Mexicans, courage!"[7]

Auh inin ça tiqujncaoa, çan popolivi: auh in ie iuhquj, in ovel motzõtec, njman ie ic teçaçaco in cioatzitzinti, in jlamatzitzin yoã in ie tlapalivi, muchintin mjmjctiloque, aocac mocauhque, ca iuhqujn qujmontlatolevito, qujmoncujtlachivito in ovallaque in techpalevizquja xochmjlcatl, in cujtlaoacatl.

Auh njman iquezqujlhujoc, ontetl in acalli quj-çaco, vncan in jiauhtenco çan mjxcavico in Espa-ñoles, ioatzinco in qujçaco, aiaac tlacatl, çan oc val-mjxcavitiaque. Auh in ie iuhquj in oconacanque imacal: njman ie ic vallalhoacaqujça: auh in oval-lalhoacaqujzque njman ie ic mjcaltivitze, tlatlequj-qujzvitivitze, tlatepuzmjvitivitze.

Auh in tiacavan cêca mopachoa tenantitlan, yoã qujmototoctitimanj in calli anoço tepantli. Auh in iautlachixquj vel yix itequjuh in canjn neovaz: auh in ie qualcã in ie inman, njman ie ic tzatzi: qujtoa. Mexicae ma ie cuel.

---

6. Part of Nonoalco. Cf. Caso, "Barrios antiguos," p. 41.

7. This phrase, repeated at the beginning of the next chapter, evidently marks an arbitrary division.

Thirty-fourth Chapter, in which it is told how the Mexicans took captives when they took fifteen [1] Spaniards.

"O Mexicans, courage!"

Thereupon there was a roar and the blowing of shell trumpets, and the sentinel brandished his shield.

Thereupon they pursued the Spaniards. They went upsetting them and taking them. Fifteen of the Spaniards were taken. Then they brought them in. And [the foe] then withdrew their boats. They went spreading out in the middle of the lake.

And when they had come forcing the eighteen there where they were to die, [a place] called Tlacochcalco,[2] they thereupon stripped them. They took from them all their battle gear and their quilted cotton armor, all which was on them; they completely disrobed them. Then, since they became slaves, they slew them. And their companions lay watching them from the middle of the lake.[3]

And at one time they intruded two of their boats there at Xocotitlan.[4] When they had beached them, they thereupon went looking into the hamlet of the people of Xocotitlan. And Tzilacatzin and still other brave warriors, when they saw the Spaniards, then quickly went forward against them. They followed pursuing them; they went casting stones at them. They came scattering the Spaniards in the water.

And once again they brought forth their boats there at Coyonacazco[5] in order to combat, in order to fight. And when they came to arrive, then some Spaniards came forth. Xicotencatl[6] Castañeda led them forth. He went with his quetzal feather ball [device]. There-

Injc cempoalli ommatlactli onnavi capitulo: vncan mjtoa in quenjn iehoantin Mexica tlamaque in qujmacique Españoles caxtolti.

Mexicae ma ie cuel:

njman ie ic tlacaoaca, yoan tlapitzalo yoan chimallaça in iautlachjxquj:

njman ie ic qujntoca in Españoles, qujmaiauhtivi yoā qujmantivi, caxtoltin in anoque in Españoles: njmā ic qujnoalhujcaque: auh in jmacal njmā ic qujtzinqujxtique, anepantla contecato.

Auh in oqujmaxitico caxtoltin omei in vncan mjqujzque itoca: tlacuchcalco: njmā ie ic qujnpepetlaoa, much qujncujlique in iniautlatquj, yoā in jmjchcavipil, yoan in jxqujch in intech catca, moch qujntepeoaltique: njman ie ic tlacoti qujnmjctia: auh in jmjcnjoan qujnvalitztoque anepantla.

Auh ceppa qujcalaqujque vntetl in imacal in vmpa xocotitlā: in oconacanque, njmā ie ic vmpa itztivi in incalla xocoteca. Auh in Tzilacatzin, yoan oc cequjntin tiacaoan: in oqujmittaque in Españoles: njman intech oalietiqujzque, qujnoallalochtocaque, qujntepachotivi, atlan qujntepeoaco in Españoles.

Auh ie no ceppa qujoalhujcaque in jmacal in vncan coionacazco injc tlaiecozque, injc mjcalizque. Auh in oacico njman ic valqujzque cequjntin Españoles, qujnvaliacan in Castañeda xicotencatl: iquetzaltemal ietinemj. Nima ie ic vallatepuzmjvia: auh

---

1. Eighteen are mentioned later. Cf. also Bustamante, *Aparicion*, p. 189 (chapter heading). The corresponding Spanish text of the *Florentine Codex* has fifteen.

2. Bustamante, *Aparicion*, p. 189: "*en que estaba una casa que era como casa de audiencia, cerca de donde agora es la iglesia de Santa Ana.*"

3. Corresponding Spanish text: "*sacaronlos los coraçones delante del ydolo que se llama Macujltotec y los otros españoles estauan mjrando desde los vergantines como los matauan.*"

4. Bustamante, *Aparicion*, p. 190: "*que es agora S. Francisco.*" Caso ("Barrios antiguos," Table V) implies that it is the same as Cihuatecpan. See also p. 34 and note.

5. Bustamante, *Aparicion*, p. 190: "*cerca del hermita de Sta. Lucía (que por otro nombre se llama Amaxac).*" Caso ("Barrios an-

tiguos," pp. 36–37) implies that Coyonacazco was a part of the *barrio* of Telpochcaltitlan, on its eastern border, in Tlatilulco. R. H. Barlow ("Cinco siglos de las calles de Tlatelolco," *Tlatelolco a través de los tiempos*, Vol. IX [1947], p. 32) places it "*no lejos de la estación del Ferrocarril de Hidalgo.*" A map in Antonieta Espejo and R. H. Barlow, "El plano más antiguo de Tlatelolco," *Tlatelolco a través de los tiempos*, Vol. I (1944), shows it in the northwest part of the city.

6. Bustamante, *Aparicion*, p. 190: "*Rodrigo de Castañeda (á quien los indios llamaban Xicotencatl, por tenerle por valiente hombre)*"; Cervantes de Salazar, *Crónica de Nueva España*, Vol. III, p. 245: "*Tuvieron cuenta . . . muy grande los mexicanos con Rodrigo de Castañeda, que fué uno de los que mejor deprendieron la lengua, y como en la viveza y orgullo parescía mucho a Xicotencatl y traía un plumaje á manera de los indios, decíanle muchos denuestos, llamándole 'Xicotencatl cuilone.'*"

upon they shot crossbow bolts. But there was only one who was pierced — in the forehead. He then died. It was Castañeda who shot at him. And the brave warriors quickly went at him; they made [the Spaniards] go into the water; they repeatedly cast stones at them. And there Castañeda would have died, but he only clung to a boat. Thus they took him to Xocotitlan.

And one boat lay at Tetenanteputzco;[7] there the walls curve. And still another boat lay there at Totecco,[8] from which the road goes direct to Tepetzinco.[9] It only lay continuously on guard in the water, but when it was already night they removed it.

And some days later once again the Spaniards determined about us.[10] Then they came. Already they found the Quauecatitlan[11] road which leads direct to the place where salt is sold. And there at Quauecatitlan on the road they were not spread out. And every Tlaxcallan, Acolhuacan, Chalcan thereupon filled in the canal.[12] And where they were not yet spread out[13] they cast in adobes, house beams; door lintels, pillars, round logs were laid down; they bound together reeds to toss into the water. And when it was filled up, then the Spaniards put themselves in place. Very softly they went marching. The standard led them. They came blowing trumpets; they came beating drums. And behind them were coming all the Tlaxcallans and all the dwellers in [allied] cities. Much did the Tlaxcallans exert themselves. Each one of the Tlaxcallans shook his head; each one beat his breast; they sang. Also the Mexicans sang. On both sides there was song. They intoned whatsoever they remembered. Thus it came about that they animated themselves.

And when [the foe] came to reach Tlalhuacan,[14] the brave [Mexican] warriors were well crouched.

ça ce in mjnoc ixquac, njman ic momjqujli: iehoatl in valtemj in Castañeda. Auh in tiacaoã itech ietiqujzque, atlan qujnnemjtique, qujntetepachoque: auh vncã mjqujzquja in castañeda: auh ça acaltitech pilcatia injc qujvicaque xocotitlan.

Auh centetl acalli onoca tetenanteputzco, vncã in colivi tetenamjtl: auh in oc centetl acalli vmpa onoca in totecco: in jpan vtli tlamelaoa Tepetzinco, çan tlatlapixtoca in atlan. Auh in ie ioa qujvica.

Auh iquezqujlhujoc ie no ceppa techcentlatalhuj in Españoles: nec vitze, ie qujoalmottilique in quavecatitlan vtli, in oallamelauhticac iztanamacoian. Auh in vncan in quauecatitlan in vtlica moiauhque. Auh in jxqujch tlaxcaltecatl, in aculhoacatl, in chalcatl: njman ie ic catzupa in acalutli: yoan in ocamoiauhque vtli: contlaça in xamjtl, yoan in calquavitl, in tecoc in tlaixquatl in tlaquetzalli, in quãmjmjlli, in acatl qujcujtlalpia in contepeoa atlan. Auh in jquac in omotzop nec valmotema in Españoles, cencã ivian in iativitze, qujniacana in quachpanjtl, tlapitztivitze, tlatzotzontivitze. Auh imjcampa onotivitze in ie ixqujch tlaxcaltecatl, yoan in ie ixqujch altepeoa, cenca muchicava moquaquacuecuechoa, meeltzotzona in tlaxcalteca, cujca, no cujca in mexica necoccampa cujco, queoa in çaço tlein qujlnamjquj, ic mellaquaoa muchioa.

Auh in oacico tlalhoacan in tiacaoã vel nepacholo, vel mopachoa vel netlatilo, qujtetetzontlaliaia, quj-

7. Corresponding Spanish text: *"cerca de aquella yglesia que se llama sãcta lucia."* Caso ("Barrios antiguos," p. 37) places it in la Garita de Peralvillo, *barrio* of Telpochcaltitlan.

8. Near la Concepción Atenantitlan, according to Caso ("Barrios antiguos," p. 36). To the N. is Calle del Canal del Norte; E., Ave. del Trabajo; S., *barrio* of Mecamalinco and an uneven line from the intersection of Toltecas and Matamoros to the intersection of Peñón and Jesús Carranza.

9. El Peñón de los Baños — east of the center of Tenochtitlan, in the lake. However, Espejo and Barlow ("Plano mas antiguo," p. 46 and map) locate it as a hill in the southeastern part of Tlatilulco.

10. Corresponding Spanish text: *"determinaron entre si los españoles de darnos guerra por alli."*

11. Quauhecatitlan acopoctli: according to Caso ("Barrios antiguos," p. 38), Quauhecatitlan was probably a *tlaxilacalli* or neighborhood in the *barrio* of Atezcapan; it was probably the Calle de Comonfort. Espejo

and Barlow ("Plano más antiguo") show it on the map as in the southwest part of the city.

12. In Bustamante, *Aparicion*, p. 190, the version is somewhat different from what appears in either the Spanish or Nahuatl texts of the *Florentine Codex*: *"por razon de los españoles que los indios habian muerto en su presencia, tornaron á pregonar guerra de nuevo, haciendo juramento solemne que la guerra no habia de cesar hasta que vengasen la muerte de sus hermanos los españoles, y no quedase hombre dellos que no muriese en sus manos: de ahí adelante comenzaron á cegar todas las acequias y caminos de canoas por donde peleaban entre las casas donde los bergantines no podian entrar, y así comenzaron a derrocar casas, y allanar todas las acequias."*

13. Read *in vtlica amoiauhque* and *in oc amoiauhque vtli.*

14. Corresponding Spanish text: *"vn barrio que se llama Tliloacan que es agora sanct mjn"* (San Martín). Caso ("Barrios antiguos," p. 35) says that it, Yacacolco, and Atezcapan were probably all on the Calle de González Bocanegra.

They were well crouched, well hidden. They each prepared for, they lay waiting for the time when they would be sent to rise against [the Spaniards], the time when they would hear the shouting, the rising against them. And when there was the shouting — "O Mexicans, courage!" — then the *tlapanecatl* Ecatzin, an Otomí [warrior], coped with them. He threw himself at them. He said: "O brave warriors, O Tlatilulcans, courage! Who are these barbarians? Come on!" Then with this he went to knock down a Spaniard. He struck him to the ground. This [Ecatzin] was first in going to knock him down, in going ahead against him. And when he had gone knocking him down, then they went dragging the Spaniard off.

chjxtoque in quemman teevitiloz, in quenman qujcaqujzque tzatziliztli, in teevitiliztli: auh in otzatzioac. Mexicae, ma ie cuel iehoatl: njman ic qujvalixti, in Tlapanecatl hecatzin, otomjtl, inca ommomotlac: qujto. Tiiacavane tlatilulcae, ma ie cuel, aqujque in in Tenjme, xivalnenemjcan: njman ic ica ce maiavito in Español, tlalli ic qujvitec: iehoatl in valiacattivia in qujmaiavito in qujvaliacatitivia. Auh in oqujmaiavito: nec convilanato in Español.

Thirty-fifth Chapter, in which it is related how once again the Mexicans took captives when they overtook Spaniards. As the Spaniards who were overtaken were counted, they were fifty-three. And also [were taken] many Tlaxcallans, Texcocans, Chalcans, Xochimilcans. And [it is told] how they slew them all there before those who were their gods.

And when this had happened, the brave warriors who had lain crouched then all together threw themselves upon [the Spaniards]. They quickly forced them to run along among the houses.[1] And when the Spaniards saw this, they were just like drunk men. Thereupon captives were taken. Many Tlaxcallans, Acolhuans, Chalcans, Xochimilcans, etc., were taken. Indeed in abundance they were made captive, in abundance they were slain. Indeed they forced the Spaniards and all the [allied] people into the water.

And the road became indeed slippery. No more could it be walked. There was only continual slipping, there was only continual sliding. And the captives were each dragged by force. In this place the banner was taken; here it was seized. Those who took it were Tlatilulcans. It was taken here where now it is called San Martín. They only ignored it; there was no heed given it.[2] And some [Spaniards] yet escaped their hands. [The Mexicans] went leaving them weary there at Colhuacatonco,[3] at the canal's edge. There [the Spaniards] went to gather themselves together.[4]

And thereupon they brought the captives there to Yacacolco. Each was forced to go. They went rounding up their captives. One went weeping; one went singing; one went crying out while striking the mouth with the palm of the hand. And when they had made them reach Yacacolco, thereupon they were put in rows. They were put in rows. One by one the multi-

Injc cempoalli on caxtolli capitulo: vncan moteneoa, in quenjn ie no ceppa tlamaque mexica in qujmacique Españoles, in juh mopouhque in axivaque Españoles, ontecpãtli ommatlactli omei: yoã no mjequjn tlaxcalteca, Tetzcuca, chalca, xuchmjlca. Auh in quenjn muchtin, vncã qujnmjctique in imjxpan inTeuoan catca./.

Auh in ie iuhquj in jxqujchtin tiiacavan, nec qujvalcentlaça in omopachotoca, caltzalantli qujvaltotocatiqujzque. Auh in Españoles in oqujttaque ça iuhqujn tlavãque: njman ie ic tlamalo, mjequjntin in axivaque in tlaxcalteca, in aculhoaque, in chalca, in xuchmjlca, &c. vel tonacatlamaloc, tonacamjcoac, vel atlan qujnnemjtique in Españoles, yoã in ie ixqujch tlacatl:

auh in vtli vel petzcauhtimoquetz, aoc vel nenemoa, ça nepepetzcolo, ça neaalaoalo. Auh in mamaltin tevivilano. Ie vncan in, in axioac in vandera, vncan anoc: iehoantin caciq̃ in Tlatilulca: vncan in macic, in ie axcan sanct Martin moteneoa: çan atle ipã qujttaque, amo õnecujtlaviloc. Auh in oc cequjntin tematitlampa qujzque: vmpa qujmõciauhcavato in colhoacatonco, acalotenco, vmpa valmomanato.

Auh njmã ie ic qujnvica in mamaltin in vmpa iacacolco, tetototzalo, qujmololhujtivi in immalhoan, in aca chocatiuh, in aca cujcatiuh, in aca motenvitectiuh. Auh in onteaxitiloc iacaculco: njmã ie ic tevipano, tevipanolo, ceceniaca oniatimanj in mumuzco, in vncan tlamjctilo, iacattiaq̃ in Españoles, coniacatique: auh ça vntlatzacujque, ontlatoqujlique

---

1. *Quivalcentlaça*, etc.: in our interpretation of the demands of the context, we read the object prefixes as if they were plural. The Spanish text corresponding to this passage reads: "*Trauose vna batalla muy recia en este dia: de manera que los mexicanos como borrachos se arrojaron contra los enemigos. y captiuaron muchos de los Tlaxcaltecas, y Chalcas, y tezcucanos, y mataron muchos de ellos, y peleando, y hizieron saltar a los españoles en las acequias.*" Consult variant versions in Sahagún, Garibay ed., Vol. IV, p. 148, and Seler, *Einige Kapitel*, p. 549.

2. It was captured by an Indian from Tlatelolco named Tlapane-

catl or Tlapanecatl hecatzin, according to the version in Bustamante, *Aparicion*, pp. 191–92; here it is said that this exploit preceded the capture of the fifty-three Spaniards.

3. A *barrio* in the Parcialidad de Sta. María la Redonda Cuepopan or Tlaquechiuhcan; now bounded N. by Calle del Organo; E., República de Chile; S., Perú; W., Allende (approximately) (Caso, "Barrios antiguos," p. 29).

4. Corresponding Spanish text: "*y los Españoles huyeron y siguieronlos hasta el barrio que llaman Coloacatonco alli se recogieron.*"

tude went to the small pyramid, where they were slain as sacrifices. The Spaniards went first; they went first. But only at the last, following, were all the dwellers of the [allied] cities. And when they had been slain as sacrifices, then they strung each of the Spaniards' heads on the [skull rack] staves. Also they strung up the horses' heads. They placed them below. And the Spaniards' heads were above.[5] As they were strung up, they were facing the sun. But [as for] all the various [allied] people, they did not string up the heads of the people of distant places. And of Spaniards overtaken there were fifty-three. And there were four horses.

And yet everywhere watch was continually kept. There was fighting. Not because of this [success] did watching cease. Everywhere the Xochimilcans went surrounding us with boats. On both sides captives were taken. On both sides there were deaths.

And all the common folk suffered much. There was famine. Many died of hunger. No more did they drink good water, pure water.[6] Only nitrous water did they drink. Many people died of it. And many people thus contracted a bloody flux; because of it they died. And all was eaten — the lizard, the barn swallow, and maize straw,[7] and saltgrass.[8] And they gnawed colorin wood,[9] and they gnawed the glue orchid[10] and the frilled flower,[11] and tanned hides and buckskin, which they roasted, baked, toasted, cooked, so that they could eat them; and sedum,[12] and

in ixqujchtin altepeoaque. Auh in ontlamjctiloc, nec qujnquaquauhço in intzontecon in Españoles: no qujçoçoque in cavallosme intzõtecon, tlatzintlan in qujtecaque: auh in intzontecon Españoles tlacpac in onoca, in çoçotoca, tonatiuh qujxnamjctoca. Auh in jxqujch nepapan tlacatl, amo qujnçoçoque in intzontecõ in veca tlaca. auh in axioaque Españoles ontecpantli onmatlactli omei, yoan nauhtetl cavallos:

auh tel novian tlatlapielo, necalioa: amo ic mocaoa in tlapieliztli, in novian techiaoalotinemj in xuchmjlca in acaltica, necoccampa tlamalo, necoccampa mjcoa.

Auh in jxqujch macevalli, cenca tlaihioviaia maianoia, mjec in mapizmjqujli aocmo quja in qualli atl, in ecatl, ça tequjxqujatl in quja ic mjec tlacatl momjqujli, yoã mjec tlacatl ic tlaelli qujtlaz ic mjc: yoan much qualoc in cuetzpalin, in cujcujtzcatl, yoan Eloçacatl, yoan in tequjxqujçacatl: yoan qujquaquaque in tzumpanquavitl, yoan qujquaquaque in tzacuxuchitl, yoan in tlaqujli, yoan in cuetlaxtli yoan in maçaeoatl, qujtletleoatzaia, qujmooxqujaia qujtototopotzaia, qujtotoponjaia injc qujquaia yoã in tetzmetl, yoan in xantetl qujtetexoaia: aoc tle iuhquj

---

5. *Ibid.*: "*los españoles mas altas...los otros indios mas baxas... los cauallos mas baxas.*"

6. Seler (*Einige Kapitel*, p. 550) reads this *yecatl*.

7. *Eloçacatl:* leaves, or straw, of maize, which Mexican cattle eat, green or dry; the plant itself after the maize grains have been harvested (personal communication, Rafael García Granados). In Sahagún, Garibay ed., Vol. III, p. 328, it is described as "*heno...es muy verde y tiene porretas como el trigo, y es blanco, cómenlo los conejos y otros animales.*" Emmart (*Badianus Manuscript*, p. 259), describing it as a diuretic and purgative, suggests "maize straw" as a name.

8. *Tequixquiçacatl:* probably pasture on saline lands, of the variety called "grama." It creeps over the ground, putting forth small roots (personal communication, Rafael García Granados). For this, Sahagún, Garibay ed., Vol. III, p. 327, has "*heno muy áspero y espinoso, que se hace en tierra salitrosa...es bueno para quemar.*" Cf. also Dibble and Anderson, *Book XI*, p. 193. Emmart (*Badianus Manuscript*, p. 223), citing Siméon, *Dictionnaire de la langue nahuatl*, calls it nitre grass or couch grass, possibly *Distichlis spicata* (L.) Greene. *Grama* (*tequixquiçacatl* in Molina, *Vocabulario de la lengua mexicana*, fol. 105v), Santamaría (*Diccionario de mejicanismos*, p. 562) identifies as *Panicum repans* L., very abundant in the Americas.

9. *Tzumpanquauitl.* According to Sahagún, Garibay ed., Vol. III, p. 331: "*es árbol mediano, tiene ramas acopadas, tiene la copa redonda y de buen parecer, tiene unas flores que se llaman* equimixóchitl*; son*

muy coloradas y de buen parecer y no tienen olor ninguno; las hojas de este árbol se llaman equímitl.*" In Dibble and Anderson, *Book XI*, p. 204, n. 9, it is *Erythrina americana*. Santamaría, *Diccionario de mejicanismos*, p. 1152, giving it the identification of *E. americana* Mill. and *E. coralloides* D. C., adds the common name (*zompancle*), and observes of the bean (*colorín*) that it is "*especie de frijolillo rojo, duro que contiene un alcaloide muy venenoso.*"

10. *Tzacuxuchitl.* Emmart (*Badianus Manuscript*, p. 309), calling it a "glue flower," notes that it is an orchid. *Bletia coccinea* Ll. and Lex., or *B. campanulata* Ll. and Lex., in Dibble and Anderson, *Book XI*, p. 211, n. 19.

11. *Tlaquilli.* In Molina, *Vocabulario de la lengua mexicana*, fol. 234r, *tlaquilli* is plaster or stucco. *Tlaquilin*, however, is given by Emmart (*Badianus Manuscript*, p. 226) as "frilled flower" — probably *Mirabilis jalapa* L., known as *maravilla*. It is medicinal. Francisco J. Santamaría, in his *Diccionario general de americanismos* (Mexico, D.F.: Editorial Pedro Robredo, 1942), Vol. III, p. 186, adds these common names: *sandiego de noche, arrebolera*, and *trompetilla*.

12. *Tetzmetl: Sedum dendroideum* Moc. and Sessé in Dibble and Anderson, *Book XI*, p. 219, n. 11. Sahagún, Garibay ed., Vol. III, p. 308, says it is like *tetzmitic*: "*hojas muy verdes y correosas y redondillas, y también mana leche, y tiene las ramas coloradas...raíces... dulces, y espesas y larguillas...lo interior de esta raíz molido*" (medicinal). Santamaría, *Diccionario de mejicanismos*, p. 973, adds *S. quitense* H. B. K. and *S. roseum* Stev.

mud bricks[13] which they gnawed. Never had there been such suffering. It terrified one, when they were shut in, that indeed in large numbers they died of hunger. And quite tranquilly [the foe] pressed us back as if with a wall; quite tranquilly they herded us.

inic tlaihioviloc, temamauhti in tzaqualoc, vel tonac in apizmjc: auh çan jvian techvalcaltechpachotiaque, çan jviã techololalique.

---

13. Cf., however, Seler, *Einige Kapitel*, p. 550: "*und Stuck und Leder und Hirschhaut, sie brieten, buken, rösteten, brannten, assen es so, und Tetzmetlgras und Lehmziegel und assen Texoatl*," which is a hot country plant used for coloring — *Miconia laevigata* (L.) D. C. in Dibble and Anderson, *Book XI*, p. 242, n. 5. Santamaría (*Diccionario de mejicanismos*, p. 1039) (*tesguate*), says it is "*nombre vulgar de varias plantas melastomáceas, como el* capulincillo *o* nigua (Conostegia xalapensis), *el* totopozole (Miconia laevigata), *y otras.*"

Thirty-sixth Chapter, in which it is told how the Spaniards for the first time came to enter the market place here in Tlatilulco.

And at one time it came to pass that four horse-[men] came to enter the market place. And when they had come to enter, then they followed a circle; they followed about the edge of the market place. They followed, they went lancing the brave warriors. They slew many. They came penetrating the market place. It was when for the first time they came to look at the market place. Then they went; they turned their backs upon it.

And the brave warriors were fearless against them; they pursued them. And when they came entering the market place for the first time, it was not expected by one; they did not warn one.

And also then was when they burned the temple.[1] They set fire to it. And when they had set it afire, it then flared up. Very high rose the flames, the tongues of fire. It was as if the flames continually crackled and continually flared up. And when [the Tlatilulcans] saw that the temple was already burning, thereupon there was weeping, there were tearful greetings. It was so thought that there would be plundering of the people.[2]

And for a long time there was fighting in the market place. The battle indeed took place at each of its edges. Gradually they abandoned the wall[3] there at Tenexnamacoyan and there at Copalnamacoyan[4] and Atecocolecan.[5] And there at Xochicalco,[6] among the houses, there was entering. In some way the brave warriors were everywhere on the wall. And all the houses of the Quauhquechollan people which lay surrounding the market place, all of them became a

Injc cempoalli on caxtolli oce capitulo: vncan mjtoa in quenjn Españoles iancujcan calaqujco tianqujzco in njcan tlatilulco.

Auh ceppa muchiuh nauhteme in cavallos in calaqujco tianqujzco. Auh in ocalaqujco, nec tlanaoatl qujtoca, tianqujztentli qujtoca in tiiacavan qujnxixiltivi, mjeq'ntin in mjcque concujtlaxeloco in tianqujztli: iquac iancujcan qujttaco in tianqujztli: njman ic iaque, ic moteputztique.

Auh in tiacaoan intech motlapaloque qujntocaq̄: auh in jquac calaqujco iancujcan tianqujzco amo tenemachpan, amo qujteimachitique:

auh yoan njmã iquac qujtlatique in teucalli, contlemjnque: auh in ocontlemjnque nec cuetlan, cenca veca eoac in tletl, in tlenenepilli, iuhqujn ihicoioca tletl yoan cuecuetlanj. Auh in oqujttaque in ie tlatla in teucalli: njman ie ic nechoqujlilo, nechoqujztlapalolli: iuh nemachoc in ca ie ontenamoieloz.

Auh vecauhtica in necalioac in tianqujzco, vel tetemman in iauiotl, aiaxcã in qujcauhque in tenamjtl, in vncan in tenexnamacoiã. Auh in vncan copalnamacoian, yoan atecocolecan, yoã in vncan xuchicalco in caltzalan, in calacoaia, vel ipã mantinenca in tiacavan in tenamjtl. Auh in jxqujch quauhquecholteca calli in tianqujztli qujiavalotoc moch tenamjtl mochiuh mjequjntin tlapanco onoca in valla-

1. Corresponding Spanish text: "*el mesmo dia pusieron hoego al cu mayor que era de Vitzilobuchtli.*"

2. *Ibid.*: "*Tomarõ mal aguero de uer quemar el cu.*"

3. *Ibid.*: "*derrocaron los españoles vnos paredones o albarradas con el artilleria.*"

4. Probably near Yacacolco, Tlilhuacan, and Atezcapan, in Tlatilulco, on the Amaxac road or *tlaxilacalli*; now Calle de González Bocanegra (Caso, "Barrios antiguos," pp. 35, 38). Tenexnamacoyan can be presumed to have been nearby.

5. Sta. Cruz Atecocolocan, now "*a la esquina noroeste de los patios de los Ferrocarriles,*" according to R. H. Barlow ("Las ocho ermitas de Santiago Tlatelolco," *Tlatelolco a través de los tiempos*, Vol. IX [1947], p. 65). Caso ("Barrios antiguos," p. 38) states that it is an area now bounded N. by Canal del Norte; E., *barrio* of Telpochcaltitlan; S., Calle de la Constancia; W., Comonfort.

6. In Tlatilulco in a *barrio* which may have had the same name; see Caso, "Barrios antiguos," pp. 38–39; "*La puerta del Norte del Templo Mayor, es decir la que daba a Tlatelolco, es entonces muy probable que fuera la de Acatlyacapan, Atecocolocan, Xochicalco....*"

wall. Many [Mexicans][7] lay upon the roof terraces; they threw stones, they cast the stones, the arrows. And the Quauhquechollan[8] people's houses all had openings at the back. They made small openings. And when the horse[men] followed after one, when they tried to kick them, when they tried to get ahead of them, the brave warriors each quickly entered.

And at one time it came to pass that the Spaniards entered Acatl yiacapan.[9] Then there was plundering of the people, then there was capturing of the poor common folk. And when the brave warriors saw it, they then repulsed the [enemy] brave warriors. A shorn one named Axoquentzin came to be standing there. He pursued his foes. He made them let the people go; he turned them about. And this brave warrior died there. There they shot him with an iron bolt in the breast; when they pierced him, the iron bolt pierced his heart. As if stretched out in sleep,[10] so he died. And then our foes sat down to rest.

And there at Yacacolco[11] similarly there was combat. The Spaniards[12] who shot iron bolts came arranged in order. The Four Lords[13] came to help them; they came to be with them; they came to close off the road. And the brave [Mexican] warriors then were crouched down in order to penetrate among them. The sun already hung low. And when this came to pass, when they already came, some of our foes climbed upon the roof terrace. And when they cried out they said: "Ho, O Tlaxcallans! Come this way! Here are your foes!" Then they cast the darts upon those who had lain crouched, [who] then crumbled.[14]

Slowly [the Spaniards] came to reach Yacacolco, where, at each edge, battle took place. There they came only hurting themselves; they could not break through the Tlatilulcans, who lay across the water. These shot arrows at them, stoned them. No ford, no bridge did [the Spaniards] take.

motla, qujoallaça in tetl, in mjtl, oallatepachoa, vallamjna, yoan moch mocujtlacoionj in quauhquecholteca calli, achitoton qujcoionjque. Auh in jquac ie no valtetoca in cavallosme, in ie no qujnxopiloznequj, in ie qujniacatzacujliznequj: vmpa cacalactivetzi in tiacavan.

Auh ceppa muchiuh in Españoles: acatl yiacapan in valcalacq̄ nec tenamoielo, nec teçaçaco in maceoaltzitzinti. Auh in oqujttaque in tiiacavan: nec qujvallaça in tiiacavan, vncan icativitz quachic: itoca Axoquentzin qujntocac in jiaovan, qujntetlaçalti, qujnmalacacho: auh inin tiacauh vncā momjqujli, vncan qujtepuzmjviq̄ yielpan, in qujtlaxilique, yiollopan in qujtlaxilique tepuzmjtl, iuhqujn necochaano inic ommomjqujli: auh njmā ic mocototztlalique in toiaovan.

Auh in vmpa in iacacolco: çan no ivi in tlaiecolo, in Espanoles in tlatepuzmjvia tecpantivitze, qujnpalevitivitze, qujntlamatilitivitze in nauhtecutli, qujtzacutivitze in vtli. Auh in tiacavan nec nepacholo, injc qujncujtlaxelozque, ie ommopiloa in tonatiuh. Auh in ie iuhquj in ie vitze: cequjntin tlapanco tlecoque in toiaovan: auh in otzatzic, qujto. huj tlaxcaltecae, xioalnenemjcan, njcan cate in amoiaovan: nec qujvallaça in mjtl, in impan in mopachotoca, nec xitinque:

yiolic onacico in iacaculco vncā motetemmā in iauiotl: çan vncā ommotzotzonaco avel qujnpetlaque in Tlatilulca, in amac onoque qujnvalmjna, qujnvaltepachoa aoc tle in panoanj, aoc tle acuepanavaztli, ocaanque.

---

7. From here on, Tlatilulco is the scene of battle. Doubtless, warriors of Tenochtitlan and Tlatilulco fought together. The term "Mexicans," from this point forward, in brackets, implies Indians of both these cities.

8. Same area as Xochicalco (n. 6); "*se dice que el Mercado estaba circundada por las casas de la gente de Cuauhquechol . . .*" (Caso, "Barrios antiguos," p. 39).

9. Bustamante, *Aparicion*, p. 194: "*Otro dia los españoles vinieron á hacer entrada al tianguez por la parte del patio donde estaba el Cú grande de Vitzilopuchtli, por el patio del mismo que se llama Acatlyacapa.*"

10. If read *necoc haano*, the passage could be translated: "It was as if [the arrow] extended on both sides, so that he perished."

11. Corresponding Spanish text: "*se retruxeron los españoles, que*

peleauā de la parte de San mjn." In Bustamante, *Aparicion*, p. 195, the fighting is said to have taken place at Zacoalco, "*que es á donde está agora la iglesia de Santa Ana.*"

12. *Espanoles*: the tilde is omitted in the Nahuatl text.

13. See Chapter 14.

14. Bustamante, *Aparicion*, p. 195: "*y siendo todos juntos los españoles y tlaxcaltecas, algunos tlaxcaltecas y españoles subieron sobre las azoteas de las tiendas que estaban en rededor del tianguez. Estos que subieron sobre las azoteas descubrieron la celada, y dieron voces á los que iban por bajo y dijeron . . . . ¡Mirad, tlaxcaltecas, que vuestros enemigos están aquí en celada! Y luego comenzaron á flechar á los que estaban en la celada, mexicanos y tlatilulcanos, y los de la celada como vieron que ya los habian visto, comenzaron á huir.*"

Thirty-seventh Chapter, in which it is told how the Mexicans worked with continual difficulty as by night they uncovered the [canal] waters where by day the Spaniards had filled them in.

And our foes came filling in the canals. But when the foe went, once again [the Mexicans] took out the rocks with which the foes had filled them in. When it dawned once again, it was even as it had been the day before. Always they did so where [the Spaniards] had filled in the canals when at once they took out the rocks, the wood, etc. Thus by a little was the war lengthened. With difficulty [the Spaniards] broke through them, and the canals were considered to be like great walls.

And the common responsibility of the Spaniards and of all the Tlaxcallans was the road, the highway, to Yacacolco, and to Tlilhuacan [and] Atezcapan.[1] And Yacacolco, Cuepopan,[2] Apauazcan,[3] and Atliceuhyan, with which went Ayacac[4] [and] Totecco, became the responsibility of the Xochimilcans, the Cuitlauacans, the Mizquicans, the men of Colhuacan, of Itztapalapan. It became their common responsibility to give battle in boats.

And those of Atliceuhyan and of Ayacac, boatmen and archers, indeed animated themselves to contend against [the Spaniards and the Tlaxcallans]. They lost no time. They were indeed their equals in the fray. It was as if it rained barbed spears; as the serpent strikes, so the arrows continued to pass over. When they cast them with the atlatl, it was as if a deep yellow was spread over the foes.

And some of the brave warriors — the *tezcacoacatl* Xiuhcozcatzin, the *tepanecatl* Quaquatzin,[5] Uitzitzin, Itzcuintzin — whose houses were in Yacacolco, lost no time. They did not abandon the beloved woman,

Injc cempoalli on caxtolli omume capitulo: vncan mjtoa in q̃nin Mexica in cohuvitiaia in qujtlatlapoaia in atl in ioaltica, in vncan catzupaia Españoles in tlaca.

Auh in toiaovan, catzuptivitze in acalutli. Auh in onoiaque in iavme ie no ceppa qujqujxtia in tetl injc otlaatzupca iaume: in otlatvic ie no ceppa iuhcan, in juhcan catca ialhoa: muchipa iuh qujchiuhque in vncã catzupaia in acalotli, in çan njmã qujvalqujxtiaia in tetl in quavitl. &c. ic achi vecaoac in iauiotl, aiaxcan in qujnvalpetlaque: auh in acalotli in, iuhq'n vei tenamjtl ipan momatia.

Auh in Españoles yoan in jxqujch tlaxcaltecatl incentequjuh in vtli, in vei vtli iacacolco, yoan in tlilhoacan in atezcapan. Auh in iacaculco, in cuepopan, in apaoazcan, yoan atliceuhian injc iaticac aiacac, in totecco intequjuh muchiuh in Xuchmjlcatl, in cujtlaoacatl, in mjzqujcatl, in culhoacatl in Jtztapalapanecatl, incẽtequjuh muchiuh in acaltica in tlaiecoaia.

Auh in atliceuhca, yoan aiacacalque in acaleque, in tlamjnanj, vel muchicaoa injc qujnnamjquj, amo moquequetza, vel moneneuhcavia, iuhqujn tzetzelivi in tlatzontectli, iuhqujn coatl motlamjna mopipiaçoa in mjtl: in jquac atlatica qujtlaça iuhqujn cozpul ommoteca in impan iaume:

auh in cequjntin tiacaoan in Xiuhcozcatzin quaquatzi, Tezcacoacatl, Tecpanecatl, Vitzitzin, Itzcujntzin: in iacaculca vel ipan mantivia in calli: amo moquequetzaia, amo qujxiccavaia in Cioatzintli, in

1. See Chap. 36, n. 4. Atezcapan was a *barrio* fronting that of Tezcatonco in Tenochtitlan: an area now bounded N., by Calle de Matamoros; E., Comonfort; S., Organo; and W., Sta. María la Redonda and the water's edge (Caso, "Barrios antiguos," pp. 29–30, 38). R. H. Barlow ("Las ocho ermitas," p. 63) locates it *"entre las calles de Jaime Nunó y de González Bocanegra."*

2. Cuepopan or Tlaquechiuhcan, an area bounded now, N., by Calle de Moctezuma; E., Gabriel Leyva; S., approx. Pedro Moreno (once a canal); and W., Lerdo (Caso, "Barrios antiguos," p. 31).

3. To the east of the Plaza de Tlatilulco (*ibid.*, pp. 37–38).

4. Atliceuhyan is classed as a street and a *tlaxilacalli* (neighborhood) in the *barrio* of Atenantitech, an area now bounded N., by Matamoros before crossing Real de Santiago and a line northward from here to a prolongation of Rivero; E., by a line which would be a prolongation to the S. of Sta. Lucía; by an irregular line reaching González Bocanegra and then Rep. del Brasil; S., by Organo; and W., by Comonfort. Ayacac is mentioned as part of the *barrio* of Atenantitlan, to the N.E. of Atenantitech (*ibid.*, pp. 35–37).

5. Seler (*Einige Kapitel*, p. 555) groups the names and titles as given here.

the child. With difficulty they went to shelter them by another canal which was in Amaxac.

And once it befell that the Spaniards came forth there at Totecco. And when they came to reach where stood the young men's house, at a place called Ayacac, they then set fire to it.

And another of the Spaniards' boats entered there at Atliceuhyan, and many were the boats of the Xochimilcans which it brought to enter with it. And the brave warrior Temilotzin, a *tlacateccatl*, stood erect on a small pyramid. He stood facing the Spaniards. And the brave warrior Coyoueuetzin put on the device of an eagle-ocelot warrior, half eagle, half ocelot. He came in a boat; from Tolmayecan he repulsed them. And many shield-boats[6] came to be with him. He said: "O brave warriors, courage! We repulse them!" Thereupon they fell upon the boats.[7] And when the Spaniards saw it, they then turned their backs. [The Mexicans] pursued them; [Coyoueuetzin and his warriors] then went direct to Atliceuhyan. And the Spaniards then withdrew their boats; they went to line them up at Amanalco. And many Xochimilcans died of the arrows. And when this had happened, when [the Mexicans] had pursued them, once more [the Spaniards] stopped. Then the brave warriors pursued them. Coyoueuetzin hid himself behind a small pyramid. Then he reversed them. He indeed went forcing them to where stood the young men's house in Atliceuhyan. Once again [the Spaniards] pursued Coyoueuetzin; they came making him jump into the water. Likewise a young Otomí [warrior], Itzpapalotzin, repulsed them. He also put on a device. Then he pursued them. As if they were mud he rolled them up. He indeed went driving them into the boats.[8] Then they departed. Thus they went defeated.

And the Cuitlauacans, when they thought that their ruler Mayeuatzin had died, that he had died with the others, were very angry. They said: "You have slain our ruler. Bring him forth! Why have you slain our ruler?" But Mayeuatzin, when he knew that his vassals were angry, was therefore angry at them. Then he said to Coyoueuetzin:[9] "O my elder brother, set forth one of our brave warriors who can shout, one of

piltzintli, aiaxcan in qujmõcaltechpachoto in oc ce acalotli itech in amaxac icac.

Auh ceppa muchiuh in vmpa totecco, vmpa oalqujzque in Españoles: auh in onacico in vncan telpuchcalli icac: itocaiocan aiacac: njman contlemjnque.

Auh in oc centetl in jmacal in Españoles, valcalac in vncan atliceuhian, yoã mjec in jmacal in Xuchimjlca in qujvalhujcaticalac. Auh in tiiacauh in Temjlotzin, tlacateccatl: momuzco in oquetzticac, qujmonjtzticac in Españoles: auh in tiiacauh Coiovevetzin: in onaquj tlaviztli quauhtlocelutl: cectlapal quauhtli cectlapal ocelutl acaltica in valla tolmaiecampa in qujvallaz: yoan mjec in acalchimalli, in qujtlamatilitivitze: qujvalitotia. Tiacavane ma ie cuel iehoatl ticcentlaça: njmã ie ic macalhujtequj. Auh in oqujttaque in Españoles: njman ic moteputztique, qujntocaque: nec vallamelaoa in atliceuhiã. Auh in jmacal Españoles: nec qujtzinqujxtia, contecato amanalco. Auh in Xuchimjlca, mjequjntin injc mjcque mjtl: auh in ie iuhquj in oq'ntocaque, oc ceppa valmomãque, nec qujnvaltoca in tiiacavan: in Coiovevetzin qujmotocti in mumuztli: njmã ic qujcuep vel qujmaxitito in vmpa icac telpuchcalli in atliceuhian: ie no ceppa qujvaltocaque in coiovevetzin atlan conchololtico: ie no cuele contlaz in telpuchotomjtl, Jtzpapalotzin in no onaquj tlaviztli, nec q'ntoca, iuhqujn çoqujtl qujmololoa, vel qujntepeoato acaacalco: njman ic iaque, ic popolivito.

Auh in cujtlaoaca in momatque ca omjc, ca otehoan mjc, in intlatocauh in Maiehoatzin, cenca qualanj: qujtoaia. Ca oanqujmjctique in totlatocauh Xiqualnextican, tleica in oanqujmjctique totlatocauh. Auh in Maiehoatzin in oqujma in ca qualanj, in jmaceoalhoan: injc qujtlaqualanjlia: njmã qujlhuj in Coiovevetzin. Nachcauhtzine, tla ce xiqualquetza in tachcavan in vel tzatzi, in tlatolchicaoac, in toz-

---

6. See Pls. 116, 117, 121.

7. Sahagún, Garibay ed., Vol. IV, p. 153: "*Inmediatamente se arrojaron a las barcas.*"

8. *Aca acalco: aca* is probably a copyist's error. Seler (*Einige Kapi-*

tel, p. 556) reads the phrase *qujntepeoa acalco.*

9. The MS is apparently corrected here to read as reproduced: *qujlhuj in coiovevetzin.*

strong speech, of strong voice." Then they called to a seasoned warrior named Tlamayocatl. Then Mayeuatzin commanded him; he said to him: "Go there; tell the Cuitlauacans, 'O Cuitlauacans, your ruler Mayeuatzin sent me! Behold him! There he is standing up on the small pyramid!'" And when the Cuitlauacans had heard it, they answered: "No! Ye have slain him!" Then he said to them: "He is not dead! Look well at him! There he already standeth!" And [Mayeuatzin] said: "I have not died! Let nothing damage my lip pendant, my greenstone, my device!" And when he had ended his words, then there was roaring [among the Spaniards' Indian allies]. Thereupon there was fighting.[10] Then they pursued [the Mexicans]. And in the market place, there at Copalnamacoyan, the battle gradually ceased; there it lasted long.

And once our foes, those of Tliliuhquitepec, those of Atetemollan[11] came to a decision about one. Already they had been shown the path which led among the houses. It was the path belonging to a nobleman named Tlacatzin. And when our foes had entered, then the brave warriors pursued them. And a personage among the brave warriors, a seasoned warrior named Tlapanecatl (his home was in Atezcapan) then contended against them. Then our foes quickly seized him. And the brave warriors then hurled themselves upon him; they went shooting arrows at our foes. Then they made those who had seized the brave warrior loose him. And our foes then wounded him in the thigh there where it is bled. Then they went; each one abandoned the fight.

cachicaoac: njman ic qujvalnotzque ce tequjoa, itoca: Tlamaiocatl: nec qujnaoatia in Maiehoatzin: qujlhuja. Tla xoniauh, tla xiqujmonjlhuj in cujtlaoaca: Cujtlavacae, onechoaliva in amotlatocauh in Maiehoatzin, xoconjttacan nechca moquetzticac mumuzco. Auh in oqujcacque cujtlaoaca, qujvalitoque. Ca amo, ca oanqujmjctique: nec qujmonjlhuja. Ca amo mjquj, vel, xocottacan ie in nechca icac: yoan qujvalitoa, ca amo njmjquj, ma itla nechitlacalhujti, in notençac, in nochalchiuh, in notlaviz: auh in ocontzonqujxti in jtlatol, nec tlacaoaca: njman ie ic necalioa, nec qujvaltoca. Auh in tianqujzco in vmpa copalnamacoian, aiaxcan in mocauh, vncā vecaoac in iauiotl.

Auh ceppa tecentlatalhujque in toiaovan in Tliliuhqujtepeca, atetemoleque: ie qujmottilique in vpitzactli in calla qujzticac, yiovi catca ce pilli: itoca, Tlacatzin. Auh in ie calaquj in toiaovan: nec qujntoca in tiiacaoan. Auh ce tlacatl tiacauh, tequjoa, itoca Tlapanecatl, atezcapā ichan catca: nec qujnoalnamjquj, njmā ic qujcujtivetzque in toiaovan: auh in tiiacavan, njmā ipan ommotepeuhque, qujnmjntivi in toiaovan: njmā ic contetlaçaltito in cacica tiiacauh. Auh in toiaovan nec qujvalmetzvitecque: vncā in jnezcoaian: njman ic iaque, ōmocacauhque in mjcali.

10. Corresponding Spanish text: "*Como dixo estas palabras el señor de cujtlaoac luego los indios amigos de los españoles comencaron* [sic] *a dar grita y a pelear contra los mexicanos.*"

11. *Ibid.*: "*en especial los otomjes de tlaxcala.*"

Thirty-eighth Chapter, in which it is told how the Spaniards set up a catapult with which they would have treacherously slain the Tlatilulcans.

And then the Spaniards set up a catapult upon a small pyramid with which to stone the common folk. And when they had arranged it, when already they were to loose it, much did they go circling it, much did they point with their fingers. They pointed at the common folk. They pointed at them where they were assembled at Amaxac.[1] All the common folk were indicated. The Spaniards extended their arms as they were to loose it, to cast it upon them, as if to use a sling upon them. Then they turned, they wound [the ropes]. Then the beam of the catapult rose upright.[2] But the stone could not go there upon the common folk. It went to fall only beyond the back of the market place at Xomolco.

And therefore [the Spaniards] disputed among themselves. Thus the Spaniards appeared as if they jabbed at each other's faces with their fingers. There was much chattering. And the catapult kept moving back and forth; it kept going from one side to the other. Slowly it went balancing itself upright. Then it could appear that the sling was at its point. Very thick was the rope. Because of its rope [the Mexicans] then named it "wooden sling."

And once again the Spaniards and all the Tlaxcallans descended upon them.[3] Thereupon they arranged themselves in order in Yacacolco and Tecpancaltitlan[4] and Copalnamacoyan. Then, there at Atecocolecan, [the Spaniards] led all who lay besieging

Injc cempoalli on caxtolli omei capitulo: vncã mjtoa in quenjn españoles qujtlalique quauhtematlatl, injc qujnpoiomjctizquja in tlatilulca.

Auh njman in iehoan Españoles, qujtlalique in quauhtematlatl in mumuzticpac, injc qujntepachozq̃ in macevaltin. Auh in oqujcencauhque, in ie qujtlaçazque, cenca cololhujtinemj, cẽca ommapiloa, qujnmapilhuja in macevalti, ommapiloa in vmpa omocenqujxtiq̃ in amaxac, in ie ixqujch macevalli, cenca qujmõmottitia, ommaçoa in Españoles, injc impan contlaçazque conmaiavizque, in juhquj qujntematlavizque: nec qujmalacachoa nec qujtevilacachoa: njmã ic meoatiquetz in quauhtemalacatl in jquauhio. Auh in tetl amo vel vmpa ia in jpã macevalli, çan ie icampa iteputzco in vetzito tianqujztli xumolco.

Auh ic vncã mjxnamjcque in juh nezque Españoles iuhqujn mjxmapilxixili, cenca chachalaca. Auh in quauhtematlatl mocuecuepa avic iaiauh, çan jvian motlamelauhcaquetztia: njman ic vel nez in jiacac catca in tematlatl cenca tomaoac in mecatl, injc mecaio: njman ic qujtocaiotique quauhtematlatl:

auh ie no ceppa qujcentlazque in Españoles: yoã in jxqujch tlaxcaltecatl, njmã ie ic motecpana in iacaculco, yoan tecpancaltitlan yoan copalnamacoia: njmã ie vmpa atecocolecan qujniacana in jxqujch techiaoalotoc, cencan ivian in onotiuj. Auh in tiia-

---

1. In the *barrio* of Tetenamitl, "*cave la Concepcion*," in the version of Bustamante, *Aparicion*, p. 209. Caso ("Barrios antiguos," p. 36) identifies it as a *tlaxilacalli* in the *barrio* of Atenantitlan, an area bounded now, N., by Calle del Canal del Norte; E., Ave. del Trabajo; S., *barrio* of Mecamalinco and a broken line from intersection of Toltecas and Matamoros to approximately the intersection of Peñón and Jesús Carranza; and W., Jesús Carranza.

2. Sahagún, Garibay ed.., Vol. IV, p. 154, differs in this passage, here quoted at length:

"*Cuando ya la habían acabado, cuando estaba para tirar, se rodearon muchos de ella, la señalaban con el dedo, la admiraban unos con otros los indios que estaban reunidos en Amáxac.*

"...*Todos los del pueblo bajo estaban allí mirando. Los españoles*

manejan para tirar contra de ellos. Van a lanzarles un tiro como si fuera una honda.

"*En seguida le dan vueltas, dan vueltas en espiral, y dejan enhiesto luego el maderamento de aquella máquina de palo que tiene forma de honda.*"

3. *Ibid.*, p. 155: "*Una vez más se replegaron en uno los españoles y todos los de Tlaxcala.*"

4. A *barrio* occupying an area bounded now, N., by Calle de la Independencia; E., a line approximately along Marroqui, prolonged southward to Plaza de S. Juan; S., approximately Pugibet; and W., Luis Moya (Caso, "Barrios antiguos," p. 11). The context would suggest, however, another place of the same name in Tlatilulco, or, possibly, Telpochcaltitlan. See *ibid.*, Maps 1 and 2.

us. Very slowly they proceeded.[5] And the brave [Mexican] warriors went taking their places. Each one indeed animated himself;[6] they indeed exalted their manhood. Not one of them lost courage; none behaved like women. They said: "Come on, O brave warriors! Who are the little barbarians, the crude little men?"[7] And the brave warriors went zig-zagging, went to each side. There was none who stood up straight, who raised himself straight up.

(And often the Spaniards disguised themselves. They did not reveal themselves. As the people here arrayed themselves, so also did they array themselves. They put on devices, they tied on capes over themselves in order to disguise themselves. They came just joining themselves to the group; just so they made themselves aware of them. When [the Spaniards] shot one with an arrow, there was crouching down, there was falling to the ground. There was much watching, there was continual attention as to whence the iron bolt came — where it went facing. Very prudent were the brave warriors, the Tlatilulcans; very cautious were they.)

And it was very slowly that [the Spaniards] went repulsing them; they went pressing them back against the houses. And at Copalnamacoyan, upon the Amaxac road, the shields went pressed against us; they went meeting [us] head on.

And a personage whose name was Chalchiuhtepeua hid himself behind a wall there in Amaxac. And this man was a Mexican from Tlatilulco. And he closely studied a horse, in order to spear it. And when he had speared the horse, then the Spaniard [riding it] was thrown down. Then each of [the horseman's] friends quickly came to seize him. Then all the brave warriors and the noblemen pursued them, emerged against them, then pursued them at their rear guard. Thus once again they went forcing them to take a stand in Copalnamacoyan, where stood the wall. Then each rested; there was the departure of each, there was the entering of each into his house.[8]

And once it came to pass that all who lay surrounding us — not the Spaniards — went to assemble

caoan valmomãtivi, vel mochichicaoa, vel moqujchquetza, aiac tlacuecuetlaxoa, aiac tlacioatlamachtia: qujtoa. Xioalnenemjcan tiiacavane, aqujque in tenjtotonti, tlalhujcatotonti. Auh in tiiacavan avic vivi, ixtlapalhujvi, aocac tlamelauhca icac, motlamelauhcaquetza

(auh mjecpa motlacacuepaia in Españoles, amo monextiaia in juh mochichioa njcan tlaca: no iuh mochichioaia, tlaviztli cõmaqujaia, tilmatli panj qujmolpiliaia, injc mjxpoloaia, çan motetoctitivitz, çan jc qujteimachitia, in oaca qujmjnque, nepacholo, tlaltech viloa, cenca tlachialo, cenca mjxpepetza in campa ie vallauh, in campa ie valitztiuh in tepuzmjtl, vel mjmati, vel motlachielia in tiiacaoan in Tlatilulca:)

Auh cencan yiolic intech xocotivi, intech caltechpachotivi. Auh in copalnamacoian in jpan vtli amaxac cenca netechpachiuhtiuh in chimalli, moquanamjctiuh.

Auh ce tlacatl itoca catca Chalchiuhtepeoa, qujmotocti tepantli, vncã in amaxac. Auh in iehoatl in ca mexicatl tlatilucatl: auh cenca qujmottilia in cavallo injc qujxiliz: auh in oqujxil cavallo: njman ic valmotzineuh in Español: njman ic caantiqujzque in icnjvan, njman ic qujnteputztique, çan much ieoãtin in tiiacavan, yoan in pipiltin, intech ietiqujzq̃ nec imjcampa qujnteputztique, ic ie no ceppa qujnquetzato in copalnamacoian, in vncan tenamjtl onoca: nec ic onceceuh, viviloac, cacalacoac.

Auh ceppa muchiuh in jxqujch in techiaoalotoc: amo no iehoan in españoles: cenqujçato in vmpa

5. Seler (*Einige Kapitel*, p. 559) translates thus: "*In Atecocolecan liegt ganz ruhig der Führer über die gesamten (Streitkräfte), die uns umringen (einschliessen)*." Garibay (Sahagún, Garibay ed., Vol. IV, p. 155) translates: "*Y allá en Acocolecan los dirigía a los que nos acosaban, lentamente iba pasando por la tierra*."

6. The context does not indicate whether Tlaxcallan or Mexican chieftains are meant; it may be speculated that the latter are referred to. See a parallel passage, *supra.*, Chap. 34.

7. See Charles E. Dibble and Arthur J. O. Anderson, trans., "The People," *Florentine Codex, Book X* (Santa Fe: School of American Research and University of Utah, 1961), p. 186.

8. The three paragraphs which follow deal with a confrontation of the Mexicans and Tlatilulcans against the Tlaxcallans: "*todos los indios enemjgos de los mexicanos que tenjan cercados a los mexicanos*," according to the corresponding Spanish text.

there at Teteuhtitlan.[9] It was yet early dawn that they went to take position. Thereupon they filled in a body of water; they filled in a pond named Tlaixcuipan.[10] It was as if they went too crowded together. They carried all [kinds of] rocks, all [kinds of] wood, pillars, door lintels, adobes, worked corner stones, etc. They went chattering; they went raising the dust. For this reason were they so doing, that thus they thought, thus they imagined that they would rob the common folk who lay on the border, who lay upon the road which went to Tepeyacac.

And when the brave [Mexican] warriors saw what they already did, what they imagined, thereupon they considered what they would do. And when they had considered well, thereupon came a boat; very cautiously they came poling it. They came to extend it at the road's edge. No war device showed; it only came covered over. Another came. In just the same way, cautiously they went poling it. And once again two boats came, so that there were four. Then there rose up two eagle warriors [and] two ocelot warriors. The first eagle warrior was Topantemoctzin; the second, Tlacotzin. And the first ocelot warrior was Temilotzin; the second, Coyoueuetzin. Thereupon there arose an ocelot warrior [and] an eagle warrior. They poled them with all their force; it was as if the boats flew. They went cautiously to Teteuhtitlan to head [the foe] off, to cut them off. And when they had gone, once again they dispatched two, another eagle warrior and another ocelot warrior. They were to spring into the midst of the enemy. And when they had already gone, then flutes were blown. Thereupon the people were robbed, but some of the brave warriors came from a distance to cut off [the foe].

And when our foes saw this, they would have fled. Many died in the water when they sank, when they were submerged. They only pulled one another. It was as if they were no longer conscious, just as if each were stunned, just as if each were suddenly soaked. Those who would in vain have fled only fell into spaces [among] the beams. There was the dragging out of each one. They were completely mud-covered, they were completely gleaming with mud, well soaked, well soaked through. There were indeed many who perished; there were indeed deaths there in large numbers. And this was the only time that

Teteuhtitlan oc ioan in momanato: njmã ie ic tlaatzupa, catzupa in atezcatl in jtoca Tlaixcujpã iuhqujn moquequeztinemj ixqujch tetl qujtquj, ixqujch quavitl, tlaquetzalli, tlaixquatl, xamjtl, tenacaztli. &c. chachalacatinemj teuhtli qujquetztinemj: in jpampa iuh qujchiuhca, ca iuh qujlnamjquja, iuh qujmopictiaia, injc qujnnamoiezque in macevalti in otentoque in onoque in jpan vtli tepeiacac iaticac.

Auh in oqujttaque tiiacaoan in ie tlein qujchioa, qujmopictia: njman ie ic qujnemjlia in quenjn vel qujchioazque: auh in ovel qujnemjlique, njman ie ic ce vitz in acalli, cencã yiolic, in qujtlanelhujtivitze, contecaco vtenco, amo valneztia in tlaviztli, çan vallapachiuhtia, ie no ce valla, çan ie no ivi in jiolic qujvallanelhujtiaque: auh ie no ceppa valla vme in acalli ic onnauhtetix. Nimã ic valmevatiquetz vntetl quauhtli, ontetl ocelutl: injc ce quauhtli, iehoatl in Topãtemoctzin: injc vme, iehoatl in Tlacutzin. Auh injc ce ocelutl iehoatl in Temjlotzin: injc vme, iehoatl in Coiovevetzin: njmã ie ic oneoa: ce ocelutl, ce quauhtli, qujntequjtlanelhuja, iuhqujn patlanj acalli, vmpa tlamattiuh in teteuhtitlan in q'niacacotonazque, in qujnviltequjzque. Auh in jquac oiaque ie no ceppa no contlazque in omentin no ce quauhtli, auh no ce ocelutl qujntlacomotlazque: auh in jquac ie vi nec tlapitzalo, njman ie ic tenamoielo: auh ceq'ntin njpa qujniacatzacujlico in tiiacaoan.

Auh in oqujttaque in toiaovan motlalozquja mjec in atlan mjc, in polacq in illacque, ça netech ommotilinjaia, iuhqujn aocmo qujmati, ça iuhqujn çoçotlaoa ça iuhqujn chachapantivetzi, in oc nen motlaloznequj ça quauhcamac activetzi, tevivilano, omach moçoqujneloque, omach moçoqujpetzcoque, vel chachaquanque, vel popolacque, vel mjec in ixpoliuh, oncan vel tonacamjcoac: auh ça yioppa in vncã ontonacamjcque in toiaovan in nepapan tlaca: auh in jquac ommjqujco in toiaovan, in jmuztlaioc, ça cactimanca:

---

9. Near Tlaixcuepan: *"Probablemente en el barrio de Telpochcaltitlan"* (Caso, "Barrios antiguos," p. 46).

10. A pond (*estanque*) in or near Teteuhtitlan (*ibid.*).

our foes, the various [native] people, died in large numbers there. But when our foes had come to die, on the next day it was quite deserted.

And thus came the Spaniards there to Amaxac. They indeed came to arrive there, there where the common folk lay finished.[11] They had indeed surrounded us. War took place at each edge, there indeed at Amaxac and upon the road which went to Tepeyacac. Then [the Spaniards] went to enter the young men's house named Ueican,[12] because there were assembled the young men. Then they climbed up to the roof terrace. And all the common folk thereupon were scattered behind the young men's house. Then there was scattering into the water. And a great brave warrior, a shorn one, called Uitzilhuatzin, placed himself upon the roof terrace above the young men's house. He yet became as a wall;[13] the common folk yet followed him a little. But the Spaniards then fell upon them, brought themselves upon them; thereupon they continually struck him, continually cut him, pounded him. Then once again the brave warriors repulsed [the Spaniards], and then the brave warriors quickly made them leave him. Then they went to take him; however, he could not die. Then [the Spaniards] went. It was indeed deserted.

And the images of the devil [the Spaniards] set fire to there. They burned each one of them.[14]

And the brave warriors still in vain went holding themselves [against the Spaniards]. Yet these did not shoot arrows at the women: only at those who came as men. And when there was a withdrawal by each one, there was only a little sun.

And upon the fourth day in just the same way it came to pass that our foes moved together. There where the common folk lay, there the Spaniards cautiously went; very slowly did they go. And the brave warrior, the *tlacateccatl* Temilotzin, was watching them in vain. He hid behind a wall. He came forth standing as an eagle warrior. His iron sword was with him; with it he would cut them off. But when he saw that nowhere could he do anything he then threw himself into the water; he went bursting into the water. There was a great roar. There once again war

auh ic vallaque in Españoles in vncan amaxac, vel vmpa acito, in vmpa tlantoque in macevaltin, vel techiaoaloque, vel motetemmã in iauiotl, in vel vncã amaxac yoan ipan vtli in tepeiacac iaticac: njmã ic calaqujto in telpuchcali: moteneoa veican: iehica ca vncan monechicoaia in jxqujch telpuchtli: njman ic tlecoque in tlapanco. Auh in jxqujch maceoalli: njman ie ic ommotepeoa in jcampa Telpuchcalli, nec atla onnetepevalo. Auh ce vei tiiacauh quachic itoca, Vitzilhoatzin tlapanco moquetz, icpac in telpuchcalli, oc iuhqujn tenamjtl muchiuh, oc ic achi contocac in macevalli. Auh in Españoles: njmã ic impã ommotepeuhque, impan ommotqujque: njman ie ic qujvivitequj, qujtlatlapana, qujtzeltilia: njman ic ie no ceppa qujvallazque in tiiacaoan: auh njman ic qujcauhtiqujzque in tiiacauh: njman ic conanato, amo tel vel mjc, njmã ic iaque, cactimoman.

Auh in diablome imjxiptlavan: vncan contlecavique, contlatlatique.

Auh in tiiacavan, oc nen valmomantivi tel amo ma qujnmjna in cioa: çan iehoantin in oqujchicativitze: auh in necacaoaloc ça achiton tonatiuh.

Auh injc navilhujtl çan ie no ivi in mochiuh cemolinque in toiaovan: in vmpa onoc macevalli vmpa tlamattivi in Españoles, cencan ivian in iativi. Auh in tiiacauh tlacateccatl in temjlotzin, oc nen qujnmopachiviaia, tepantli qujmotocti Quauhtli ipan qujzticac, itepuzmaquauh ieticac, injc qujncotonazquja: auh in oqujttac in aoccampa veli, njmã ic atlan valmomaiauh, axotlatiuh, cenca tlacavaca: vncan ie no ceppa motetemmã in iauiotl, çan vncan acito: vel cemjlhujtl in manca iauiotl.

11. Corresponding Spanish text: "*donde esta la yglesia de la Cõcepcion.*"

12. *Ibid.*: "*finalmente llegaron a donde estaua el vagaxe de los mexicanos.*"

13. *Ibid.*: "*vn capitan que se llamaua Vitziloatzin con muchos soldados que estaua sobre los tlapancos comēçaron a restir [sic] a los españoles ponjendose por muro para que no pasasen a dõde estaua el vagaxe.*"

14. *Ibid.*: "*y otro dia los españoles pegaron hoego aquella casa en la qual auja muchas estatuas de los ydolos.*" See Anderson and Dibble, *Book II*, p. 168 (Coacalco).

took place at each edge. Only there did it go reaching. Indeed all day did the battle take place.

And when it dawned, when it was already the fifth day, our foes the Spaniards indeed attacked; and they all lay surrounding us. They indeed all moved together; they indeed wound around us, they were wrapped around us, no one could go anywhere. There was indeed continual jostling; there was indeed continual crowding. Indeed many died in the press; there was continual trampling. And when they reached close to us a woman threw water upon them; she threw water into their faces; she made water run from the faces of our foes.[15]

And the ruler Quauhtemoc and the brave warriors Coyoueuetzin, Temilotzin, Topantemoctzin, Auelitoctzin the *mixcoatlailotlac*, Tlacotzin, [and] Petlauhtzin then seized upon a great brave warrior named Tlapaltecatl opochtzin. His home was in Coatlan. Thereupon they arrayed him, they set him, in the quetzal-owl garb.[16] It had been the device of Auitzotl. Quauhtemoc said: "This device was the device of my governor, my beloved father Auitzotl.[17] Let this man wear it. May he die with it. May he display himself with it proudly before [our foes]; may he make himself seen with it by them. May our foes behold it; may they marvel at it."[18] And when they had put it on him, he was indeed terrifying, he indeed looked marvelous. And they commanded four [others] to go helping him, to go being with him. They gave him the darts[19] which were the devil's, the rod-darts with the flint tips.[20]

And when they had done this, it was as if he became one of the number of the Mexicans' rulers. The *ciuacoatl* Tlacotzin said: "O Mexicans! O Tlatilulcans! Is there nothing of which Mexico was, of which the Mexican state consisted? What is said is that here is the natural condition of Uitzilopochtli,[21] that which

Auh in otlatvic, in ie ic macujlilhujtl: ie no ceppa vel qujcētlaz in toiaouh in Españoles: yoan in jxqujch in techiaoalotoc, vel cemolin, vel techiavaloque, techololhujque, aocac campa vel huja vel nexoxocolo, vel nepapatzolo, vel mjequjntin patzmjcque, nequequeçaloc. Auh in cenca ie in techonaci, ce civatl qujvallatequja, qujmjxatequja, qujmjxapapatza in toiaovan.

Auh in tlatoanj in Quauhtemoctzin yoan in tiiacavan in Coiovevetzi in Temjlotzin, Topantemoctzin, Auelitoctzin. Mixcoatlailotlactzin. Tlacutzin, Petlauhtzin. Nimā ic conanq̄ ce vei tiacauh, itoca Tlapaltecatl opuchtzin coatlan ichā njman ie ic qujchichioa, conaqujque, in quetzalteculotl: itlaviz catca in Aujtzotzin: qujto in Quauhtemoctzin. Jnjn tlaviztli, itlaviz catca in notechiuhcauh in notatzi Aujtzotzin, ma iehoatl conjtquj ma ipan ommjquj ma cōtemaviçolti ma ipan tetlattiti ma qujttacan in toiaovan ma qujmaviçocan. Auh in oconaqujque vel temamauhti, vel maviztic in neci: auh navinti in qujnnavatique in qujvalpalevitiazque, in qujvallamatilitiazque, qujvalmacaque in jmjuh catca tlacateculotl, tlacumjtl, iacatecpaio.

Auh injc iuh qujchiuhque in, iuhqujnma intlapoal muchiuh in tlatoque in Mexica: qujto in Civacoatl tlacutzin. Mexicae tlatilulcae, atlei injc mexico ocatca, injc ommanca mexicaiutl: in mjtoa in vncan inavatil in vitzilobuchtli in tepā qujtlaça ca çan iee in xiuhcoatl, in mamalhoaztli in otepā qujtlaztinenca

---

15. Corresponding Spanish text: *"las mugeres tambien peleauan cegando a los contrarios con el agua de las acequias arrojandosela con los remos."*

16. Bustamante, *Aparicion*, p. 211: *"un buho (hecho de plumajes ricos y espantable)."*

17. While the first edition of *Book XII* was in press, Dr. Anderson wrote the following comment from Florence, Italy: "The word is almost illegible in the MS. Examination of the original (Med.-Palat. 218–220, Laurentian Library, Florence), in connection with researches in Europe made possible by the John Simon Guggenheim Memorial Foundation, suggests that *notechiuhcauh* (my maker or begetter) is meant."

18. Corresponding Spanish text: *"Estando ya los mexicanos acosados de todas partes de los enemjgos acordaron de tomar pronostico o aguero si era ya acabada su ventura o si los quedaua lugar de escapar de aquel grā peligro en que estauā: y hablo el señor de mexico que se llamaua*

Quauhtemoctzin, y dixo a los p'ncipales que con el estauā . . . hagamus esperiencia a uer si podemos escapar deste peligro ē que estamos venga uno de los mas valientes que ay entre nosotros y vistase las armas y diujsas que eran de mi padre Auitzotzin: luego llamaron a vn mancebo valiente hombre que se llamaua Tlapaltecatl opuchtzin que era del barrio de coatlan donde es agora la perrocha de s.ª catalina en el tlatilulco."

19. The Nahuatl text may read *inj injuh. In jmjuh* is probably meant.

20. Sahagún, Garibay ed., Vol. IV, p. 158: *"Le dieron aquello en que consistía la dicha insignia de mago. Era esto:*
"Era un largo dardo colocado en vara que tenía en la punta un pedernal."

21. *Ibid.*: *"La voluntad de Huitzilopochtli."* Seler, *Einige Kapitel*, p. 564: *"Man sagt, (dass es da ist) wo der Befehl Uitzilpochtlis ist."*

he cast at one. It is just the fire serpent, the fire drill, which he went casting at one, upon our foes — that which you grasp, O Mexicans, the dart of his natural condition. Immediately you will make it look there toward our foes. You will not just drop it on the ground; you will cast it strongly at them. And if one or two of them should be shot, and if perhaps one or two of our foes should be struck, he is truly of our number. For yet a while we will find favor. What will our lord yet require?" Thereupon the quetzal-owl went; the quetzal feathers went as if spreading.

And when our foes saw him, it was as if a mountain crumbled. All the Spaniards indeed were terrified; he terrorized them; it was as if they marveled at something. Then the quetzal-owl climbed to the roof terrace. And some of our foes, those who could see him, arose. Then they turned him back, they pursued him. Once again the quetzal-owl pursued them. Thereupon he took from them [their] quetzal feathers and gold.[22] And then he dropped from the roof terrace. He did not die; our foes did not take him. Also, already three of our foes had been taken. Finally, the battle just stopped; thus silence reigned; nothing took place. Then our foes departed. All was quiet and nothing more took place. Thus night fell.

And upon the next day nothing at all took place. There was no one who spoke aloud. The common folk only lay destroyed. And the Spaniards also did nothing. They only lay [still]; they lay looking at the common folk. Nothing was taking place. They only lay very [quiet].

And here are told all the brave warriors, the great warriors indeed able in war, who commanded in war, who presided over war: the *tlacochcalcatl* Coyoueuetzin, the lord of Tzilacan, Temilotzin — those were Tlatilulcans; and those of Tenochtitlan were these: the *ciuacoatl* Tlacotzin, the *uitznauatl* Motelchiuhtzin. These are the ones who were the great brave warriors of Tlatilulco and hence Tenochtitlan.

in toiaupan in ie anconcuj Mexicae in jnaoatil in mjtl: çan njmã vmpa anqujtlachieltizque in ïvicpa toiaovan, amo çan tlalpan anqujmaiavizque cenca intech in anqujtlaçazque: auh intla ce, anoço vme momjnaz: auh in ano ce, anoço vme in maçiz toiaouh ca nel totlapoal, oc achitzin tinacazitztiazque, oc quenjn qujmonequjltiz in totecujo: njman ie ic iauh in quetzalteculotl, in quetzalli iuhqujn xexeliuhtiuh.

Auh in oqujttaque in toiaovan, iuhqujn tepetl vitomj vel muchintin momauhtique in Españoles, cenca qujnmauhti, iuhqujnma itla ipan qujttaque: njman ic tlapanco tlecoc in quetzalteculotl. Auh in cequjntin toiaovan in ovel qujttaque moquetzque: njman ic qujvalcuepque, qujvaltocaque: ie no ceppa no qujncuep qujntocac in quetzalteculotl, njman ie ic qujnamoia in quetzalli, yoan in teucujtlatl: auh njman ic vmpa valhuetz in tlapanco, amo mjc, amo qujvicaque in toiaovan: ie no ieintin in axivaque in toiauvã ça iccen ontzotzon in iauiotl ic cactimoman, aoc tle muchiuh: njman ic iaque in toiaovan, cactimoman, aoc tle muchiuh injc oniovan.

Auh in jmuztlaioc, çan njmã aoc tle muchiuh, aocac navati, ça pachiuhtoc in macevalli. Auh in iehoantin Españoles aoc no tle ay, ça onoque, qujmonjtztoque in macevaltin aoc tle mantoc, cencã ça onoq̃.

Auh njcan moteneoa in jzq'ntin tiiacavan, in vevei oqujchtin, in vel imjxco catca iauiotl, in iautecaia in jpan icaca iauiotl. Tlacuchcalcatl, Coiovevetzin, Tzilacatecutli Temjlotzin: in iehoantin in ca tlatilulca. Auh in tenuchca, iehoantin in. Cioacoatl tlacutzin, vitznaoatl Motelchiuhtzin: oca iehoãtin in, in veveintin tiiacavan catca in tlatilulco, yoan injc tenuchtitlan.

---

22. This is explained in the Spanish text: "*subio otra vez en el tlapanco donde los tlaxcaltecas tenjan quetzales y cosas de oro robadas.*"

Thirty-ninth Chapter, in which it is told how, when indeed [the Spaniards] had gone forcing them to the wall, there appeared to the Mexicans, there was seen, a bloodstone.[1] It was as if it came from the heavens. And it appeared like a great, blazing coal.

And when night had fallen, it thereupon rained at intervals; it sprinkled at intervals. It was already deep night when a fire appeared. As it was seen, as it appeared, it was as if it came from the heavens like a whirlwind.[2] It went continually spinning about; it went revolving. It was as if the blazing coal broke into many pieces, some very large, some only very small, some just like sparks. It arose like a coppery wind. Much did it rustle, crackle, snap. It only circled the ramparts at the water's edge; it went toward Coyonacazco.[3] Then it went into the middle of the water. There it went to disappear.

No one shouted, striking his lips with his hand. No one spoke aloud.

And on the next day likewise nothing was done. There was only lying [quiet]. Our foes also lay [quiet].

And the Captain was watching from a roof terrace in Amaxac, Aztauatzin's roof terrace, from a canopy. It was a many-colored canopy. He was looking forth from there at the common folk. The Spaniards were crowded about; they were crowded taking counsel among themselves.

And Quauhtemoc and the rest of the rulers[4] — the *ciuacoatl*[5] Tlacotzin, the *tlillancalqui*[6] Petlauhtzin, the *uitznauatl*[7] Motelchiuhtzin, the *achcauhtli*[8] of Mexico, the lord of priests;[9] then the rulers of Tlatilulco: the *tlacochcalcatl* Coyoueuetzin, the *tlacatec-*

Injc cempoalli on caxtolli onnavi capitulo: vncã mjtoa in quenjn iehoantin Mexica in jquac ovel qujncaltechpachoto in nez in mottac Eztetl: iuhq'nma ilhujcacpa valla. Auh injc valneztia iuhqujn vei tlexuchtli.

Auh in ovalioac: njman ie ic qujqujiavi, avachqujqujiavi, ie tlaquauhiova in nez tletl: in juh mottac, in juh nez, iuhqujn ilhujcacpa valla, iuhqujn ecamalacutl, momamalacachotiuh, motevilacachotiuh, iuhqujn cuecuepocatiuh tlexuchtli, cequj vevei, cequj çan tepitoton, cequj ça iuhqujn tlemoiutl, iuhqujn ecatepuztli, moquetza, cenca icoioca, tetecujca, titicujca, çan qujiavalo in atenamjtl: coionacazco in valitztia: njmã ic ia in anepantla, vmpa popolivito,

aiac motenvitec, aiac navat:

auh in jmuztlaioc, aoc no tle muchiuh, ça onoac, ça no onoque in toiaovan.

Auh in capitan tlapãco vallachixtica in amaxac, Aztavatzin itlapanco, cevalcalco, tlatlapalli in cevalcalli, qujmonjtztica in macevaltin, cololhujtoque in Españoles, mononotztoque.

Auh in Quauhtemoctzin; yoan in oc cequjntin tlatoque. Civacoatl tlacutzin. Tlillancalquj. vitznaoatl. Petlauhtzin. Motelchiuhtzi mexicatl. Achcauhtli, Tecutlamacazcatzin. Niman in iehoantin in tlatilulco tlatoque. Tlacuchcalcatl. Coioveuetzin. tla-

1. Seler (*Einige Kapitel,* p. 566) translates *extetl* (corrected *eztetl*) as *Blutfeuer.* See, however, Siméon, *Dictionnaire de la langue nahuatl,* p. 136.

2. Seler, *Einige Kapitel,* p. 566, has *ein Windbeil (?).*

3. See Chap. 34, n. 5.

4. We have rearranged the first few of the series as Seler does in *Einige Kapitel,* p. 567, for the sake of more logical reading.

5. *Ciuacoatl:* cf. Clark, *Codex Mendoza,* Vol. III, fol. 3; also Juan de Torquemada, *Segunda parte de los veinte i un libros rituales i monar-*

chia indiana (Madrid: Nicolas Rodrigo Franco, 1723), Vol. II, p. 352; Chimalpahin, *Annales,* p. 195.

6. *Tlillancalqui:* cf. Clark, *Codex Mendoza,* Vol. III, fol. 65. For *tlillancalcatl,* Torquemada, *Segunda parte,* p. 178, has *sacristan mayor.*

7. *Uitznauatl:* cf. Clark, *Codex Mendoza,* Vol. III, fol. 67.

8. *Achcauhtli:* cf. Arthur J. O. Anderson and Charles E. Dibble, trans., "The Origin of the Gods," *Florentine Codex, Book III* (Santa Fe: School of American Research and University of Utah, 1952), p. 53.

9. *Tecutlamacazcatzin:* cf. Clark, *Codex Mendoza,* Vol. II, p. 117.

catl[10] Temilotzin, the *tiçociauacatl*[11] Topantemoctzin, the *mixcoatlailotlactzin*[12] Auelitoctzin, the *uitznauatl* Uitziliuitzin, the *tepanecatl*[13] Uitzitzin, all of whom were rulers — were assembled at Tolmayecan. They were grouped consulting among themselves as to how to accomplish what we should pay as tribute and how we should submit to [the Spaniards].

Thereupon they took Quauhtemoc in a boat. There were only two; two [companions] took him with them, went with him, Tepotzitoloc, a brave warrior, and Yaztachimal, Quauhtemoc's page. And the one who went poling them was named Cenyaotl.

And when they were already taking Quauhtemoc, thereupon all the common folk wept. They said: "Already the noble youngest son, Quauhtemoc, is going! He already is going to give himself up to the gods, to the Spaniards!"

cateccatl. Temjlotzin. Ticociavacatl. Topantemoctzin. Mixcoatlailotlactzin. Auelitoctzin, vitznaoatl. vitzilivitzin. tepanecatl vitzitzin: in muchintin in tlatoque, in ocentlaliticatca tolmaiecan mononotztoca in quenjn muchioaz in tlein tictequjtizque: auh in quenjn intlan toncalaqujzque.

Niman ie ic qujvica in Quauhtemoctzin, acaltica, çan ommote: vmětin in convicaque, itlan ietiaque. Teputzitoloc tequjoa, yoan Jaztachimal ixolouh in Quauhtemoctzin. Auh ce qujtlanelhujtia itoca Ceniautl:

auh in jquac ie qujvica in Quauhtemoctzin: njmā ie ic mochoqujlia in ixqujch macevalli qujtoque. Je iauh in tlacatl xocoiotl in Quauhtemoctzin ie iauh qujnmomacaz in teteu in Españoles.

---

10. *Tlacochcalcatl, tlacateccatl*: cf. Anderson and Dibble, *Book VIII*, p. 43.

11. *Tiçociauacatl*: cf. Clark, *Codex Mendoza*, Vol. III, fol. 65. The cedilla is omitted in the *Florentine Codex*.

12. *Mixcoatlailotlactzin*: cf. Clark, *Codex Mendoza*, Vol. III, fol. 68.

13. *Tepanecatl*: cf. Chimalpahin, *Annales*, p. 342. Cervantes de Salazar, *Crónica de Nueva España*, Vol. III, p. 289, mentions capture at the same time as Quauhtemoc of the ruler of Tacuba (Tlacopan); so does Ixtlilxochitl, *Décima tercia relación*, p. 48.

Fortieth Chapter, in which it is told how the Tlatilulcans and those of Tenochtitlan and their rulers submitted to the Spaniards,[1] and what came to pass when they were already among them.

And when they had gone taking him, when they had gone disembarking him, thereupon all the Spaniards watched. They drew him forth. The Spaniards drew him forth by the hand. Thereupon they took him up to the roof terrace; they went to stand him before the Captain, the war commander. And when they had gone to stand him before [Cortés], thereupon he looked at, he presented himself to, he continually stroked Quauhtemoc. Then they seated him near [Cortés] and fired the guns. They struck no one with [the shots]; they only fired them above; [the shots] only passed over the common folk.[2] Then they brought a [gun], put it into a boat; they took it there to Coyoueuetzin's house.[3] And when they had arrived, then they climbed [with it] to the roof terrace. Thereupon once again they slew people; many died there. And [the Mexicans] only ran off. Just so did the war go to its end.

Then there was shouting. They said: "Enough! Let there be leaving! Eat the greens!" When they heard this, the common folk thereupon departed; they thereupon went, only into the water.

But when they had gone to leave upon the great road, once again they there slew some [of the allies of the Spaniards].[4] The Spaniards were angered by this when, besides, just some of them took with them their obsidian-bladed swords and their shields. Those who lay in the groups of houses went direct to Amaxac; they went direct to where the road could fork. There the common folk variously separated. All went toward Tepeyacac, all went toward Xoxouiltitlan, all went toward Nonoalco; but no one went there toward Xoloco, toward Maçatzintamalco.

Injc ompoalli capitulo vnca mjtoa in quenjn iehoantin tlatilulca yoã tenuchca yoan in intlatocauh in intlan oncalacque Espanoles: auh in tlein muchiuh in jquac ie intlã cate./.

Auh in oconaxitito in ocontlalhoacaqujxtito: njman ie ic much vallachia in Españoles, qujvalanque, imatitech qujvalanque in Españoles njman ie ic qujtlecavia in tlapanco ixpan conquetzato in Capitan in iautachcauh. Auh in oixpan conquetzato, njmã ie ic qujtta, qujmoottitia, qujpepepetla in Quauhtemoctzin: njman ic itlan qujtlalique yoan contlazque in tlequjqujztli, aiac ic qujmotlaque, çan impan qujqujxtique çan jmjcpac qujz in macevalti: njman ic cẽtetl convicaque, concalaqujque in acalli: vmpa cõvicaque in jchan Coiovevetzin. Auh in oacique: njmã ic tlecoque in tlapanco: njman ie ic no ceppa temjctia mjec in vncan mjc: auh çã choloque, çan jc vmpolivito in iauiotl:

nec valtzatzioa: qujtoa. Ie ixqujch ma qujxoa, xicmoqualtitin in qujltzintli: in oiuh qujcacque in njman ie ic oneoa in macevalli: njman ie ic vi, çan atlan.

Auh in oqujçato vei vtli ipan, ie no ceppa cequjn vmpa qujnmjctia, ic qualãque in Españoles in oc no çan cequjntin qujtquj in immaquauh yoan inchimal: in calla onoca qujvalmelauhque in amaxac vallamelaoa, in vncan vel vmaxac: vncan xexeliuh in macevalli, ixqujch tepeiacac itztia, ixqujch xoxoviltitlã itztia, ixqujch nonoalco itztia. Auh in xollocopa, yoan in maçatzintamalcopa, aiac vmpa itztia.

---

1. *Espanoles*: the tilde is omitted in the Nahuatl text.

2. Probably an artillery salvo, without projectiles; we know that Cortés used this system to impress the Indians. Perhaps this time it was in joy over the end of the war (personal communication, Rafael García Granados).

3. Seler (*Einige Kapitel*, p. 568) implies that they brought a cannon

(whence *centetl*). See also Sahagún, Garibay ed., Vol. IV, p. 161. What appears to be the corresponding Spanish text reads: "*quando esto acontecio salieron dos canoas de mexicanos y entraron en la casa de vn principal que se llamaua Coioueuetzin.*"

4. Corresponding Spanish text: "*donde quijera q̃ topauã a algunos indios de los amjgos de los españoles matauãlos.*"

And all who were in boats and those who [lived] upon platforms [in the water] and those at Tolmayecan[5] just went through the water. On one the water went reaching to his stomach; on one to his chest; on one it went reaching to his neck. And one indeed submerged there where it was deep. The little children were each carried on people's backs. There arose a tearful cry. Some went rejoicing, each one; some went content, each one, as they went joining the road. And those who had boats, all who owned boats, went forth only at night, but yet, even by day, they went forth. It was as if [the boats] struck against one another as they went.

And everywhere on the roads the Spaniards robbed the people. They sought gold. They despised the green stone, the precious feathers, and the turquoise. [The gold] was everywhere in the bosoms, in the skirts of the poor women. And as for us who were men: it was everywhere in their breech clouts, in their mouths.

And [the Spaniards] seized, they selected the women — the pretty ones, those whose bodies were yellow: the yellow ones. And some women, when they were to be taken from the people, muddied their faces, and clothed themselves in old clothing, put rags on themselves as a shift. It was all only rags that they put on themselves.

And also some were selected from among us men — those who were strong, those soon grown to manhood, and those of whom later as young men they would make messengers, who would be their messengers, those known as *tlamacazque*. Of some they then burned [branded] the cheeks; of some they painted the cheeks; of some they painted the lips.

And when the shields were laid down, when we fell, it was in the year count Three House; and in the day count it was One Serpent.

And when Quauhtemoc went to give himself up, then they took him to Acachinanco, when already it was night. And upon the next day, when already there was a little sun, once again the Spaniards came. There were indeed many. They likewise came still spent.[6] They came in battle array, [with] iron cuirasses, iron helmets, but not their iron swords, and not their shields. Only all of them pressed against their

Auh in jxqujch acaltica onoca yoan in tlapechco catca, yoan in tolmaiecan çan atlan in iaque: in aca ixillan acitiuh in atl, in aca ielchiqujpan, in aca iquechtlan acitiuh: auh in aca vel polaquj, in vncan vecatlan: in pipiltzitzinti temamamalo, tlachoqujztleoa: cequjnti mopapaqujltitivi, maavieltitivi: in oconnepanoto vtli Auh in acaleque, in jxqujch acale ça ioaltica in qujz, yoã tel cemjlhujtl in qujzque iuhqujn moquequeztivi injc vi.

Auh in jzqujcan antica tetlatlaçaltiaia in Españoles in teucujtlatl qujtemoa amo tle ipan qujtta, in chalchivitl, in quetzalli yoan in xivitl: novian nemja in inxilla in incuetitlan, in cioatzitzinti. Auh in toqujchtin novian nemj in imaxtlatitlan, yoan in incamac

yoan qujmanaia, qujnpepenaia in Cioa in chipavaque, in Cuztic innacaio in cuztique. Auh in cequjntin cioa injc motetlaçaltiaia, mjçoqujvique, yoan tatapatli in qujmocuetiq tzotzomatli in qujmovipiltique, çan moch tzotzomatli in intech qujtlalique.

Auh no cequjntin pepenaloque in toqujchtin iehoantin in chicaoaque in iniolloco oqujchtin yoã in qujn telpupuchtotonti in qujntitlanjzque, in intitlanvan iezque, in moteneoa intlamacazcaoan: cequjntin njmã qujncamatlatiq cequjntin qujncamaicujloque: cequjntin qujntenjcujloque.

Auh in omomã chimalli: injc tixitinque, in xiuhtonalli ei calli. Auh in cemjlhujtlapoalli ce coatl:

Auh in jquac in õmotemacato in Quauhtemoctzin: njmã qujvicaque in acachinanco in ie ioa. Auh in jmuztlaioc in ie achiton tonatiuh, ie no ceppa vallaque in Españoles: vel mjequjntin, no çan iuh tlantivitze, in moiauchichiuhtivitze, tepuzvipilli, in tepuzquacalalatli: auh aoc tle in intepuzmaquauh, yoan aoc tle in inchimal, ça muchintin valmoiacapa-

---

5. Caso ("Barrios antiguos," pp. 36–37) mentions *"Atliceuhyan calle o barrio al que se llegaba por agua y donde había un telpochcalli que menciona* [Sahagún] *en Ayacac...."* It was in the *barrio* of Atenantitlan, whose location is given above in Chap. 37, n. 4.

6. Garibay (Sahagún, Garibay ed., Vol. IV, p. 163) translates the phrase: *"También era su final"*; Seler, *Einige Kapitel,* p. 570: *"Ebenso am Ende ihrer Kräfte (wie die Mexikaner)."*

noses with fine white cloths; the dead sickened them — they already smelled offensive; they already stank.

All went walking on foot; they went holding Quauhtemoc, Coanacochtzin, [and] Tetlepanquetzatzin[7] by their capes. Only the three went held. And there were the *ciuacoatl* Tlacotzin, the *tlillancalqui* Petlauhtzin, the *uitznauatl* Motelchiuhtzin, the *achcauhtli* of Mexico, the lord of priests Coatzin, the *tlatlati* Tlaçolyaotzin, those who guarded all the gold.

Then they went direct there to Atactzinco,[8] there to the house of the brave warrior, the *tlacochcalcatl* Coyoueuetzin. The Spaniards[9] were in file; already two lines stretched; far off did they go ending, far did they go reaching. And when they came to reach Coyoueuetzin's home, then they climbed up to the roof terrace, to the platform. Then they sat down. They placed a canopy of a varicolored large cape for the Captain. Then the Marquis sat there. Near him sat Marina.

And Quauhtemoc was near the Captain. He had bound on himself the shining maguey fiber [cape], each half of different color, with hummingbird feathers in the style of the people of Ocuillan. It looked dirty. He had only this. Then there was, after him, Coanacochtzin, the ruler of Texcoco. He was bound in no more than a maguey fiber cape with a flowered border, with a design of radiating flowers. It also looked dirty. Then there was, after him, Tetlepanquetzaltzin, ruler of Tlacopan. Likewise he was bound in a maguey fiber cape. It was also very dirty, very dirty. Then there was, after him, the *mixcoatlailotlac* Auelitoctzin. Last was Yopicatl popocatzin, a nobleman. To the side were those of Tenochtitlan: Tlacotzin, Petlauhtzin, Motelchiuhtzin, the *achcauhtli* of Mexico, the lord of priests, Coatzin, the *tlatlati* Tlaçolyaotl.[10]

chotiaque iztac canaoac ica qujntlaieltiaia in mjmjcque in ie iyaia, in ie potonj:

muchintin vallacxipanvitiaque, qujvalqujtzqujtiaque itilmatitech in Quauhtemoctzin, Coanacotzin, Tetlepanquetzatzin, çan ieixtin valmantiaque. Auh in Cioacoatl tlacutzin: Tlillancalquj. petlauhtzin, vitznaoatl, motelchiuhtzin mexicatl. Achcauhtli, Tecutlamacazquj, Coatzin, tlatlati, tlaçuliautl, in iehoantin in qujpiaia in jxqujch teucujtlatl:

njman vmpa tlamelauhque in atactzinco, in vncan ichan in tiiacauh in tlacuchcalcatl, in Coiovevetzin: pipilivi in Espanoles, ie vmmecatl motilinja, veca tlantivi, veca acitivi: auh in oacito in jchã coiovevetzin, njmã ic tlecoque in tlapanco, in tlapechco: njman ic motlalique, tlatlalpalquachtli in qujcevalcaltique capitan, njmã ic oncã ommotlali in Marques, itlan ommotlali in Malintzin:

auh in Quauhtemoctzin itlan ca in Capitan: in qujmolpilia quetzalichpetztli, tlatlacuhujtectli, vitzitzilin hivio injc ocujltecaio, omach catzaoac, çan qujxcavitica: njmã contoqujlitica in Coanacutzin, tetzcucu tlatoanj: in qujmolpilitica, çan vel ichtilmatli, xoxochiteio, xochimoiaoac, omach no catzaoac: njmã cõtoqujlitica. Tetlepanquetzatzi, tlacuban tlatoanj, çã no iuhquj in qujmolpilitica in ichtilmatli, ono vel catzactix, ouel catzaoac: njmã contoqujlitica. Mixcoatlailotlac, avelitoctzin: tlatzacutica Jopicatl, pupucatzin, pilli: cectlapal onoque in tenochca. Tlacutzin. Petlauhtzin. Motelchiuhtzin mexicatl, achcauhtli, tecutlamacazquj, coatzintlatlati, Tlaculiautl.

---

7. Rulers of Tlacopan and of the Tecpaneca, respectively, according to Bustamante, *Aparicion*, p. 232.

8. *"Donde ahora está edificada la iglesia de Santa Lucía, aquí en Tlatilulco"* (ibid.).

9. *Espanoles*: the tilde is omitted in the Nahuatl text.

10. *Tlaculiautl*: the cedilla is omitted in the Nahuatl text. In this passage, *coatzintlatlati* appears to be run together. Cf., however, Molina, *Vocabulario de la lengua mexicana*, fol. 139r, and Siméon, *Dictionnaire de la langue nahuatl*, p. 606 (*tlatlati*).

Forty-first Chapter, in which are told the words with which Don Hernando Cortés admonished the rulers of all the cities here in Mexico and Texcoco [and] Tlacopan, when the shields had been laid down. He questioned them as to the gold which they had scattered in their haste there in the Tolteca canal when they had left, had fled Mexico.

Thereupon the Marquis, the Captain, admonished the rulers. He said to them: "What of the gold? That which was guarded in Mexico?" Thereupon was taken out of the boats all the gold — the golden flags, the golden conical caps, the golden arm bands, the golden bands for the calf of the leg, the golden helmets, the golden discs. They laid all before the Captain. Indeed all of it the Spaniards removed.

Thereupon the Captain said: "Is only this all the gold? That which was guarded in Mexico? You will show it all. For our lords seek it diligently!"

Thereupon Tlacotzin spoke: "May our lord the god hear! It came to be taken to our palace. We walled it up with many adobes. Did not, in truth, our lords take it all with them?"

Then Marina said: "The Captain saith, 'It is so. We took all. It was all gathered together, and it was all marked. But they forced us to abandon it there at the Tolteca canal. They forced us to drop it there. You will produce it all.'"

Thereupon the *ciuacoatl* Tlacotzin answered: "May the god, the Captain, hear! The men of Tenochtitlan truly hold back from boats. It is not their accomplishment; it is only the attribute of the Tlatilulcans, who combat in boats, who went to stop our lords. Did not in truth the Tlatilulcans take it all?"

Thereupon Quauhtemoc spoke. He said to the *ciuacoatl*: "What art thou saying, O *ciuacoatl*? Even if the Tlatilulcans took it, were not those who merited it therefore made captive? Did they not produce it all? Was it not gathered together in Texopan? And what did our lords take? Was it not this?" Quauhtemoc pointed to the gold with his finger.

Then Marina said to him: "The Captain saith, 'Is this quite all?'"

Injc ompoalli oce capitulo vncã mjtoa in tlatolli injc qujnnonotz do hernando Cortes in jxqujchtin altepetl ipã tlatoque in njcan Mexico: auh tetzcucu, tlacuba, in jquac ie omoman chimalli, in qujntemoliaia in cuztic teucujtlatl, in vncan qujcenmantiqujzque tulteca acaluco, in jquac qujzque, choloque mexico.

Niman ie ic qujnnonotza in Marques in Capitan in tlatoque: qujmjlhuja. Catli in teucujtlatl? in omopiaia Mexico: njman ie ic vallaqujxtilo in acalco in jxqujch in teucujtlatl, in teucujtlapanjtl, in teucujtlacopilli, in teucujtlamatemecatl, in teucujtlacotzevatl, in teucujtlaquacalalatli, in teucujtlacomalli: muchi ixpan contecaque in capitan, çã much iehoan in Españoles in vallaqujxtique:

njman ie ic qujtoa in Capitan, çan ie ixqujch in in teucujtlatl? in omopiaia Mexico, muchi anqujnextizque? ca vel qujtemoa in totecujovan:

Nimã ie ic ontlatoa in Tlacutzin. Tla qujmocaqujti in totecujo in teutl, ca oipan maxitico in totecpan, ca much ticxaxantzacque, amo nel much qujmotqujlique in totecujovan?

njman qujvalito in Malintzin, qujmjtalhuja in Capitan, Quemaca ca much ticcujque, muchi omocentlali, yoan muchi omumachioti: auh ca much techtlaçaltique in vncã tulteca acaloco, much oncã techtepevaltique, much qujnextizque:

njmã ie ic tlananqujlia in Cioacoatl tlacutzin, tla qujmocaqujti in teutl in Capitã. Ca vel acalco moquetza in tenuchcatl, ca amo ichivil, ca çan ineixcavil qujchiuh in tlatilulcatl, in acaltica tlaiecoque, in qujniacatzacujlito in totecujovã amo nel iehoantin muchi qujcujque in tlatilulca:

njmã ie ic vallatoa in Quauhtemoctzin: qujvalilhuj in Cioacoatl, tlein tiqujtoa Cioacoatle: maço qujcujõ in tlatilulca, amo ic çaçacoque in tlamaceuhque? amo muchi qujnextique? amo texopan in monechico? auh tlein oconmocujlique in totecujovan amo iehoatl in? commapilhuj in teucujtlatl in Quauhtemoctzin:

njmã qujvalilhuj in Malintzin qujmjtalhuja in capitan. Çan ie ixqujch in?

125

Then the *ciuacoatl* said: "Perhaps someone of the common folk took it away. But it will be sought. Our lord the Captain will see it."

Then once again Marina spoke: "The Captain saith, 'You will produce two hundred pieces of gold this size.'" She measured it with her hands; she moved her hands in a circle.[1]

Once again the *ciuacoatl* answered. He said: "Perhaps some poor woman put it in her skirt. It will be sought. He will find it."

Thereupon the *mixcoatlailotlac* Auelitoctzin spoke. He said: "May the nobleman, our lord the Captain, hear! When there was yet Moctezuma, when there was a conquest, the Mexicans, the Tlatilulcans, the Tepanecans, the Acolhuans moved together. All the Tepanecans, all the Acolhuans, and those of the floating gardens — all of us moved together when we conquered. And when the city fell, thereupon there was turning back; all separately found their cities. And later came the people of the cities, the people already conquered. They brought their tribute; their goods went to become [the victor's]: the green stone, the gold, the precious feathers, and still other precious stones, the fine turquoise, the lovely cotinga, the roseate spoonbill. They gave it to Moctezuma. It arrived there together. All the tribute, the gold was together there in Tenochtitlan."

njman ic conjto in cioacoatl, aço aca qujqujxti in Macevalli, atel motlatemoliz, a qujmottiliz in totecujo in capitan:

njmã ie no ceppa qujvalito in Malintzin, qujmjtalhuja in Capitan Matlacpoalli anqujnextizque in teucujtlatl ixqujch in: qujvaltamachiuh imatica, qujvaliavallali in jma:

ie no ceppa ontlananqujli in civacoatl: qujto. Aço ça aca ipan mocueti in civatzintli, a motemoliz, a qujmottiliz:

njman ie ic ontlatoa in Mixcoatlailotlac, avelitoctzin: qujto. tla qujmocaqujti in tlacatl in totecujo in Capitan, in oc vnca Motecuçoma, in jquac ontepevaloia cana, ca cemolinj in Mexicatl, in tlatilulcatl, in tepanecatl in aculhoa: in jxqujch tepanecatl, in jxqujch aculhoa yoan in jxqujch chinampanecatl, ca ticemolinj, in tontepeva: auh in onia altepetl, ca njmã ie ic valnecuepalo, ceceniaca cõmati in jmaltepeuh. Auh çatepan valhuj in altepevaque in ie pevallaca, qujvalitquj in intlacalaqujl, intlatquj valmuchiuhtiuh in chalchivitl in teucujtlatl, in quetzalli yoan in oc cequj tlaçotetl, in teuxivitl, in xiuhtototl, in tlauhquechol: qujoalmacaia in Motecuçoma, çan cẽ vmpa valaci, çã vmpa valmocemaci in tenuchtitlan in jxqujch tlacalaqujli in teucujtlatl.

---

1. Corresponding Spanish text: "*Otra uez dixo Marina el señor capitan, dize que busqueys docientos tesoelos de oro tan grandes, como* *asi: y señaloles con las manos, el grandor de vna patena de caliz.*"